the food and cooking of THAILAND

the food and cooking of

THAILAND

Explore an exotic cuisine in over 180 authentic recipes shown step by step in more than 700 photographs

JUDY BASTYRA AND BECKY JOHNSON

southwater

This edition is published by Southwater
an imprint of Anness Publishing Ltd
info@anness.com
www.annesspublishing.com

If you like the images in this book and would like to investigate using them for publishing, promotions or advertising, please visit our website www.practicalpictures.com for more information.

A CIP catalogue record for this book is available from the British Library.

Publisher: Joanna Lorenz
Managing Editor: Linda Fraser
Senior Editor: Susannah Blake
Copy Editor: Jenni Fleetwood
Editorial Readers: Penelope Goodare and Jay Thundercliffe
Photographer: Nicki Dowey
Food Stylist: Lucy McKelvie
Stylist: Helen Trent
Designer: Nigel Partridge
Jacket Designer: Adelle Morris
Production: Ben Worley

COOK'S NOTES

For all recipes, quantities are given in both metric and imperial measures and, where appropriate, measures are also given in standard cups and spoons. Follow one set, but not a mixture, because they are not interchangeable.

Standard spoon and cup measures are level.
1 tsp = 5ml, 1 tbsp = 15ml, 1 cup = 250ml/8fl oz

Australian standard tablespoons are 20ml. Australian readers should use 3 tsp in place of 1 tbsp for measuring small quantities of gelatine, cornflour, salt, etc.

Medium (US large) eggs are used unless otherwise stated.

Bracketed terms are intended for American readers.

Contents

HISTORY

Thailand lies in the heart of South-east Asia, dropping down in a long, narrow peninsula to meet Malaysia at its southern tip. The top of the country borders Myanmar (formerly known as Burma) in the north and west, Laos in the north and north-east, Cambodia in the east and south-east, and the Gulf of Thailand in the south.

The history of Thailand covers a broad area of South-east Asia, rather than the defined area that we now know as Thailand. Over the centuries numerous peoples settled in the region and the borders between today's South-east Asian countries were blurred.

As the various peoples moved and migrated, the shape, identity and the name of the country changed. These influences can still be seen clearly in Thailand today. The Thai religion is an adaptation of Indian Buddhism, the language is an amalgam of several tongues, and the alphabet is based on the Mon, Khmer and Indian scripts.

Until recently, prehistoric Thailand was regarded as a cultural backwater but archaeologists have now discovered evidence of a Bronze Age society in the areas around the city of Udon Thani in the north-east. Among the finds were ceramic pots, some dating as far back as 3000BC. Thailand's more recent history, which helps to define the country that we know today, can be divided into five distinct periods.

Below: Thailand's history includes not only the country itself, but the surrounding areas of South-east Asia.

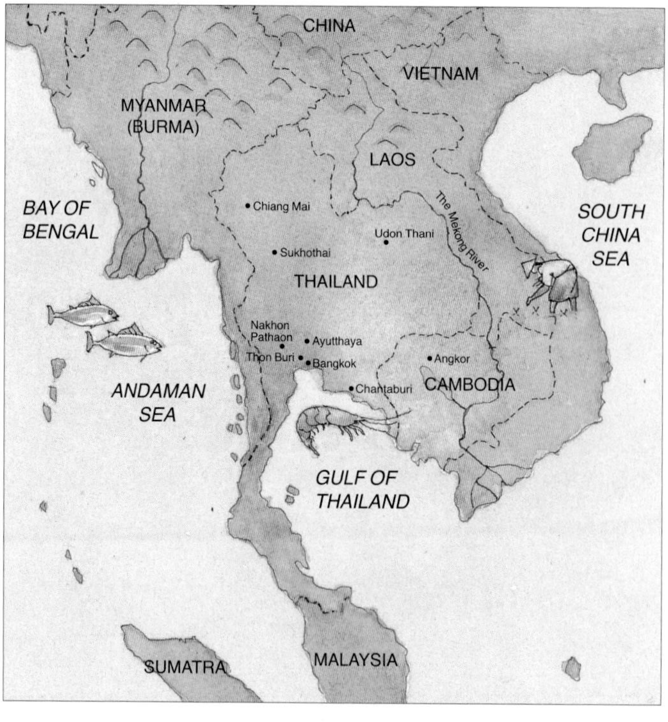

TAI AND NAN CHAO PERIOD

At the beginning of the 1st century, southern China was home to various tribal settlements. The two most important of these were the Tai and the Nan Chao, who were to migrate and settle in northern Thailand.

Gradually, the Nan Chao extended their power over neighbouring states. In response, China attacked the Nan Chao tribe in an attempt to bring it under Chinese domination and ensure protection of the western trade route. Eventually, however, Tibetan aggression from the west in a series of political wars, was to lead to the Nan Chao and Chinese becoming allies.

It is thought that the Tai people migrated further south to remain free and independent of the Chinese. The majority of the Thai people today are descendants of this early tribe.

Most of the area now recognized as Thailand was occupied by various tribes, including the Tai and Nan Chao. The most influential of these tribes were the Burmese Mons and the Cambodian Khmers. By the 10th century, the Mons had established themselves in central Thailand and had formed small Buddhist kingdoms in the area from Nakhon Pathaon, on the Korat Plateau, up to Chiang Mai.

By the 11th century, the Khmers had overpowered the Mons. Their growing influence stretched across Cambodia, southern Laos and Thailand, and Angkor became their capital city. At the same time, the Chinese were experiencing fierce opposition from the Mongols (from central Asia) who conquered many of the Chinese states.

By the 13th century, the Nan Chao had also come under the power of the Mongols. This caused floods of Nan Chao immigrants to join forces with the Tai tribes in northern Thailand. The Tai people adopted many of the military skills of the Mongols and using these, along with their superior organizational abilities, took control from the Khmers. This led to the independent Kingdom of Sukhothai being founded in 1238.

SUKHOTHAI PERIOD

The Tai people had, by now, become known as Thai. The Thais referred to the area as the Kingdom of Sukhothai, while the Chinese called the area Siam and referred to the people as Siamese. These terms were then adopted and used by other foreigners.

Sukhothai's rulers referred to this period as the dawn of happiness, and it is often considered to be the golden era of Thai history. It was considered to be a perfect state in a land of plenty, governed by paternal and benevolent kings. One of the most important archaeological finds illustrating this is the tablet on which is inscribed:

This Sukhothai is good:
In the water, there is fish
In the fields, there is rice
Whoever wishes to trade
May trade
The King does not take advantage
Of his subjects
The faces of his people shine
Bright with happiness
This is prosperity.

The most famous of Sukhothai's kings was Ramkamhaeng the Great, who is credited with creating the first Thai alphabet. His rule also saw the beginning of international commerce.

The Kingdom of Sukhothai was to thrive until 1350 when a Mon leader, Ramatibodi, broke away towards the south and founded the Kingdom of Ayutthaya. Ayutthaya's power gradually grew, eventually leading to the conquering of the Khmer capital of Angkor and reduction of the Kingdom of Sukhothai to a subservient state.

AYUTTHAYA PERIOD

From the very beginning, the kings of Ayutthaya adopted Khmer cultural influences. No longer the paternal and accessible rulers that the kings of Sukhothai had been, Ayutthaya's sovereigns were absolute monarchs and assumed the title *devaraja* (god-king).

The early part of this period saw Ayutthaya extend its sovereignty over neighbouring Thai principalities and come into conflict with its neighbours. A Burmese invasion in 1767 succeeded in capturing Ayutthaya.

However, despite their overwhelming victory, the Burmese did not manage to retain control of the kingdom for long. A young general named Phya Taksin and his followers escaped to Chantaburi. Only seven months after the fall of Ayutthaya, Taksin and his men sailed back to the capital and expelled the Burmese and restored the kingdom.

Above: A statue of Buddha sits among the ruins of Wat Mahathat at Sukhothai, Thailand's first capital city.

THON BURI PERIOD

After his victory, General Taksin proclaimed himself king and he established Thon Buri, which was nearer to the sea, as the new capital. This facilitated foreign trade, ensured the procurement of arms, and made defence and withdrawal easier in case of a renewed attack from Burma. However, the lack of central authority since the fall of Ayutthaya led to the disintegration of the kingdom and Taksin's reign was spent reuniting the provinces.

RATTANAKOSIN PERIOD

After General Taksin's death, General Chakri acceded to the throne in 1782, becoming the first king of the Chakri dynasty, Rama I. His first action as king was to transfer the royal capital across the river from Thon Buri to Bangkok (originally named Krung Rattanakosin) and build the Grand Palace. Rama II, Phraphutthaloetla Naphalai (1809–1824), continued the work that had been begun by Rama I.

King Nang Klao, Rama III (1824–1851), reopened relations with Western nations and developed trade with China. King Mongkut, Rama IV (1851–1868), concluded treaties with European countries, avoided colonization and established modern Thailand. He made many social and economic reforms during his reign. King Chulalongkorn, Rama V (1868–1910) continued his father's tradition of reform, abolishing slavery, and improving the public welfare and administrative system. King Vajiravudh, Rama VI (1910–1925), introduced compulsory education and other educational reforms.

During the reign of King Prajadhipok, Rama VII (1925–1935), the country changed from an absolute monarchy to a constitutional monarchy. The king abdicated in 1935 and was survived by his nephew, King Ananda Mahidol, Rama VIII (1935–1946). The country's name was changed from Siam to Thailand in 1939, marking the advent of a democratic government and King Bhumibol, Rama IX, acceded to the throne in 1946.

TRADITIONAL BEHAVIOUR

Left: Monks pray with their feet tucked under them to avoid pointing their feet at the statue of Buddha.

Thai attitudes towards social behaviour, dress, religion and authority figures are generally more conservative than those found in the West. The Thais' social customs and etiquette are closely linked to the foundations and teachings of Buddhism. They are blessed with a very gentle religion and this guides their behaviour and the way they live their lives. Thai society is extremely non-confrontational, and loud, public disagreements are seen as a weakness and lack of control.

Thai people are extremely polite and expect polite behaviour in return. Displays of anger towards a Thai person will only embarrass them and make them far less likely to be helpful. Although Thais are generally extremely tolerant, it is important to avoid embarrassment and misunderstanding by respecting their social customs.

SHOWING RESPECT

Visitors to the country should dress respectfully because Thais find revealing clothing such as low-cut dresses, bare shoulders and short skirts or shorts offensive. In temples, long skirts or trousers and covered shoulders are acceptable, but often entry is prohibited if your dress is deemed inappropriate. When entering a temple or a Thai house, shoes are removed.

In Thai culture the head is seen as the most sacred part of the body. For this reason it should never be touched. Thai people will take great offence if a person pats them on the head, even if it is intended as a friendly gesture. Standing over someone older and wiser than yourself is also considered rude because it implies social superiority.

The feet are the least sacred part of the body. If sitting on the floor, the feet should never point at anyone, as this is a highly offensive gesture. Nor should they point towards a religious effigy or shrine. As a result of this, most Thais tuck their feet underneath them when they sit on the floor.

Touching is seen as an invasion of personal space so handshaking is not employed in Thailand. The traditional Thai greeting is the *wai*. The hands are placed together and raised upwards towards the face while the head is bowed slightly. When greeting monks, dignitaries and other people of high status, the hands should be raised higher, to the bridge of the nose. For children, it is necessary only to nod; the *wai* is not appropriate. The *wai* is a useful gesture for visitors unfamiliar with Thai etiquette. If you feel you may have offended someone, a *wai* in their direction should result in forgiveness.

Public displays of affection between men and women are also frowned upon. You may see young Thai couples holding hands in public but this is as far as it goes in polite society.

Right: A young woman brings her hands together and lowers her head in the traditional Thai greeting, the wai.

THE REGIONS

Thailand can be split into four distinct geographical regions: north, north-east, central and south – all of which have their own distinct characteristics.

THE NORTH

Bordered by Myanmar and Laos and characterized by forested mountains and fertile river valleys, northern Thailand lies within the fabled Golden Triangle. The region has only really become integrated with the rest of Thailand within the last one hundred years and, in the case of the hill tribes, integration is still taking place.

There are many different tribes living in the north; the most well known are the Karen, Akkha, Lisu, Yao, Meo, Lahu and Hmong. Each tribe has its own culture, dialect and distinctive costume. In the past many tribespeople earned their living through opium farming but today they are cultivating strawberries, peaches, potatoes and fruit trees. They are famous for their handicrafts, specializing in colourful textiles and silver jewellery, and have become a great tourist attraction, with tours and treks to their settlements.

THE NORTH-EAST

This region is a high, semi-arid plateau, used mainly for cattle and growing crops such as rice and maize (corn). It is the poorest, most undeveloped region of Thailand but is an area of spectacular natural beauty, with forested mountains, national parks and rolling farmland. Known as *I-San* by the Thais, the region is bordered to the north and east by the Mekong River and Laos, and to the south by Cambodia. Many of the residents of north-eastern Thailand are ethnically Laotian.

CENTRAL THAILAND

This mainly flat and fertile region stretches from the rugged western mountains bordering Myanmar to the plateau to the east. Its northern extent is Nakhon Sawan, where the Ping, Wang, Nan and Yom rivers unite to form the Chao Phraya River (River of Kings), which flows through Bangkok before entering the Gulf of Thailand. To the south, the area stretches to Thailand's narrowest point between the western mountains and the Gulf of Thailand. The region is rich in historical sites and is home to Bangkok, Thailand's capital and major point of entry.

The Chao Phraya River irrigates the central plain, which is the main rice growing area of Thailand, producing a considerable proportion of the global supply. The best fragrant rice is grown here. The Chao Phraya is the main artery of the country, sustaining an intricate network of canals that irrigate bountiful orchards and market gardens. It is host to floating markets, and supports a unique, waterborne way of life. The central plain is the area where Thailand's finest fruits and vegetables are grown, including durians, mangoes, guavas, pomelos, papayas, cabbages, mushrooms, cucumbers and pumpkins.

THE SOUTH

Geographically, southern Thailand extends through the Kra Isthmus from Chumphon, south of Bangkok, to the Thai-Malaysian border, with the Gulf of Thailand to the east and the Andaman Sea to the west. The region is generally hilly and mountainous with rich mineral deposits. Lush jungle covers craggy limestone mountains fed by rain that falls for eight months of the year. The south is also home to rubber and coconut plantations, remote national parks, forested mountains, waterfalls and historic cities. It also includes the lush tropical islands with palm-fringed beaches that lie off the region's shores.

Below: The many waterways of central Thailand have created a waterborne way of life with much of the travel, transport and trade carried out in boats.

The Thai Cuisine

Founded on simple ingredients of excellent quality, the Thai cuisine relies on five primary flavours that are used in differing proportions to produce a wonderful range of dishes. The cooking of each region, while using these basic flavours, has its own characteristics and produces an interesting array of local specialities. The Royal Palace tradition also plays an important role in the preparation of Thai dishes, particularly in their carefully crafted presentation.

THE FIVE FLAVOURS

In Thai cooking, the five key flavours that are used are salty, sweet, sour, bitter and hot. The secret to all Thai food lies in the subtle differences in the proportions of ingredients used, which can add layers of flavour and aroma.

Salty

This flavour enhances and brings out the tastes of the other ingredients. It is not usually added in the form of table salt, but through the addition of salty ingredients. One of the most important and widely used of these is *nam pla*, which is a sauce made from fermented fish, while *kapi*, a salty shrimp paste, is used to add its own distinctive flavour to dishes. Other condiments that can add the salty element to Thai dishes include Thai oyster sauce (milder and more "oystery" than its Chinese counterpart); light soy sauce; dark or light yellow bean sauce; dried fish or shrimp (which can be ground and added to soups or salads); salted plums; and salted preserved vegetables, such as cabbage or mooli (daikon).

Sweet

Thai food often has a subtle sweetness. Sweet ingredients such as palm sugar and coconut sugar are often added to savoury dishes to enhance the flavours of spices and herbs. Other commonly used sweetening agents include sweet black soy sauce, which is made by fermenting soy sauce with treacle (molasses); sweet pickled garlic; and brown rice syrup. Honey is sometimes also used as a sweetener.

Sour

Lime juice is one of the most popular sour flavourings because it not only adds a sour taste but also helps to accentuate other flavours. Sour tamarind, often sold as wet tamarind, is also used as a souring agent. Both ingredients have a tenderizing effect on meats and fish. Various vinegars such as coconut, white distilled or the less sharp rice vinegar are also employed.

Bitter

The bitter flavour of Thai dishes is produced by ingredients such as herbs or dark green vegetables. These are generally one of the main ingredients of the recipe, so the bitterness must be balanced by adjusting the other four primary flavours.

Hot

Despite the fiery reputation of the Thai cuisine, not all dishes are overpoweringly hot. However, Thais do have a great tolerance to spicy dishes, acquired from a lifetime's experience. The main source of heat is the chilli, which is sold fresh, dried or in pastes and sauces (*priks*). Before the chilli was introduced to Thailand, heat was obtained from peppercorns, which are still used. Heat can also be introduced through ginger, onions and garlic.

Chilli-based condiments such as crushed dried chillies and chilli paste are usually placed on the table so that diners can season the dish further, adding heat to their own taste.

Left: A Thai cook prepares a classic stir-fried dish in her kitchen.

Left: Throughout the southern region, the villages along the coastline send out their boats every day to catch fish.

THE NORTHERN CUISINE

Unlike the rest of Thailand, where jasmine rice is favoured, northerners prefer sticky glutinous rice, which can be rolled into balls and dipped into sauces or curries. The curries are often thin because coconut milk, which is used as a thickener elsewhere, is not readily available. The dishes also tend to be less spicy than in other regions. Unusual ingredients found in the north include buffalo meat and giant beetles.

The influence of Myanmar and Laos can be found in many typical northern dishes. The classic chicken and noodle curry, *koi soi*, and the popular *gaeng hong lae* (pork curry) originated in Burma. *Nam prik nuum*, a smoky, not-too-spicy dip served with poached freshwater fish and crisp fried pork, shows a Laotian influence.

The traditional entertainment is the *kantoke* dinner (*kan* means bowl). Guests sit on the floor around a low table and serve themselves to various dishes, which are constantly replaced by the host.

FOOD IN THE NORTH-EAST

North-eastern Thais have a reputation for adventurous eating. Some of the more unusual delicacies include ant eggs, grubworms, grasshoppers, snail curry and pungent, fermented fish. While many people in Thailand look down on the eating habits of the north-easterners, restaurants in Bangkok prepare many north-eastern specialities such as *som tam* (green papaya salad), *laap*, a dish of spiced raw minced (ground) meat, and *haw mok pla*, a fish custard steamed in banana leaves.

North-eastern cooking is usually very hot and spicy, using more chilli than is favoured in other regions. The cuisine also shows a strong Laotian influence. A classic delicacy from Laos, which is served at celebrations, is *khanom buang* – crispy pancakes stuffed with dried shrimp and beansprouts.

EATING IN THE CENTRAL REGION

The traditional food of this region, particularly in the outlying villages, is often plainer than that eaten elsewhere. A typical dish will consist of rice with stir-fried vegetables, fish from a nearby river, canal or paddy field, and a salad made from salted eggs, chillies, spring onion (scallion) and lime juice.

In the bustling hub of Bangkok, however, you can experience not only Thailand's regional cuisines, but also many international dishes. The city is a paradise for food lovers. Everywhere there is food on display and there are innumerable cafés and restaurants, as well as the street or river vendors.

SOUTHERN COOKING

Fish and shellfish are abundant in the south, which is almost completely surrounded by coastline. Many dishes feature rock lobsters, crabs, mussels, squid, prawns (shrimp) and scallops. They may be used in soup, grilled (broiled), steamed, or added to a curry.

Many different cultures and countries have influenced the cuisine of this region, and there is a strong Muslim presence, which can be seen in the food. Mussaman-style curry shows an Indian influence, while satay originates from Indonesia. The dishes of Songkhla and the island of Phuket, where the population is largely Chinese, show a definite Chinese influence.

Coconuts grow plentifully everywhere, providing milk for thickening soups and curries, and oil for frying. Fresh coconut is used in savoury and sweet dishes. Cashew nuts and pineapples also grow here. In general, the food is chilli-hot.

THE ROYAL PALACE TRADITION

The tradition of food decoration and presentation originates from the court of the Grand Palace in Bangkok. Living within the walls of the inner palace was a large community of women who existed almost independently from the outside world. Aristocrats and noblemen vied for their daughters to be taken into the palace where they would receive training in the running of an elegant household, honing and refining skills that would impress potential husbands. An integral part of their training was learning to prepare food. Importance was laid equally between flavour and aesthetic appeal. Many hours were spent on painstaking preparation, perfecting the flavour and appearance of each dish.

One of the most visually impressive skills passed down through generations of these women was that of vegetable and fruit carving. The women learned to transform various vegetables and fruits into the most intricate creations. Huge watermelons and tiny chillies were turned into elaborate blossoming flowers, and pumpkins and ginger roots were cut into complicated abstract designs or pretty birds.

As times and attitudes changed, the Grand Palace gradually evolved and the polygamous environment was finally abolished under the reign of King Rama VI. Many of the women living inside the palace were reluctant to be relocated and up until 1960, at least one still resided within the palace.

What was once a teeming city within a city, complete with streets, houses, artificial lakes and shops is now a ghost of its former self, shut off from most outsiders. Some of the surviving palace women still visit the palace daily and sit in the beautiful gardens.

Despite the changes that have occurred inside the palace, outside the walls many of the palace traditions still thrive. The art of vegetable and fruit carving is seen as a symbol of good food throughout Thailand and the recipes and dishes that were perfected and refined within the palace walls are commonplace today in one variation or another on the Thai dining table.

One of the more memorable dishes that survives is *foi thong*, a blend of egg yolk and sugar, which is manipulated into golden threads. Other traditional dishes include *look choop*, a mixture of bean paste and coconut milk that is moulded into imitation fruits, the colours blended to match the real thing, and *mae grob*, a savoury dish of crispy rice noodles and shrimp topped with sweet-and-sour sauce.

Another tradition of the Royal Palace that can still be seen today is the art of making floral decorations. Scented and colourful blooms were threaded together to make elegant wreaths and garlands. Today, these colourful and fragrant garlands have become a symbol of refinement and elegance, and they can be seen throughout Thailand, especially Bangkok, where they are often used to decorate restaurants, shops and homes.

Left: The intricately decorated Grand Palace in Bangkok was home to a huge community of women, who studied and developed the art of food presentation.

Eating Thai-Style

For the Thai people, eating is always a pleasure and is an important feature of everyday life. Lunch may be a quick bowl of noodle soup bought from one of the many street vendors, or it may be a meal eaten at home with the rest of the family. Whatever the meal, eating is always a time for enjoyment.

At home, meals are generally shared and are based on rice (*khao*). The thai word "to eat" is actually *kin khao* (to eat rice). A bowl of rice is usually placed at the centre of the table surrounded by the other dishes and condiments. It is considered polite to begin the meal with a single spoonful of rice symbolizing the importance of the grain within the Thai culture and way of life.

The host will serve himself or herself with rice first, before offering it to guests. It is important to only take small helpings of each dish. When the meal is over, food should always be left on the plate and in the serving dishes, to emphasize the generosity of the host.

The influence of the Buddhist tradition can be seen in the Thai approach to meat. Thais do not believe that meat should be served in large portions. It is, therefore, always served in small amounts, usually cut into bitesize pieces or shredded.

Because meat is always chopped small before cooking, knives are redundant at a Thai table. Meals are usually eaten with a spoon and a fork. The fork is held in the left hand and is used to push food on to the spoon. The food is then conveyed to the mouth using the spoon; it is considered rude to put a fork in one's mouth. Chopsticks are only used when eating Chinese-style noodles. In the northern territories, sticky, glutinous rice is rolled into balls and eaten with the right hand – they swear it tastes better. However, licking your fingers is considered impolite. Blowing your nose at the table is also considered very rude.

TRADITIONAL MEALS

Thai meals are generally an informal affair and there are no particular rules as to what time meals should be eaten. Food is separated into a savoury course and a sweet course, but within these categories all dishes are served at the same time and not in any particular order. Guests are expected to help themselves from the selection of dishes.

The main meal is usually the last one of the day. A traditional Thai meal includes a variety of dishes, which are served as soon as they are cooked. Steamed rice is generally served with clear soup (which may be eaten either at the beginning or end of the meal), a steamed dish, a fried dish, a salad and a spicy sauce such as *kruang jim, nam pla* or *nam prik*. Condiments usually include crushed dried chilli, chopped fresh chilli, pickled garlic, cucumber, tomatoes and spring onion (scallion).

Once the main course has been cleared, fresh fruit and a dessert are usually served. Desserts in Thailand are quite different from those found in the West. Usually based on fruit or coconut and rice or flour, they are often very sweet with a delicate, scented flavour.

Above: A Thai woman enjoys a bowl of rice at a bustling floating market.

On very special occasions such as weddings or festivals the sweet dishes are generally more elaborate and incorporate *foi thang* (golden threads of spun sugar) or banana leaf cups of *takaw* (a sugary confection made from tapioca, flour, sugar and coconut).

Of course, on ordinary days, Thai people do not eat as much as this. For breakfast they may eat *khao tom*, which is rice cooked in twice the normal amount of water, leaving it with a soft soup-like consistency similar to the Chinese *congee*. Small pieces of cooked chicken, pork or fish can be added to this rice dish, or it may be served plain with egg, salt fish and pickles. Lunch is generally a light meal of either noodles or fried rice. Dinner is still the most substantial meal of the day but is a much more modest version of the traditional meal.

STREET FOOD

Wherever you go in Thailand, you will inevitably come across the famously noisy and energetic food vendors who prepare and cook their dishes on the side of the street, on the rivers and waterways, and in markets. Although the dishes and snacks on offer may be as varied as the terrain and culture, hawker food in Thailand is renowned for its freshness and flavour. Street food is part of the Thai way of life and is eaten and enjoyed by everyone, regardless of social standing and income.

Navigating the streets and walkways of most Thai cities is an exhilarating journey for the senses. Street vendors advertise their produce loudly, banging spoons against metal pots, ringing bells, striking gongs, shouting the names of the strange and exotic-sounding delicacies while their woks and cooking vessels emit the heady aromas of a variety of spices and sauces.

The noise of the street vendor in Thailand is as common as the *tuk-tuk* drivers' habitual horn-blowing. Some of the reasons their produce is so appealing are the speed of preparation, the freshness of the ingredients and the low cost. Nevertheless, many politicians have attempted to have hawker food abolished, citing reasons such as lack of hygiene and street obstruction. Despite this, however, hawker food has become such an integral part of the Thai tradition and culture that street and river food continue to thrive.

FOOD STALLS

Thailand boasts a huge variety of mobile restaurants, from stands and braziers to trolleys and bicycles. These functional stalls are often family businesses. The commonest, and simplest, is the *hahp* – a bamboo pole, with a basket balanced at each end that the hawker uses to carry not only the ingredients but also cooking equipment and a brazier. The vendor carries the pole over his shoulder, allowing great freedom of passage down small narrow walkways and ease of mobility on the boats that travel up and down the river systems.

From the *hahp*, the next step up is the pushcart or trolley. After this are the more permanent stalls that are often found under awnings on the roadside, or in night markets. These stalls are complete with tables and chairs and offer more substantial meals.

Trade and commerce used to be exclusive to the rivers. Today, in places with extensive waterways such as the former capital Ayutthaya, you will often encounter *gueyteow rua* (noodle boats).

Above: A street hawker prepares a snack for a customer over the brazier carried in one basket of his hahp.

Hawkers, particularly those with very simple stalls, often specialize in one particular dish or delicacy. The food is generally rich in flavour and variety, with recipes often having been passed down through generations.

SNACKING

The Thais are keen snackers, and tasty morsels can be found on virtually every street. Freshly sliced fruit including *sapparof* (sweet pineapple), *ma-muang* (tart green mango) and *farang* (crispy guava) is a popular snack that can be bought coated in sugar, salt or dried crushed chilli flakes.

Khao poot (corn) is a very common snack. It is often cooked in a giant aluminium steamer and the buyer can choose to have it on the cob or dunked in salty water and the kernels sliced off and eaten separately. The steamed cobs can also be cooked over a brazier.

Salapao, which are steamed rice flour dumplings stuffed with pork or a sweetened bean paste, are also very popular. Vendors who specialize in *salapao* often also make *khanom jip*, a steamed snack made from minced (ground) pork or shrimp wrapped in wonton skins. *Salapao* vendors are frequently seen roaring down the streets on motorbikes with sidecars filled with piles of the small, white puffy snacks.

Below: Glass-sided carts filled with wedges of freshly prepared fruit are a common sight throughout Thailand.

Above: A selection of skewered snacks are displayed on banana leaves, ready to be cooked over a brazier.

Another quick bite is *bah jang*, a mixture of sticky rice and peanuts combined with pork, mushrooms, Chinese sausage or salty eggs. The mixture is wrapped in banana leaves, tied together with straw string, and hung in rows from vendors' carts.

The north-east is well-known for its titbits of crunchy, salty grasshoppers, grubworms, ant eggs and potent fermented fish, which are eaten in much the same way as peanuts and potato crisps (US potato chips) are in the West.

You can also buy refreshing drinks including *ka-fe dam yen* (ice-cold coffee) or *nam pol-lamai* (fruit juices), which are sold in small, cleverly tied plastic bags with a loop on one corner for easy carrying and a straw poking out of the other for drinking. A pinch or two of salt is usually added to the freshly made fruit juices.

MAIN MEALS

As with all Thai food, neighbouring countries have influenced street food: rich sauces from Myanmar, fish and shellfish dishes from Malaysia, and charcuterie from Laos. In Chiang Mai, locals eat *khanom jin* (noodles with spicy fish); in the north-east *gai yang* (chicken cooked over a charcoal brazier and accompanied by glutinous rice and green papaya salad) is popular.

One of the most popular street food dishes is *kuay tiao phad thai*, which is cooked in woks on pushcarts that have bottles of sauces and seasonings balanced around the edges. For this dish, noodles are flash-fried with prawns (shrimp), eggs, spring onions (scallions), beansprouts and garlic, then various other ingredients are added before the final sprinkling of crushed peanuts. Another popular dish is *kuay tiao nam gai*, which is similar to *phad thai* but is served in a seasoned stock with roasted chicken and flavoured with fresh coriander (cilantro).

SWEET TREATS

For those with a sweet tooth, Thailand's hawker food offers everything from small, bitesize confections to desserts. Many of the sugary snacks are prepared by the vendor at home, then displayed in glass cases out on the street. The assortment of offerings varies from lengths of sugar cane to *kluay ping* (honey-dipped bananas). Other popular dishes include *khan Korea* (coconut desserts cooked in clay vessels over hot charcoal) and *sangkaya fuk thong* (steamed pumpkin custard).

THE MARKETS

Throughout the cities and rural areas of Thailand, you will find loud, colourful and crowded markets, which may sell anything from fresh produce, flowers and delicious snacks to clothes and exotic and unusual creatures. These markets are the hub of Thai life and you can witness Thais at their most excitable and enterprising. The markets are an unforgettable experience for any visitor to Thailand.

FRESH PRODUCE

Thai markets are often found in narrow streets and are filled with tightly packed stalls. The bustling atmosphere fuels the intensity of the environment. You will find it almost impossible to simply pop into a Thai market because, on entering, you are quickly swept into the flow of pedestrian traffic.

Walking through markets takes time. They are often an eclectic mixture of hawker food, bright containers overflowing with fragrant fresh herbs and spices, and Thai men and women gossiping loudly and expressively while sitting at small Formica-topped tables tucking into steaming bowls of food.

Below: The floating markets of Bangkok are a splendid sight, full of rich colours and intriguing sounds and aromas.

You will almost certainly come across items and produce with which you are unfamiliar – but vendors will be happy to give vivid mimed explanations. Allow your senses to take in the amazing and unusual products on offer.

There is a huge array of fresh foods available. On meat stalls you will find piles of bloodied entrails and row upon row of plucked chickens lined up, ready for cooking. Seafood is a popular commodity and many stalls have large bins filled to the brim with live crabs, turtles and fish. Hanging from the tops of the stalls on brightly coloured clothes pegs (pins), like old, faded Christmas decorations, are rows of squid, dried and flattened until paper thin.

One of Thailand's most famous markets is the floating market, situated in the former capital of Thon Buri. Although the produce is standard to all Thai markets, here the stalls are all on water. At the break of dawn each morning, farmers from the surrounding areas row their boats to the market to trade their home-grown vegetables and fruits. Their low, flat boats groan under the weight of mountainous piles of freshly picked produce. The bright colour and crisp, succulent stems and leaves of the fruits and vegetables can only be explained by the speed with which they were transported from the soil to the floating market. Other items are also available, including clothes, fresh drinks and piping hot dishes to be enjoyed immediately. Customers can only access the market by boat.

Above: Stalls are filled with the brightly coloured, scented garlands that are a common sight throughout Thailand.

The flower market near the Grand Palace in Bangkok is a fiesta of colour and fragrance. It is a wholesale market for flower shop owners and garland makers who flock to the market early in the morning to purchase freshly cut flowers for their day's trading.

Fresh flowers are an important feature in the Thai culture. They are made into bouquets and garlands to decorate homes and shrines. Garlands are often presented to wedding guests and to people of importance to signify respect or gratitude. Large wreaths are used at funerals and cremation ceremonies.

The flower market in Bangkok is a spectacular visual feast where exotic and colourful flowers of varying shapes and sizes can be purchased. Often intricate, unusual and artistic garlands or bouquets are on display here, and visitors may also see some of these being made, as the male and female vendors sit gossiping at their stalls.

When buying food and fresh produce in markets, there is no need to barter over price. Quantities are requested either in monetary value by asking for, for example, "ten baht" of a product, or by the Thai measurement – the handful. The quantity is then weighed on hand-held scales or larger fixed ones.

Fresh foods such as vegetables and fruits, and raw meat and fish are usually packaged in plastic bags, as are ready-made foods such as biscuits (cookies) and confectionery. It is common to be given liquid produce such as freshly squeezed fruit juices and spicy sauces in a plastic bag knotted at the top.

OTHER MARKETS

As well as the markets selling fresh food and produce, there are also markets that sell clothes, live animals, porcelain and many other things.

Jatujak (Chatuchak) is one of the most famous general markets in Thailand. It is not for the faint-hearted but is undoubtedly where you will find the most bizarre merchandise. The market was originally situated in Sanam Luang but was relocated in 1982 to ease congestion in central Bangkok. Now it can be found next to Jatujak Park at the end of the sky train line, 10 minutes from Bangkok city centre.

Jatujak is a weekend market, which is ideal for antique collectors or those looking to buy silks, porcelain, clothes and second-hand books. It is one of the largest markets in Asia, where hours can be spent navigating the complex maze of alleys and back streets – a confusing combination of houses and stalls are linked together haphazardly under canvas awnings.

The animal section is an unusual and unique spectacle, and is one of the reasons why the market has received such notoriety. A huge variety of animals, from turtles and terrapins to rodents and rattlesnakes, are crammed together in tiny cages. Some of these animals are for sale as domestic pets while others await a more sinister fate.

Thailand is also host to many tourist markets, which are open during both the day and night. One of the most renowned is the night market in the infamous Patpong district of Bangkok. Patpong is the sex show capital of the world and tourists flock to see the more unusual sights of Bangkok.

The night market, situated on the main strip, is lit up below the crude flashing neon signs of the sex clubs and is alive to the sound of dance music. Here you can wander around and take in the heady, electrifying atmosphere of Patpong. It is a noisy, colourful and fast-paced market where you can buy fakes of every kind of designer goods, from watches and clothes to handbags and jewellery.

In these markets, bartering is not only possible but expected by the vendor and is always a good-humoured affair. In most of the tourist markets, vendors will approach visitors who show an interest in their goods with a calculator. They will display their initial price and offer it to the customer who will type in what they are prepared to pay. The calculator is passed back and forth until a price is agreed. The Thais enjoy and encourage bartering, and this exchange is often a source of great joviality.

Below: A seller displays his produce at one of the many Thai street markets.

FESTIVALS AND CELEBRATIONS

Theravada Buddhism is the prevalent religion in Thailand and is a guiding force in the Thai culture and way of life. The influence of Buddhism can be seen clearly in Thailand's many festivals and celebrations, and in the foods that are enjoyed at these times. Buddhists like to prepare savoury food and desserts for monks and guests at these celebrations.

Buddhist monks are bound by their religion only to accept food as donations and gifts. As a result, the tradition of merit-making (offering food to monks) has become an inherent part of most ceremonies and celebrations. The food is always carefully prepared and includes freshly cooked rice, various savoury dishes, fresh fruit and desserts.

The names of many traditional Thai desserts reflect this ethos of giving and are intended to bless those who receive them with prosperity and good luck. *Khanom chan* is a many layered dessert, representing the levels of success in one's work; *khanom mong koot* means high success in one's work; and *kha noon*, which is a dessert made from jackfruit seeds, means constant support for one's business.

Another popular theme in these celebratory desserts is gold (*thong*). The names *thong yib, thong yod, foy thong, thong ex, thong plu, thong prong* and *thong muan* all mean to wish with gold.

The multitude of festivals and events that fill the calendar are varied in their origins. Some are religious, others celebrate the annual rice-farming cycle or express gratitude for produce from the land, and some are held in honour of the monarchy. The characteristics of each festival vary widely depending on the reason for the celebration. Many are set to fixed dates but religious festivals tend to be determined according to the lunar calendar, which means their date can change from year to year.

The main national festivals are large all-encompassing affairs that focus on the ideals of fresh beginnings and discarded problems or sins. They are often a good excuse for large groups of family and friends to gather together to celebrate and enjoy traditional meals. Some events include colourful, bright displays and processions filled with merriment, while others may be more sombre and humble ceremonies, with themes of poignancy, remembrance and appreciation.

The Thai urge for fun and celebration is an infectious one and festivals are often an opportunity for the community to pull out ali the stops. Food plays an important part at these celebrations, with large meals serving traditional and beautifully displayed food. Hawkers selling delicious meals and snacks also always appear at these large gatherings. Traditional national festivals such as *Songkran* will have Singha beer available on draught as well as the infamous Thai whisky. *Ya dong*, a type of moonshine, may also be available, and will often include medicinal varieties containing barks, herbs, roots and even snakes' blood.

Left: Orange-robed monks gather outside a temple in Bangkok to collect morning alms from Thai Buddhists.

ORDINATION

Buddhist ordination is considered a right of passage for all young Thai men. It is not considered a lifetime commitment and can be done for short periods of time; the minimum is usually just three months.

Ordination is especially prevalent in the rural areas and boys under twenty can be ordained as novices, and those over twenty may receive higher ordination as a fully-fledged monk. Monks can choose to enter either a forest temple and study meditation, or a more urban setting to learn the Buddhist scriptures and doctrines.

One of the most striking festivals celebrating ordination is the *Poi Sang Long*, which is thought to be unique to Mae Hong Son in northern Thailand. The festival lasts for three days, and involves a colourful procession in which offerings, which include food, candles and incense, are carried.

NEW YEAR CELEBRATIONS

Nowadays, the coming of the new year is celebrated three times in three different months. The international celebration marked on 1 January has been welcomed from the West, the Chinese New Year falls in February and the traditional lunar celebration, *Songkran* (also known as *Trut*), in April.

Thai New Year's Day is 13 April but the festival is celebrated over three days. People make pilgrimages and practise merit-making, which is done either at the temples or at designated areas set up by the government. The preparation, exchange and sharing of food is central to the festival. Other New Year celebrations include boat racing and performances of traditional dance.

Water is an important feature of New Year celebrations, symbolizing cleansing and renewal, and statues of Buddha are bathed. More high-spirited antics include the annual water fight known as *ofsat nam*. On 13 April, the streets are filled with children and adults alike, armed with water missiles and water guns, which are hurled and fired at passers-by, with the exception only of monks and uniformed police officers.

Dance and Drama

Performance and dance are a great Thai tradition and often feature as part of celebrations. The classical type of dance is the *lakhon*, which incorporates the use of dance and drama to tell folk stories and plays. There are said to be over one hundred different types of *lakhon*, which originated from various parts of Thailand. Many forms of dance are believed to derive from the classic Khmer court dances, which come from Javanese traditions.

The dancers are usually barefoot and wear elaborate costumes, most often based on the court dress of the Ayutthaya period. The dance itself is quite static with emphasis on the movements of the arms and hands.

The most classic form is *lakhon nai* (theatre of the inside), which was originally performed by the women of the inner palace. The more popular *lakhon nok* (theatre of the outside) is more specifically associated with Buddhist temple fairs. Traditionally, male actors performed *lakhon nok* but today, women are permitted to take the female roles. In southern Thailand the ancient form of *lakhon manora*, *nora* or *chatri* is still performed. It has Indian, Malaysian and Indonesian influences.

FESTIVAL OF LIGHT

The *Loy Krathong* ceremony, better known as the Festival of Light, takes place on the eve of the full moon in November. *Loy* translates to mean float and *krathong* means leaf cup.

The festival begins when the full moon is in the sky. People carry *krathongs* (small lotus-shaped banana leaf boats containing candles, incense and coins) to nearby waterways. After lighting the candles and incense and saying a blessing, the *krathong* is set afloat for the spirits and Goddess of the water. Throughout the country, the waterways are illuminated by thousands of tiny *krathongs* as they float away.

The origin of the festival is unknown although many believe that the floats symbolize the carrying of misfortune and sin away from the owner and into the darkness of the water. Lovers often try to predict the future of their romance by casting their *krathongs* together. If the small banana leaf boats remain together on their journey down the river, then their romance will result in a life-long partnership.

MAKKHA PUJA FESTIVAL

Also known as the *Makkha Bucha* festival, this is usually held on the full moon of the third lunar cycle. It commemorates the speech given by Buddha to 1250 enlightened monks who came to hear him without prior summons. The festival is marked around the country by the making of offerings and chanting, culminating in a walk around *wats* (temples).

PHI TA KHON

This festival takes place primarily in the Den Sai district of Loei, on the border of Laos, around June or July. It is part of a Buddhist merit-making holiday known locally as *Bun Pha Ves*. The origins of the festival go back to the time of Prince Vessandorn, Lord Buddha's penultimate incarnation. Legend has it that he was a particularly charitable and generous prince who gave away two of the village's prize elephants, causing great irritation amongst the villagers.

The villagers drove the prince away and he took his wife and children on a pilgrimage through a nearby forest where he gave his two children away to a poor beggar to become slaves. The ghosts and spirits of the forest were so impressed by his generosity that, when he decided to return to his village, they formed a procession to bid him farewell.

Today, the festival is held to celebrate the last incarnation of Lord Buddha and is usually held over two days. The local children, dancers and entertainers dress up in grotesque masks made from coconut husks and dance through the streets, teasing onlookers, on their way towards the main temple. In the past, the masks were thrown in the Man river at the end of the festival to ward off any real ghosts, but today they are often sold to tourists as souvenirs.

Below: A Buddhist man wears brightly coloured clothing to celebrate the Makkha Puja *festival.*

HARVEST AND THANKSGIVING FESTIVALS

The Thai people place great importance on giving thanks for the food that nature provides them with. This is marked by many festivals that occur throughout the year to celebrate the land's produce. Changes in the climate and seasons are celebrated and glorified. Homage is paid, in particular, to rice because of its importance in the Thai diet. Individual fruits and vegetables are also celebrated in the form of fairs, marking the arrival of the new produce coming into season.

Bun Bung Fai

Before the monsoons, around the second week of May, the skies of the north-eastern regions of Thailand are ablaze with the light and explosions from the launch of thousands of large fireworks. This is the *Bun Bung Fai* or rocket festival that marks the beginning of the rice-planting and ploughing season. The rockets are released to encourage a plentiful rainfall and a good harvest in the coming season.

Bun Bung Fai is a good opportunity for the local farmers and rice workers to have fun and indulge themselves before the arduous task of rice-planting begins. During the festival, there is a whole host of entertainments, which encourage high-spirited antics along with the more serious tradition of merit-making.

During the festival, the streets are filled with floats carrying elaborately decorated rockets that will later be fired into the sky. The street procession provides the stage for local people who dress in colourful costumes. Groups of the infamous "lady-boys", beautifully dressed and made-up, sometimes also perform dances. It is a time for eating and drinking and the streets are filled with hawkers selling meals and snacks.

Above: Coconuts are an essential ingredient in Thai cooking, and are one of the many fruits celebrated in the various thanksgiving fairs.

The Rice Ploughing Ceremony

At around the same time as *Bun Bung Fai*, there is a rice-ploughing ceremony in Sanam Luang, Bangkok. The event is presided over by the King or another member of the Royal family. It is an ancient Brahmin ceremony that aims to bless the farmers with bumper crops in the coming year.

At a certain point in the ceremony, *Phraya Raek Na* – the Farming Lord, who, today, is usually the Permanent Secretary of the Ministry of Agriculture – will plough an area of land near the palace to mark the start of the season. The cows are offered an assortment of different foods, including grass, rice, corn, beans, liquor and water. The foods that the cows choose are used to predict the success of the harvest in the coming year.

The Sart Festival

This event, which marks the beginning of the rice-harvesting season, was originally a Brahmin festival celebrated in India at the end of the tenth lunar month. It is now celebrated in the Buddhist temple but, in Thailand, the tenth lunar month is not the normal harvest time, so farmers plant a special type of flat rice, *khow mow*, that can be harvested at this time of year. *Khow mow* is used to prepare *krayasart*, which is a sweet confection made from rice and peanuts that is usually eaten with small bananas. *Krayasart* are offered to the monks through merit-making before others enjoy them.

Regional Food Fairs

In December, Chiang Mai hosts many food and agriculture festivals and fairs. Between 8 and 12 December is the Chiang Mai Food Festival, which celebrates the art of Thai cuisine. Among many things, it features fruit and ice carving, demonstrations of food preparation and dessert-making, and cultural shows. Over one hundred local restaurants, bakeries and food suppliers set up stalls under the night sky and sell a wonderful selection of inexpensive local cuisine. Mouthwatering cakes and confectionery sit side-by-side with classic local dishes such as *phat thai* and the spicy salad, *som tam*.

Fruit Fairs

As well as rice, fruit is also of great importance to the Thai people and this is marked countrywide by numerous fruit fairs and festivals. Sometimes the festival merely marks the start of a new season, but some fruits such as the mango (*mamuang*), have much deeper significance. It is believed that Buddha was presented with a mango tree below which he could sit, finding rest, solace and calm. As a result, the mango has achieved high status among Buddhists as a fruit of veneration to be given only to those of high worth. Mangoes are popular among Thais who use them in a variety of dishes such as *yam mamuang*, a spicy salad made from shredded, unripe mangoes. Unripe mangoes are also pickled and used in chutneys and relishes. The mango season begins in April and lasts only two months, so Thais make the most of them while they are available.

In the eastern Thai province of Chantaburi, many of their annual fruit fairs double up as celebrations of the durian harvest. Chantaburi, which is the durian capital of the world, produces about half of Thailand's crop. During the fruit fair, which takes place in June, it is possible to buy up to five different varieties of durian. The fair also incorporates other fruits such as rambutans, jackfruit and mangosteens. There is a street parade on the first day of the ten-day celebration, which consists of large floats decorated with a multitude of colourful and exotic fruits.

Thailand plays host to a variety of other regional fruit festivals and fairs, from the Palm Sugar Festival in the Pisanulok Province at the beginning of May to the Lychee Festival in the Payao Province and Chiangrai Province.

August fairs mark the picking season of longans in Lamphun in the north, and rambutans in Surat Thani in the south. These fairs also include street floats and traditional performances and ceremonies. In Surat Thani, the first rambutan tree was planted in 1926, and today the fruit is enjoyed throughout Thailand. The fair provides an open market to promote local produce. Some of the highlights include agricultural exhibitions of local produce and ornamental plants, and coconut-picking demonstrations by trained monkeys.

Vegetarian Festival

This festival is held on the island of Phuket in southern Thailand in October. It is a nine-day commitment by the islanders to eat only vegetarian food. It was originally a Chinese festival, first celebrated in Phuket in 1825. It begins on the first day with a parade of white-clothed participants and numerous colourful displays. These include lion dances, barefoot walking on hot coals and various forms of body piercing. It is a fascinating, though sometimes gruesome, experience for vegetarians and meat-eaters alike.

Right: Thanks are given with prayers, incense and offerings of food and beautiful garlands of flowers.

THE THAI KITCHEN

The Thai cuisine is founded on simple ingredients of excellent quality. Fresh fish from the sea, rice from the fields, aromatic herbs and spices and locally grown fruits and vegetables are just a few of the wonderful ingredients that are enjoyed throughout Thailand. Each region has its own specialities based on locally grown and harvested produce but there are common flavourings and culinary techniques that are used throughout the country, creating a wonderfully varied cuisine.

RICE

The most important ingredient in Thai cooking is rice. In fact when people are called to the table, the phrase used – *gkin kao* – literally translates as "a time to eat rice". All the other foods that make up a meal – meat, fish and vegetables – are regarded as accompaniments and are referred to as *ghap kao* or "things eaten with rice".

The average Thai eats 158kg/350lb of rice every year, which is almost a pound a day. It is consumed in various forms, from basic steamed rice to rice noodles, crackers and cakes.

Two distinct types of rice are popular in Thailand. The first is a delicately scented long grain variety, which is used as a staple with all meals. It comes in several qualities, and is white and fluffy with separate grains when cooked. In northern Thailand, a starchy glutinous rice is preferred. When cooked, the grains stick together.

The best quality rice is harvested in December, when the cool, dry weather allows the grains to ripen slowly. At other times of the year, the vagaries of the climate can cause problems. If the weather is too hot, the grains may ripen prematurely; if it is too wet, there is a chance that the rice may develop mould on the husks.

Although in some areas newly harvested rice is regarded as something of a delicacy, the grain is usually aged for a year before it is sold. This allows the rice to dry out a little. It is quite tricky to cook "new" rice before it has aged. The grains are delicate and it is difficult to gauge how much water is required for cooking. If too much is used, the rice will become soggy.

Rice Mother

The traditional rice-growing communities in Thailand have a high regard for *Mae Pra Posop*, the "Rice Mother". Elaborate ceremonies are performed in her name during various stages of rice cultivation so that she may bless the fields with bountiful harvests from year to year.

Above: Jasmine or Thai fragrant rice has tender, aromatic grains and is the preferred rice throughout the central and southern parts of the country. It is widely available in supermarkets and Asian stores in the West.

JASMINE RICE

Khao chao

Also known as fragrant or scented rice, this long grain variety is the staple food of the central and southern parts of Thailand. As the name suggests, it has a delicate aroma. The flavour is slightly nutty, and it resembles Basmati rice from India. The uncooked grains are translucent and, when cooked, the rice is fluffy and white. Most of the crop comes from a region between central and north-eastern Thailand where the soil is a combination of clay and sand. Newly harvested rice from this region is prized for the delicate texture of the grains.

GLUTINOUS RICE

Kao niow

Commonly referred to as sweet or sticky rice, this is the mainstay of the diet in the northern and north-eastern regions of the country. It is delicious and very filling. Its name is derived entirely from its sticky texture, as rice does not contain any gluten. Easily cultivated on the hillsides and high plateaux of these regions, glutinous rice requires less water during the growing period than the wet rice of the central lowlands.

Glutinous rice comes in both short or round grain and long grain varieties. Thai people prefer the long grain

Below: Glutinous rice, which may be black (although, more accurately, it is a very dark red), white or a hybrid known as "jasmine sweet", is most widely used in north and north-east Thailand.

Above: On deep-frying, rice squares puff up into crispy crackers.

variety; the short grain rice is more commonly used in Japanese and Chinese cooking. Some of the long grain varieties have a delicate, aromatic flavour, and these high-grade hybrids are sometimes labelled "jasmine sweet" or "jasmine glutinous rice", the adjective "jasmine" echoing the description used for their fragrant cousins in the non-glutinous rice family.

What makes this type of rice unusual is the way in which the grains clump together when cooked, enabling it to be eaten with the hands. Bitesize chunks are pulled off, one at a time, and rolled to a ball between the fingers and palm of the right hand. The ball is then dunked in a sauce or stew before being eaten. The process isn't as messy as it sounds; if done correctly, the grains stick to each other but not to the fingers or the palm. At the end of a meal, rolling the last piece of rice can actually have a cleansing effect, as the rice mops up any remaining juices or grease on the hand.

The starchiness of glutinous rice gives the uncooked grain a distinct opaque white colour, which is different from the more translucent appearance of regular rice grains. When soaked and steamed, however, the reverse is true. Glutinous rice becomes translucent, while regular rice turns opaque.

Although it is in the north and the north-eastern regions of Thailand that glutinous rice is most popular, it is also eaten elsewhere in the country, most frequently in sweet snacks or desserts. The rice is sweetened and flavoured with coconut milk, and is especially popular in the mango and durian season, when huge amounts of the coconut-flavoured rice are sold to eat with these precious fruits.

BLACK GLUTINOUS RICE

Kao niow dam

This wholegrain rice – that is, with only the husk removed – has a rich, nutty flavour that is distinctly different from the more subtle taste of white glutinous rice. It is generally sweetened with coconut milk and sugar and eaten as a snack or dessert, rather than being used as the staple of a savoury meal. It does tend to be quite heavy, filling and indigestible if eaten in quantity, so it is usually nibbled as a sweetmeat snack in the mid-afternoon or later in the evening, after the evening meal has been digested. A popular version of roasted glutinous rice, flattened into a cake, is *khao mow rang*, which is sold at all markets throughout Thailand.

In spite of its name, black rice isn't actually black in colour. If the grains are soaked in water for a few hours, the water will turn a deep burgundy red, showing the rice's true colour.

Rice Products

Fermented Rice

Khao mak

Made by fermenting cooked glutinous rice, this is a popular sweetmeat, sold on market stalls and by street vendors.

Rice-pot Crust

Khao tang

In several cultures, the crust that forms on the base of the pan when rice is cooked in a particular way is highly prized. In Thailand, the crust is lifted off the base of the pan in sheets and is then dried out in the sun before being sold. *Khao tang* is lightly toasted or fried before being eaten.

Above: Rice flour is finely ground and thoroughly pulverized. As a result, it has a very light texture and is used in desserts such as pancakes.

To make *khao tang* at home, spread a layer of cooked rice about 5mm/¼in thick on a greased baking sheet. Dry it out in a low oven, 140°C/275°F/Gas 1, for several hours. Leave to cool, then break into pieces. Deep-fry when required for just a few seconds until puffed, but not browned. Lift out using a slotted spoon or wire basket and drain on kitchen paper.

Dry Rice Squares

These can be purchased at Asian food stores. When fried in hot oil, they puff up into crispy rice crackers in the same way as prawn (shrimp) crackers, which they resemble in appearance.

Rice Flour

Paeng khao jao and *paeng khao niao*

This flour may be made from either glutinous or non-glutinous raw rice that has been very finely ground. It is used to make the dough for fresh rice noodles and is also used to make desserts such as pancakes. Rice flour is readily available in Asian food stores. When the source is non-glutinous rice it is called *paeng khao jao* and when it is made from glutinous rice it is known as *paeng khao niao*. Store it as you would wheat flour.

Preparing and cooking rice

Rice is a staple of Thai cooking and it should be cooked to perfection. Jasmine (or Thai fragrant) rice is best cooked using the absorption or covered pan method, which maximizes its fragrant flavour. Glutinous rice, in contrast, requires a slightly different cooking method involving long soaking followed by steaming.

Rinsing

Jasmine rice should always be rinsed thoroughly before being cooked as this helps to remove excess starch and any dust that may have accumulated during storage.

1 Put the jasmine rice in a large bowl and pour in sufficient cold water to cover. Gently swirl the grains between your fingers. As you do so, the water will become slightly cloudy.

2 Leave the rice to settle, then tip the bowl so that the water drains away. Alternatively, strain the rice and return it to the bowl. Cover the rice once more with cold water, then swirl the grains again, leave to settle and drain. Repeat the rinsing several times – at least three – until the water runs clear. Drain well before cooking.

Cooking by the absorption method

Also known as the covered pan method, Jasmine rice is cooked in a measured amount of water until all the water has been absorbed. The proportion of rice to water, and the cooking time, will depend on the type of rice used, but as a guide, you will need about 600ml/1 pint/2½ cups for every 225g/8oz/generous 1 cup rice.

1 Put the rice into a pan and pour in the measured water. Do not add salt. Bring to the boil, then reduce the heat to the lowest possible setting.

2 Cover tightly and cook until the liquid has been absorbed, up to 25 minutes.

3 Remove the pan from the heat. Do not remove the lid and leave to stand in a warm place for 5 minutes until tender.

Adding flavourings

If you want to add a little flavour to the rice, the absorption method provides the perfect opportunity. Simply add herbs or spices, such as lemon grass or fresh root ginger, with the liquid.

To add even more flavour to the rice, substitute either coconut milk or stock for the water – or use a mixture.

Cooking rice to perfection

- When cooking rice, it is essential that the pan is covered tightly. If the lid of your pan is loose, cover the pan with foil or a clean dishtowel before fitting the lid, making sure that any excess fabric is kept well away from the heat source.
- The rice must be cooked on a very low heat – don't be tempted to increase the heat during cooking to speed the process or the water may evaporate before the rice is fully cooked.
- Leave rice to stand for 5 minutes after cooking and before serving to "rest" it and complete the cooking process. If it isn't completely tender, re-cover the pan and leave for 5 minutes more.
- Remember that rice absorbs water as it cooks. If you use too much water with the absorption method, or cook the rice for too long, it will become soggy.
- If cooked rice is required for a fried rice dish, cook it by the absorption method, cool quickly, then chill it before frying. Not only will it behave better, but food safety will not be compromised.

Microwave method

Although no faster than conventional cooking, using the microwave is a very convenient way of preparing Thai rice.

1 Using the same quantities of rice and liquid as for the absorption method, put the jasmine rice in a heatproof bowl or microwave container. Add the boiling measured liquid. Do not add salt.

2 Cover the bowl with microwave-proof clear film (plastic wrap) and cook on full power for 10–15 minutes. (Check the time recommended in your microwave manufacturer's instruction book.) Leave the rice to stand, without stirring, for 10 minutes before using.

Food safety
Never keep cooked rice warm for more than a short time, or you may risk food poisoning. Rice is susceptible to a bacterium *bacillus cereus*, which is killed by cooking, but can leave behind spores that germinate if cooked rice is insufficiently reheated or kept warm for long periods.When buying fresh rice products store carefully and use within 12 hours.

Using an electric rice cooker

Put the rice into the cooker and add the required amount of water as indicated in your instruction booklet. Do not add salt. Cover the cooker with the lid and switch it on. The cooker will switch itself off automatically when the rice is ready, and will keep the rice hot until you are ready to serve.

Steaming

This is a combination of two cooking methods: the rice is partially cooked in a pan of simmering water or other liquid, then drained and steamed. This method is used for plain boiled/steamed jasmine rice. It is also suitable for some, but not all, glutinous rice dishes.

1 Cook the rice by the absorption method for about three-quarters of the normal cooking time. Drain the partially cooked rice in a sieve or colander.

2 Tip the rice into a sieve, lined with muslin (cheesecloth), set over a pan of simmering water. Cover tightly and steam for 5–10 minutes. If the grains of rice still feel slightly hard in the centre, steam for a little longer.

Making jasmine rice pudding

This is a quick, easy and delicious dessert for four. First, cook 50g/2oz/ generous ¼ cup jasmine rice in 475ml/16fl oz/2 cups boiling water, using the absorption method until the water has evaporated and the rice is tender. Leave the rice to stand for a few minutes, then stir in 120ml/4fl oz/ ½ cup milk and a little caster (superfine) sugar to taste. Finally, stir in 60ml/4 tbsp coconut cream, if you like. Serve the pudding hot, with fresh fruit.

Cooking glutinous rice

Glutinous rice should be soaked before cooking for at least 1 hour and up to 4 hours. An even longer soaking time is recommended in some recipes. After being well drained, the rice is best cooked by steaming. There is no need partially to cook the rice first, as for jasmine rice. Simply tip the soaked rice into the lined sieve and steam for 10–15 minutes until softened.

Making glutinous rice pudding

Glutinous rice can be simmered with coconut milk and sugar to make a delicious dessert for four.

1 Put 75g/3oz/scant ½ cup glutinous rice in a large bowl. Add cold water to cover and leave to soak for 3–4 hours. Drain well and return to the pan.

2 Pour in 300ml/½ pint/1¼ cups milk or coconut milk. Bring to the boil, then lower the heat, cover and simmer for 25–30 minutes, stirring frequently.

3 Add sugar and coconut cream to taste, with any flavourings. Cook for 5–10 minutes more, uncovered, until the rice reaches the consistency you like. Serve with slices of exotic fruits.

Storing rice

Packets of rice can be kept in a cool, dark place for up to three years if unopened. Alternatively, store the rice in an airtight container. It should be kept perfectly dry; otherwise the rice could turn mouldy. Cooked rice can be stored for up to 24 hours if cooled quickly, covered and kept in the refrigerator. The cooled rice can also be frozen for up to 3 months.

NOODLES AND WRAPPERS

NOODLES

Second only to rice in importance in the Thai diet, noodles are consumed in large quantities and are cooked in a vast number of ways. Noodles are eaten at any time of day, including breakfast, and if hunger strikes unexpectedly, one of the many roadside noodle carts will furnish a tasty snack. For the local population, soup noodles are easily the most popular dish, but tourists tend to plump for *Pad Thai* (fried noodles).

There are basically five main varieties of noodles used in Thai cooking: *sen ya, ba mee, sen mee, sen lek* and *wun sen.* Most of these can be bought fresh in Asian stores, but it is more likely that you will find them dried. Noodles come in several sizes, from tiny transparent threads to large sheets. Many of them are made from rice, which serves to further emphasize the importance of the grain in the Thai diet. Other types of noodles are based on wheat flour or flour made from ground mung beans.

Unfortunately, the names of noodles are not standardized and the same type of noodle may go under several different names, depending on the manufacturer or which part of the country they come from. Noodles made without eggs are often labelled "imitation noodles" or "alimentary paste". The most reliable way to check what they actually are is to read the list of ingredients.

> **Noodle know-how**
> Both dried and fresh noodles have to be cooked in boiling water before use – or soaked in boiling water until pliable. How long for depends on the type of noodle, their thickness and whether or not the noodles are going to be cooked again in a soup or sauce As a rule, once they have been soaked, dried noodles require about 3 minutes' cooking, while fresh ones will often be ready in less than a minute and may need to be rinsed under cold water to prevent them from overcooking.

Below: Dried vermicelli rice noodles should be soaked, not boiled.

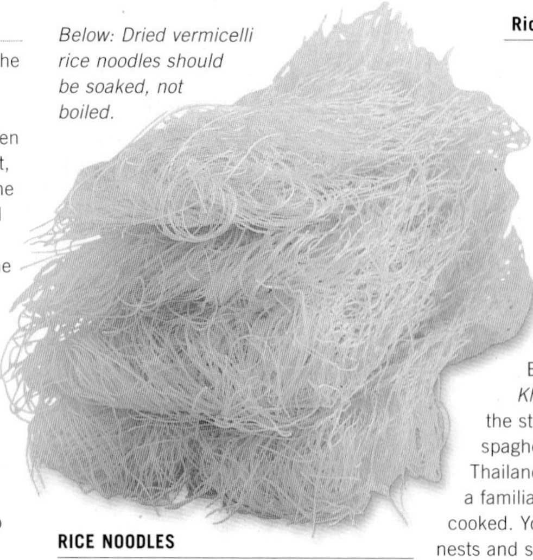

RICE NOODLES

Kui teow

Both fresh and dried rice noodles are available in Thai markets. Fresh ones are highly perishable and must be cooked as soon as possible after purchase. Rice noodles are available in a wide range of shapes and widths.

Vermicelli Rice Noodles

Mee

These noodles are usually sold dried and must be soaked in boiling water before use. When dried, rice vermicelli is called *sen mee* or rice stick noodles.

Medium Rice Noodles

Kui teow sen lek

Resembling spaghetti, these noodles are usually sold dried. The city of Chanthaburi is famous for *sen lek* noodles, which are sometimes called *Jantoboon* noodles after the nickname for the town.

Rice Stick Noodles

Kui teow sen yai

Also known as rice river noodles, these are sold both dried and fresh, although the latter form is more popular. When fresh they tend to be rather sticky and need to be separated before being cooked.

Rice Noodle Nests

Khanom Chine

Although the Thai name of these fresh thick round rice noodles means Chinese noodles, these are actually a Thai speciality, made of rice flour. In the Lacquer Pavilion of Suan Pakkad Palace there is a panel showing the making of *khanom chine* as part of the preparations for the Buddha's last meal.

Khanom chine are white and the strands are a little thicker than spaghetti. At most markets in Thailand, nests of these noodles are a familiar sight. They are sold freshly cooked. You buy them by the hundred nests and should allow four or five nests per person. Buy the cheaper ones, because they taste better although they are not so white as the more expensive noodle nests. Fresh noodles are highly perishable, so, even though they are cooked, it makes sense to buy them early in the day, and steam them again when you get them home.

They can be served with *nam ya, nam prik, sow nam* and a variety of curries.

Below: Rice stick noodles are flat, not unlike Italian tagliatelle.

Right: Spring roll wrappers are made from a wheat and water dough.

Preparing rice noodles

Rice noodles need only to be soaked in hot water for a few minutes to soften them before serving. Add the noodles to a large bowl of just-boiled water and leave for 5–10 minutes, or until they soften, stirring occasionally to separate the strands. If they are soaked for too long, they will become soggy. Their dry weight will usually double after soaking, so 115g/4oz dry noodles will produce about 225g/8oz after soaking.

Making deep-fried rice noodles

Rice stick noodles puff up and become wonderfully crisp when deep-fried. To prepare, place the noodles in a large mixing bowl and soak in cold water for 15 minutes. Drain them and lay them on kitchen paper to dry.

Heat about 1.2 litres/2 pints/5 cups vegetable oil in a large, high-sided frying pan or wok to 180°C/350°F. To test if the oil is ready, carefully drop in a couple of noodle strands. If they puff and curl up immediately, the oil is hot enough. Very carefully, add a handful of dry noodles to the hot oil. As soon as they puff up, after about 2 seconds, flip them over with a long-handled strainer and cook for 2 seconds more. Transfer to a large baking sheet lined with kitchen paper and leave to cool. Repeat this procedure with the remaining noodles, frying just a handful at a time. When the fried noodles are cold they can be transferred to a sealed plastic bag and will stay crisp for about 2 days.

Below: Egg noodles are available dried and fresh in the West.

EGG NOODLES

Ba mee

These noodles owe their yellow colour to the egg used in their manufacture. Sold fresh in nests, they must be shaken loose before being cooked. They come in both flat and round shapes. Very thin ones are known as egg thread noodles. The flat noodles are generally used for soups and the rounded type are preferred for stir-frying. Egg noodles freeze well, provided they are correctly wrapped. Thaw thoroughly before use.

Cooking egg noodles

Cook egg noodles in boiling water for 4–5 minutes, or according to the packet instructions. Drain and serve.

CELLOPHANE NOODLES

Wun sen

These thin, wiry noodles, also called glass, jelly or bean thread noodles, are made from mung beans. They are the same size as *mee* but are transparent. They are only available dried.

Preparing cellophane noodles

Cellophane noodles are never served on their own, but always as an ingredient in a dish. Soak them in hot water for 10–15 minutes to soften them, then drain and cut into shorter strands.

WRAPPERS

These are used throughout Thailand to wrap around a filling. Some may be eaten fresh while others are deep-fried.

WONTON WRAPPERS

Baang giow

Originally Chinese, these thin yellow pastry squares are made from egg and wheat flour and can be bought fresh or frozen. Fresh wrappers will last for about five days, double-wrapped and stored in the refrigerator. Simply peel off the number you require. Frozen wrappers should be thawed before use.

RICE PAPER

Banh trang

These brittle, semi-transparent, paper-thin sheets are made from a mixture of rice flour, water and salt, rolled out by a machine until very thin and then dried in the sun. Packets of 50–100 sheets are available. Store in a cool, dry place. Before use, dip in water until pliable, then wrap around a filling to make fresh spring rolls, or deep-fry.

SPRING ROLL WRAPPERS

Bang hor

These wafer-thin wrappers are used to make classic Chinese spring rolls. The sizes available range from 8cm/3¼in to 30cm/12in square, and they usually come in packets of 20. Once opened, they will dry out quickly, so peel off one at a time and keep the rest covered.

VEGETABLES

AUBERGINES/EGGPLANT

Makhua ling

Although aubergines are treated and eaten as vegetables, they are, in fact, fruit, and are related to (bell) peppers and tomatoes. Those fruit vegetables are indigenous to America, but the aubergine is thought to have originated in India, spreading very early on to China, Thailand and the rest of South-east Asia. Aubergines may be oval, tubular or round. Asian aubergines tend to be smaller than the common European varieties. Some are very tiny, not much larger than a pea, while others are about the size of tennis balls. Colours range from white to pale green, orange, purple and black. Four varieties are used in Thai cooking today.

Aubergines imported from Thailand are available from specialist Asian supermarkets and stores. Select specimens that feel heavy and firm to the touch, with uniformly smooth skin that is free from blemishes and bruises. When bought in prime condition, aubergines will keep for 3–4 days in the salad compartment of the refrigerator. If no Asian varieties are available, you can substitute the large, soft purple/black Western aubergine instead.

Long Aubergines

Makhua yaew

This elongated variety is similar in appearance and flavour to Japanese long baby aubergines. However, the Thai ones are usually pale green, but can also be purple or white. These aubergines are usually served grilled (broiled) or in green curries.

Left: Thai aubergines are usually small and fairly round in shape.

Apple Aubergines

Makhua khun

These small round aubergines are pale green, yellow or white. They are eaten raw with the ubiquitous chilli sauce, *nam prik*, or cooked in curries. They have little flavour, but when raw have an interesting texture. They discolour rapidly once cut, so drop them into salted water if you are preparing them in advance.

Pea Aubergines

Makreu puang

These pea-size berries, which grow in small clusters, have a bitter flavour that is a good foil to the richness of the spicy curries in which they are most often found. They are also used as a flavouring for *nam prik*.

Hairy Aubergines

Maeuk

Difficult to find outside Thailand, these aubergines are orange in colour and have to have the hairs thoroughly scraped off before being pounded to flavour *nam prik*. They have a sour taste. If you can't find them, any sour fruit can be used as a substitute.

Right: Bamboo shoots are available fresh, but sliced, canned shoots are easier to find.

Above: Tiny pea aubergines are bright green and grow in clusters.

Preparing aubergines

Wash the aubergine and remove the stalk, then cut into slices, strips or chunks. It is seldom necessary to peel an aubergine and the smooth skin not only adds colour, but also provides texture and flavour. Some recipes recommend salting layers of aubergine slices for 30 minutes before cooking. This is not necessary if the vegetables are young and tender.

To prevent the aubergine from absorbing too much oil during cooking, dry-fry slices or strips for 4–5 minutes before frying in oil. This method allows them to retain their succulent texture.

BAMBOO SHOOTS

Nor mai pai tong
The creamy white shoots of some species of the bamboo plant are sold diced, chopped, shredded or whole in cans. Some markets sell the same processed shoots in bulk, usually from large plastic buckets filled with water. Fresh bamboo shoots are rarely seen outside Asia. They can be toxic if not properly pre-boiled, which is a long process. Before using the canned shoots, drain and rinse them well.

BEANS

Long Beans

Thua fak yao
Also called yard-long beans, snake beans, asparagus beans or Thai beans, long beans resemble green beans but are much longer. They don't quite reach the yard (92cm) mark, but many grow up to 40cm/16in. The two common varieties are pale green and dark green, the latter being the more delectable. When choosing long beans, the thinner ones with underdeveloped seeds are the best. These young beans are tender and slightly sweet. They do not have strings, and preparation consists simply of trimming and chopping them into short lengths. As they mature, long beans can become quite tough. Try to use long beans within 3 days of purchase, before they turn yellow.

Below: Long beans are similar in flavour to, but much longer than, green beans.

Winged Beans

Tua phuu
The "wings" that give this pretty vegetable its English name – they are also known as wing beans – are frilled edges that extend along four sides of the long, flat pod. Young pods are crisp and green, becoming tougher and changing to a yellowish-green as they mature. Usually only the young pods are eaten. They can be blanched and served with coconut milk, cooked in oil and eaten with *nam prik*, or sliced finely and used as an ingredient in *tod man, keing phed* and spicy salads. The young shoots and flowers are fried, or may be added to sour spicy soup. The tubers are also edible. Preserved in sugar, they are made into sweetmeats. If the beans are not available, substitute regular green beans or asparagus.

Twisted Cluster Bean

Parkia or *sa-taw*
The seeds of a huge tree that grows in southern Thailand, these beans are about the size of broad (fava) beans. The bright green pods that house them are flat and wavy. The beans themselves have a peculiar smell and nutty taste that give a distinctive flavour to regional dishes. The beans are usually eaten as a vegetable, and they taste good in a sweet-and-sour stir-fry. They are also sometimes roasted and eaten with *nam prik*, and are made into pickles.

BEANSPROUTS

Thua ngok
Many types of bean can be sprouted, but the sprouts most often used in Thai cooking are the small "green" sprouts from mung beans and the larger "yellow" sprouts from soya beans. Soya beansprouts have a stronger flavour than mung beansprouts, but both are relatively delicate, with a pleasant and unique crunchy texture.

Fresh beansprouts are widely available in supermarkets, health-food stores and Asian food stores, or you can easily sprout your own beans at home. Avoid canned beansprouts as they are flaccid and tasteless.

Above: Mung and soya beansprouts are widely used in Thai cooking.

Preparing beansprouts

To prepare fresh beansprouts, rinse them in cold water to remove the husks and tiny roots. They can be eaten raw, blanched or briefly stir-fried. It is important not to overcook them or they will be limp and fibrous, and the characteristic crisp texture will be lost.

Mung beans
These tiny beans are usually green, although some varieties are yellow or black. They are available from Asian shops, supermarkets and health-food stores. They are a good source of protein and vitamins and are used in both savoury dishes and desserts. Soften the dried beans by soaking them in water before cooking.

To sprout mung beans, soak about a quarter of a cup of beans in water overnight. Next day, drain the beans and spread them in a single layer on a piece of wet muslin (cheesecloth) in a roasting pan. Put them somewhere dark and warm, such as the oven when it is not in use. Keep the sprouts at an even temperature of 13–21°C/55–70°F. Make sure that they are kept damp, but not sodden. They will be ready to eat in about 5 days when the shoots are 5cm/2in long.

Above: Baby corn cobs are tender and sweet – the first choice for stir-fries.

BABY CORN COBS

Khaao phot on

Corn is a popular vegetable in Thailand and roasted cobs are often on sale from street vendors. For stir-fries and soups, Thais prefer baby corn cobs, which have a musty sweet flavour, as well as a crunchy texture. They are available fresh and canned. Fresh baby corn cobs are best eaten soon after purchase but can be stored for up to 1 week in the salad drawer of the refrigerator.

Preparation and cooking techniques

If using canned corn cobs, rinse them under cold water and drain them well. They can usually be used whole but if they are quite large, cut them in half lengthways or slice them diagonally into chunks. Take care not to overcook them as they will lose their crisp texture. Blanch fresh corn cobs for 1 minute in lightly salted, boiling water and drain before stir-frying.

PAK CHOI/BOK CHOY

Hua ka-lum pee

This is the most popular variety of cabbage eaten in Thailand. Despite its other name – Chinese white cabbage – pak choi is not uniformly white. The ribbed stems are a beautiful greenish white, which stands out starkly against the lush dark green leaves.

In Thailand, cabbage is often eaten raw with a chilli dipping sauce and is also cooked in stir-fries and soups. Pak choi is usually either thinly sliced or cut into squares and is best cooked briefly.

Right: Pak choi has a wonderfully crisp texture and delightful peppery flavour.

CHINESE LEAVES/CHINESE CABBAGE

Phak kaet khaao-plee

Also known as celery cabbage, this vegetable has soft green and white leaves with a mild, sweet flavour and crisp texture. It is widely available in supermarkets and is easily recognized by its fat, cylindrical shape and tightly packed leaves. When buying, choose specimens that are heavy and firm. Before use, discard any damaged outer leaves and trim the root. Do not worry if the leaves have small black spots on them; they are harmless. This type of cabbage keeps well and can be stored in the salad compartment of the refrigerator for several weeks. It is used in stir-fries, salads and soups.

FLOWERING CABBAGE

Phak kwaang tung

The Chinese name for this type of cabbage is *choi sum*. It is widely grown in the West and is often available from farmers' markets, as well as Asian food stores. The stalks, leaves and yellow flowers of this plant are all edible and have a delicate flavour. The cabbage is usually cut into short lengths and used in soups and noodle dishes, but it may also be stir-fried.

Above: Chinese leaves have a mild and delicate flavour.

CHINESE CELERY

Kean ghai

This is similar to Western celery, but the stems are thinner and much more loosely packed, and their flavour is more pronounced. When choosing Chinese celery, select a head with fat, wide stalks as these will be the most tender. Chop them more finely than you would Western celery, as they tend to be stringy, and use them sparingly or the pungent flavour will dominate. The leaves are often used in soups.

ANGLED LOOFAH

Buap liam

Also known as silk gourd, silk squash or Chinese okra, this dark green vegetable looks like a long, thin courgette (zucchini) or a very large okra pod, and has angular ridges down its length. A close relative, the smooth loofah is paler in colour, larger and more cylindrical, with a slightly thicker base. Both have a

Above: Angled loofah has a sweet, delicate flavour when young.

very mild taste, similar to cucumber, which can be used in its place in most cooked dishes.

The gourds are eaten young, while they are still sweet. They become unpleasantly bitter as they mature. Loofah is used in stir-fries and soups, and is often boiled and eaten with *nam prik*. It goes well with foods that will not overwhelm its delicate flavour, such as chicken, fish and shellfish. It is also a popular ingredient in a large number of vegetable dishes. When a loofah is young, all you need to do is wash and slice it. They seldom need peeling, but sometimes the ridges toughen as the vegetables ripen. If this is the case, remove the ridges, but leave the skin in between, so that the loofah is striped green and white. If the skin is very tough, it is best to peel it completely. Loofah is always eaten cooked, but be careful not to overcook it.

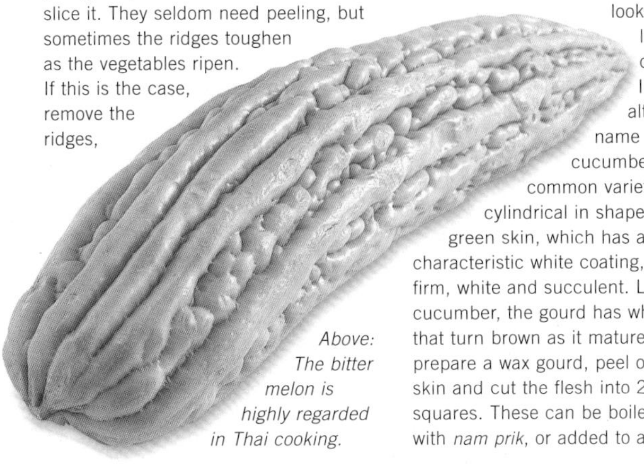

Above: The bitter melon is highly regarded in Thai cooking.

BITTER MELON

Mara

Also known as Chinese bitter gourd, this resembles a knobbly cucumber, with about 10 ridges running along its length. Before it ripens, the melon is pale green in colour, and it is at this stage that its flesh is particularly prized. The Thais believe that it is very good for the kidneys and blood.

When buying bitter melons, look for small, firm specimens that are still green. Do not peel them, simply scrub gently, but thoroughly, cut in half lengthways and scoop out the pulp and seeds. The flesh can be cut into slices or chunks. If the flesh is excessively bitter, layer with salt in a colander and then set aside for 30 minutes. Rinse thoroughly, and pat dry with kitchen paper and add to soups or curries. Alternatively, blanch the slices or chunks in lightly salted, boiling water for about 2 minutes before use.

WAX GOURD/FUZZY MELON

Taeng

These gourds come in several shapes, from a short stubby variety to one that looks like a long, fuzzy cucumber. In fact, an alternative name is hairy cucumber. The most common variety is roughly cylindrical in shape. Under the green skin, which has a characteristic white coating, the flesh is firm, white and succulent. Like a cucumber, the gourd has white seeds that turn brown as it matures. To prepare a wax gourd, peel off the outer skin and cut the flesh into 2.5cm/1in squares. These can be boiled and eaten with *nam prik*, or added to a soup, such as *kaeng liang*, which is flavoured with pork bones. When cooked, wax gourd keeps its shape, but the texture softens so that it has the consistency of soaked bread. It is fairly bland in flavour.

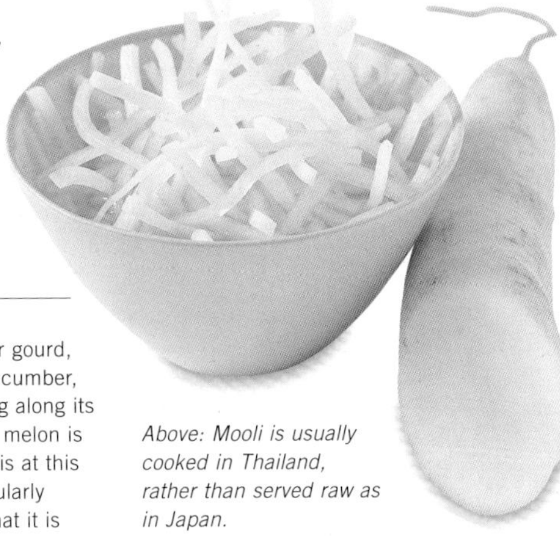

Above: Mooli is usually cooked in Thailand, rather than served raw as in Japan.

MOOLI/DAIKON

Hua phak kaak

Thais value this vegetable, believing that it aids digestion, cools the body and improves blood circulation. Also called giant white radish or winter radish, it is a long white root that resembles a slender, smooth-skinned parsnip in appearance. It can be up to 40cm/16in long, although the Thai variety is often considerably smaller. Large specimens tend to be fibrous and should be avoided. When raw, the flavour of mooli is cool, sharp and peppery, and the texture is crisp. Thais don't often eat it this way, but the grated flesh is sometimes used to tenderize seafood. When the vegetable is cooked, the characteristic texture is retained, but the flavour becomes quite sweet. It resembles turnip, which can be used as a substitute.

To prepare mooli for soups or stews, peel off the outer layer and slice thinly or cut into thin batons. Alternatively, grate the peeled mooli into a bowl, add a few pinches of salt and toss gently, then leave for 2–3 minutes. Tip into a colander, rinse under cold water and squeeze dry before combining with other ingredients in your chosen recipe.

LOTUS ROOT

Rak bua

Fresh lotus roots grow in sausage-like links, each one about 18–23cm/7–9in long. (Strictly speaking, they are rhizomes rather than roots.) Once the mud that coats them has been washed off, a pale beige-pink skin is revealed. When buying fresh lotus roots, choose ones that feel heavy for their size, as this is an indication that they are full of liquid. The crisp flesh has very little aroma, but tastes sweet and has an attractive, crunchy texture. Lotus root is also available canned and frozen, although neither is quite so crunchy as the fresh root.

Before cooking, the thin skin must be peeled, and the root cut into thin discs. Each of these will have a pretty, lacy pattern, resulting from channels in the flesh, and will be sticky with sap. Immediately add them to water that has been acidulated with lemon juice to prevent them from discolouring. For salads and stir-fries, lotus root must first be blanched in boiling water, although it can be added directly to soups or stews. As it cooks, it will sweeten the liquid and turn it a pale pink. Thin slices of lotus root can also be deep-fried to make crisps (US chips). Dry the rounds very thoroughly before adding them to the hot oil.

Below: Fresh lotus roots have pinky beige skin and look like large, linked sausages.

WATER CHESTNUTS

Haew

Nothing beats the crisp texture and nutty, sweet flavour of a fresh water chestnut. The corm of a grass-like plant, water chestnuts are encased in dark brown skin which must be peeled before the familiar white vegetable is revealed. In Thai cooking, water chestnuts are used in salads, stir-fries and even in desserts. Their greatest attribute is the fact that they stay crunchy when cooked.

When buying fresh water chestnuts, squeeze them gently and select only those that feel firm. Canned whole water chestnuts are widely available from Asian stores and supermarkets.

Left: Water chestnuts can be bought fresh as dark brown corms, or canned.

YAM BEAN

Mun kaew

In the Americas, where it originated, this popular vegetable is known as jicama. How it got its other name is perplexing, since it is not related to the yam, nor is it a bean. The vegetable looks like a large brown turnip. The flesh is sweet and crunchy and the flavour is a cross between apple and potato. Yam bean is best eaten raw with a spicy dip, although it is also used in stir-fries and in desserts. It may be eaten as a fruit.

When buying yam beans, choose heavy specimens with unblemished, smooth skins. To prepare, peel off the outer skin, then slice off the fibrous matter until you reach the translucent white flesh beneath. At this stage, the prepared yam bean can be stored in a plastic bag in the refrigerator. It will keep for up to a week. Slice into thin batons for salads or stir-fries.

Right: Despite its name, yam bean is neither a type of yam nor a bean.

TARO

Puak

This root grows wild on the banks of streams in Thailand and is particularly popular in the north of the country. The swollen tuber is full of starch and is eaten in the same manner as potatoes.

Right: Taro is a rough-skinned tuber.

The young leaves can also be eaten. Wear gloves when peeling taros.

ONIONS

Hua hom

Onions are not so popular as shallots in Thai cooking and those that are on sale tend to be fairly small. Yellow in colour, they are quite pungent, with a sweet, peppery flavour. Many Thai dishes are garnished with crisp-fried onion flakes. You can buy these ready-fried onions in tubs from Thai grocery stores.

SPRING ONIONS/SCALLIONS

Ton horm

Spring onions are used in Thai cooking for stir-fries and in soups. They are also popular for garnishes, either sliced or cut into tassels, then curled in iced water.

SHALLOTS

Horn dang

Thai shallots are smaller and much more pungent than those used in the West. Pinkish purple in colour, they are used extensively in Thai cooking to flavour relishes, soups, stews and curries and are also sliced into rings and deep-fried as a garnish (*see right*). Shallots are sweeter, much milder and not so juicy as onions, and they are often used with other aromatic ingredients, such as fresh chillies, garlic and dried shrimp, to make the spice pastes for which Thailand is so famous.

Making crispy shallots

It is very important to deep-fry the shallots slowly or they will not cook evenly. If the oil begins to splatter, reduce the heat and add a few pinches of sea salt.

1 Peel 10–15 Thai shallots, slice them paper-thin and separate the slices into rings.

2 Heat 475ml/16fl oz/2 cups of vegetable oil in a deep frying pan over a medium heat for a few minutes until it is hot, but not smoking. Add the shallots and cook very gently for 15–20 minutes, stirring constantly until the shallots turn golden brown.

3 Remove from the heat and cool slightly, then carefully strain the oil into a large metal bowl. Spread the shallots out on a baking sheet lined with kitchen paper and leave to cool completely. When cold, transfer the shallot rings to a sterilized glass jar and store at room temperature. The shallots should last for up to 1 month. Keep the strained flavoured oil to use in stir-fried dishes.

Above: Shallots from Thailand are small, pinky purple in colour and quite pungent and not so juicy as onions.

Above: Chinese chives have a strong, pungent garlic flavour and are eaten both raw and cooked.

Above: Morning glory, which has a flavour that is reminiscent of spinach, is widely eaten throughout Thailand.

CHINESE CHIVES

Kui chai

These pungent herbs look more like long, flat spring onions than their Western equivalent. The leaves are peppery, crunchy and chewy. They are eaten raw and cooked and are prized for both their texture and flavour. Spring onions can be used as a substitute but they will not have the distinctive garlic taste of Chinese chives.

MORNING GLORY

Pakk boog

This popular leafy plant, also known as water convolvulus or water spinach, is actually a herb. It grows in marshy areas, near rivers and canals, and is related to the morning glory that riots over walls and fences in many European gardens. It has slender, hollow green stems and thin ovate green leaves which are pointed at the ends. In some parts of Asia, the stems are pickled, but in Thailand, only the leaves and tender shoots are eaten. The flavour is similar to that of spinach. In Thailand, the tender tips are often eaten raw, on their own or with other raw vegetables, and served with a selection of hot sauces. When cooked, the stem tips stay firm, but the leaves rapidly become limp. Morning glory is highly perishable and must be used promptly.

MUSHROOMS

Many different varieties of both fresh and dried mushrooms – *hed* – are often used in Thai cooking. As well as cultivated mushrooms, wild mushrooms are gathered during the rainy season, especially in the north of Thailand. These include ceps, chanterelles and russulas, which are used for salads, soups and sauces.

STRAW MUSHROOMS

Hed fang

These delicate, sweet-flavoured mushrooms have acquired their English name because of the method of cultivation on beds of straw. They look like miniature helmets and are the most popular variety of mushroom in Thai cooking. Straw mushrooms are used extensively in soups, salads and curries, and taste particularly good with prawns (shrimp) and crab meat. Canned straw mushrooms are widely available from Asian stores and many supermarkets. They have neither the exquisite flavour nor the texture of the fresh mushrooms, but can be an acceptable substitute. Fresh straw mushrooms are highly perishable and so are not often available in the West. If you do locate them, use them as soon as possible after purchase.

Right: Shiitake mushrooms are available both dried, as preferred by Thai cooks, and fresh.

Below: Canned straw mushrooms, though not as tasty, can be used in place of fresh ones as these are not often available in the West.

SHIITAKE MUSHROOMS

Hed hom

Fresh shiitake mushrooms are available, but Thai cooks prefer to use them dried as they have a stronger flavour and more texture. Both types are available in supermarkets and Asian stores. Dried shiitake mushrooms must be reconstituted in water before being used. The stems are usually discarded and the caps sliced or chopped for adding to soups or stews. The soaking water can be strained and used in a soup or stock as it takes on the flavour of the shiitake. The dried mushrooms will keep well if stored in a sealed plastic tub or bag in a cool, dry place.

DRIED WOOD EAR, TREE EAR OR CLOUD EAR

Hed hunu heang

Although often described as dried mushrooms, these should more accurately be called fungi. They look like dried leaves. When soaked in boiling water, they revive, puff up and stretch into shiny black, rubbery caps. When soaked, the fungus expands to six or eight times its volume, so be sure to use plenty of water. After soaking, leave the mushrooms to cool, then pinch off and discard the hard stems. Drain, rinse well, then drain again, discarding any hard roots and bits of grit. The mushrooms can be cooked whole or thinly sliced for soups and stir-fries. They have a crunchy, chewy texture and a distinctive woody aroma, but will also readily absorb other strong flavours. All these mushrooms are available in Asian supermarkets and some organic stores.

Above: Dried wood ears are valued for their texture. They readily absorb the flavours of other ingredients.

Reconstituting dried mushrooms

To reconstitute dried mushrooms, soak them in boiling water for 20–30 minutes, depending on the variety and size, until tender. Drain and rinse well to remove any grit and dirt. They can now be stir-fried, braised, steamed or used in soups. Dried mushrooms often need to be cooked for a little longer than fresh ones.

Preserved and Pickled Vegetables

Pickles and preserves are usually served in small amounts as a side dish. They are available from Asian stores.

PICKLED GARLIC

Kratiem dorng
In Thailand, peeled heads of garlic are preserved whole in vinegar. Whether eaten whole, thinly sliced or chopped, the crunchy garlic has a complex flavour: sweet, sour, salty and pungent. Both sweet and tart varieties of this pickle can be found in jars or cans, for eating as a relish or for adding flavour to meat, noodle dishes and sauces. The pickling liquid is often added to soups or salad dressings as well. It will keep for several months in the refrigerator.

PICKLED GINGER

King dorng
As well as being an attractive garnish, the sweet taste and crunchy texture of pickled ginger makes it a good choice for adding interest to spicy Thai dishes. Very fine slices or pieces of tender young ginger, often intricately carved, are first soaked and cured with sea salt and fresh lime juice. This transforms the natural off-white colour of the flesh to a startling pink. The ginger is then pickled in a mixture of sugar and vinegar before being bottled. There are two varieties available, one is pale pink, which is the best type, and the other is bright red.

Below: Pickled mango has a lovely crisp texture and salty, sweet flavour.

Above: Bamboo shoots pickled in brine have a salty, sour taste and a pleasant chewy, yet crunchy, texture.

PICKLED CABBAGE

Pat gat dorng
Chopped crunchy white cabbage is pickled in vinegar, salt and sugar for a minimum of 3 days. It is served as a relish or added to dishes while cooking to give a salty, slightly sour flavour.

SALTED CABBAGE

Pak kad khem
Sometimes called preserved cabbage, and used to flavour Chinese Thai dishes, this condiment can be made from several different types of cabbage, which are shredded and preserved with salt and garlic. The most popular Thai salted cabbage, *Tang Chai*, originated in the Chinese district of Tianjin. The cabbage was originally stuffed into squat, round clay crocks, but the Thai variety is now packaged in a clear plastic jar. It keeps for a long time and is used to add flavour and texture to soups, noodles or egg dishes.

PICKLED BAMBOO SHOOTS

Nor mai dorng
In Thailand, bamboo shoots are only available fresh in the rainy season (May–October). During the dry season, pickled (or canned) bamboo shoots are used. Once open, jars of bamboo shoots should be stored in the refrigerator for up to 1 month. Before use, rinse the bamboo shoots in several changes of cold water and drain well.

SALTED MOOLI/DAIKON

Ho chai pok
These look like long beige rubber tubes. When sliced into long strands, they reveal a crunchy texture that adds interest to soups and noodle dishes. There are two varieties: one very salty, the other slightly sweetened. Before use, rinse the mooli in water to moderate the saltiness. Store unused mooli in its wrapper in the refrigerator.

SALTED PLUMS

Giem bouy
These dried shrivelled plums are about the same size as olives. They are greyish brown and covered in a fine layer of salt. They are sold in decorative clear plastic containers or wrapped in cellophane. Salted plums are used to flavour steamed fish or other Thai dishes. The plums and juice are used to make a sweet and sour dipping sauce.

PICKLED MANGO

Ma muang dorng
Mango, either peeled or unpeeled, may be placed in salt water for a few days until discoloured. Salted, sun-dried mango slices (*ma muang khem*) are thought to help prevent sickness.

Below: Salted plums, which are used to as a flavouring, are found in the confectionery section of Asian stores.

FRUIT

BANANAS

Kluai

Indigenous to Thailand, bananas have been cultivated for thousands of years. The banana plant is actually a huge herb. The fruit grows in bunches, which point upwards through the fan-like leaves. The leaves can be used as plates, or folded into containers for food. The stem makes a delicious curry and the buds, when cooked, taste like artichokes. Small wonder that bunches of bananas are left as offerings to the spirits, or used in religious ceremonies.

Over 30 different varieties of banana grow in Thailand, from small rice bananas to the large, bright yellow Cavendish Gros Michael. Colours range from palest cream to red, and shapes from slender fingers to plump lozenges to boomerang curves. The flavour of the flesh varies, too, from mild to sweet and fragrant.

Dessert bananas can be eaten as they are. The mashed fruit is easily digested and is particularly good for babies or the elderly. Bananas can also be cooked in their peel over a brazier, baked or made into sweetmeats. Thais transform them into delicious desserts, including bananas cooked in coconut milk (*kluat buat chi*) and a tasty delicacy made from ripe bananas wrapped in a mixture of moist glutinous rice and flour (*kluithod*).

Cooking bananas, or plantains, have firm pinkish flesh. They must be cooked before being eaten. In Thailand they are used in curries and are also made into a popular snack in which they are peeled, dipped in a coconut milk and rice flour batter, then deep-fried.

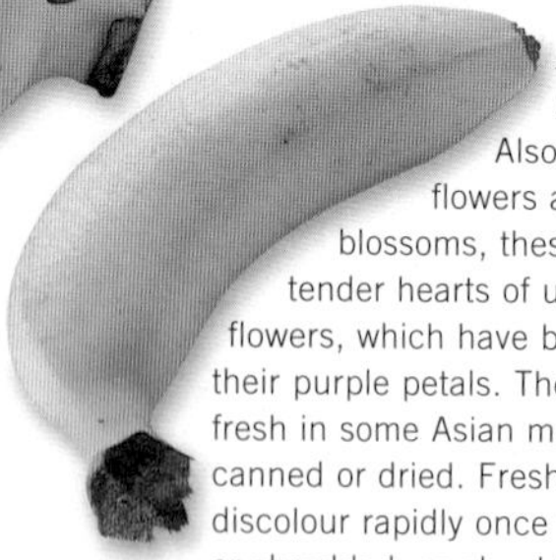

Above: Tiny Lady Finger bananas, or sugar bananas as they are also known because of their sweet flesh, are often no more than 7.5cm/3in long.

BANANA BUDS

Hua plee

Also called banana flowers and banana blossoms, these are in fact the tender hearts of unopened banana flowers, which have been stripped of their purple petals. They are available fresh in some Asian markets and also canned or dried. Fresh banana buds discolour rapidly once they are sliced or shredded, so should be brushed with lemon juice to prevent this. Banana buds are used in northern Thailand to make a tasty, squash soup. They are also a popular salad ingredient, tasting rather like artichokes.

Right: When very ripe, small apple bananas have a faint taste and aroma of fresh apple.

Above: At the heart of the banana flower lies the delicate banana bud.

Banana leaves

These large pliable green leaves are used extensively in Thai cooking to wrap food for steaming, roasting and grilling (broiling). During the cooking process the leaves impart a mild smoky flavour to the food. Sometimes they will tinge it a very light green, as well. The leaves are also used for presentation, as mats, for lining dishes, as platters and to make attractive containers that can be secured with bamboo picks.

Below: Banana leaves are not eaten but have many uses.

PAPAYAS

Malako

Native to South America, the papaya, or paw-paw, has been adopted by Thai cooks. The two main varieties available in Thailand are *khak nuan*, a blunt cylindrical papaya with a yellow skin and sweet orange flesh, and *wuak dam*, also cylindrical but with a pointed end. Its skin and sweet flesh is reddish.

Ripe papaya is often served simply sprinkled with lime juice. The unripe fruit is usually treated as a vegetable, and may be boiled or enjoyed raw in salads or as a relish.

Choose ripe fruit that is uniformly orange or, if you do not plan to use it straight away, slightly firm fruit with green skin that is turning orange. The fruit will continue to ripen in a dark place. Avoid bruised or shrivelled fruit and handle with care, as papayas are easily damaged. Ripe papayas will keep for about 1 week in the refrigerator.

To prepare, simply cut the fruit in half and scoop out the black seeds.

MANGOES

Ma muang

There are several varieties of mango available in Thailand, some grown as dessert fruit; others for eating or cooking while still green. *Ok-rong* is a dessert fruit with a pale yellow skin. It is a small variety that fits easily in the palm of the hand.

Above: Papayas are widely used in both sweet and savoury dishes throughout Thailand.

Although it is somewhat stringy, the very sweet and fragrant flavour makes *ok-rong* an excellent companion for coconut sticky rice. Another popular variety is the *nam dawg mai* (meaning "nectar of flowers"), a delightfully fragrant, juicy mango. The skin is smooth and thin, enclosing delicate, string-free flesh around a thin seed. The mango most often eaten green is *ma-muang mun*. This has a nutty taste, unlike the very sour young green mangoes used in sauces and salads.

A ripe mango should yield when pressed. Ripe mangoes can be stored in the refrigerator for several days.

GUAVAS

Farang

Many varieties of this fruit are found in Thailand. The most popular is the lemon guava. This round greenish-yellow fruit weighs about 225g/8oz and has a hard white flesh with small whitish-brown seeds that are generally discarded before eating. The Thais eat the fruit before it becomes over-ripe and develops its characteristic acidic, scented flavour. At this stage, the flesh is crisp and tastes rather bland, but is good dipped in a chilli sauce.

Above: Guavas are scented with a sweet-sharp flavour.

When buying guavas, look for firm (not hard) fruits, that are apple green to yellow in colour. Make sure that the skin is intact and handle them carefully, as they are quite fragile. Guavas will keep at room temperature for 3–4 days or in the refrigerator for about 1 week.

To prepare the fruit, cut it in half, remove the seeds, squeeze over a little lemon juice, then scoop out the flesh with a teaspoon. Alternatively, the flesh can be cut into segments or slices and served with salt or ground chillies for dipping. For a simple dessert, sprinkle slices with sugar, cover closely and leave to stand overnight.

RAMBUTANS

Ngoh

These fruits are so popular and such an important crop that the Thais dedicate a special day to the rambutan in August. It looks a little like a sweet chestnut, but with a hairy, red, green, yellow or even orange skin, depending on the variety. The flesh, which surrounds a large stone (pit), is a transluscent white with a sweet flavour. The sweetest variety is the *rongrian*. When buying rambutans, look for brightly coloured fruits with hairs that are tipped with green. They keep for up to a week in the refrigerator.

Below: Rambutans have a distinctive skin covered in soft spiky hairs.

Left: Longans are a very common fruit in Thailand and clusters of the little brown fruits can often be seen piled up in markets.

Above: Mangosteens have a fragrant, delicate flavour and are best eaten raw.

LYCHEES

Lin-chi

Another import from China, there are about 20 different varieties of lychee cultivated in Thailand and they are an important export crop. The knobbly, reddish, brittle skin encloses a white, juicy flesh that is slightly fibrous. In the centre of the fruit is a relatively large mahogany-coloured shiny seed. Lychees have a wonderfully scented aroma and a flavour similar to that of a muscat grape; they make a refreshing end to a meal. When buying lychees, look for firm, unmarked shells. They can be stored at room temperature for about 3 days, or in the refrigerator for up to 1 week.

Above: Lychees have a wonderful sweet, scented flavour.

LONGANS

Lamyai

This fruit was first introduced to Thailand at the end of the 19th century from China, although it is probably a native of Southern India. It is closely related to the lychee and the flesh has a similar, appearance and texture, though less pronounced flavour. Longans are small and round with a light brown, brittle skin. When they are in season, clusters of the little brown fruits are piled on the pavements (sidewalks), ready to be sold by vendors. Buy fruit on the stalk, if possible, and check that the skins have no defects. Because of their high sugar content, the fruits go off quite quickly. Longans can be kept in the refrigerator for 4–5 days. Surprisingly, they can also be frozen successfully.

LANGSATS AND DUKUS

Langsat and *long gong*

These two fruits are both classified as *Lansium domesticum* although they can be easily distinguished from one another. Both fruits are egg-shaped and grow in bunches. The duku is slightly larger than the langsat, with a thicker skin. It has only about ten fruits to a bunch, whereas the langsat has about 20 fruits in a cluster. The flesh of both fruits is generally white, but in some varieties of duku it may be pink. The taste ranges from sour to sweet, and it is juicy and refreshing. Both fruits can be eaten raw and they are also preserved in sugar. They are sometimes served on a bed of ice. Select clusters of fruit with smooth, yellowish, taut skin. Both langsats and dukus can be stored in the refrigerator for about 5 days.

MANGOSTEENS

Mangkhut

The mangosteen is a native of South-east Asia and is grown commercially in Thailand. It's rather clumsy-looking exterior belies the wonder of the fruit inside. Mangosteens are quite small, about the size of a plum, with a thick, deep purple skin that encloses segments of creamy, pink-veined flesh. The flesh is very sweet, and has a mouthwateringly sharp, scented flavour, suggestive of peaches and grapes.

Until recently mangosteens were not widely available in the West. Choose firm large fruits that have a slight give to them when pressed. They will keep for up to 2 weeks in the refrigerator.

PASSION FRUIT

Saowarot

The fruits of the passion flower vine have been cultivated in Thailand for only about 60 years. They are about the same size as a large plum. The leathery skin is either brown or yellowish orange. Inside are edible dark seeds in a sweet, fragrant jelly-like pulp with a slightly lemony tang. In Thailand passion fruit juice is a popular drink. The seeds are eaten, too, usually with a sprinkling of salt. Older fruits tend to become very wrinkled, so look for fruits with smooth unblemished skin. They will keep in a cool place for 1 week.

CUSTARD APPLES

Noina

Originally from Latin America, custard apples, also known as cherimoyas, were introduced to Thailand some 300 years ago. Externally the fruit looks like a small cluster of tightly packed green grapes. It splits easily into two segments to reveal white flesh interspersed with hard, inedible, glossy brown seeds. When ripe, the flesh is sweet and creamy, which is how the fruit acquired its name. Custard apples are used in ices, drinks and desserts.

When buying custard apples, choose fruit that gives slightly when squeezed. They can be stored in the refrigerator for 5–7 days.

ROSE APPLES

Chomphu

Thailand has several different varieties of this fruit, which is also known as the water apple. It is prized for its thirst-quenching nature, rather than for the flavour, which tends to be rather bland. The *tubtimjan* rose apple is oblong and skinless. The skin is red and the flesh crisp and sweet. The *phetch* rose apple is bell-shaped with a seed in the centre. The firm, juicy flesh is sweet and slightly tangy. Rose apples are seldom sold outside their native land.

CARAMBOLAS

Mafuang

Known as the star fruit in the West, the carambola is a bright yellow fruit with a bland, slightly sharp flavour. The fruit has a waxy-looking skin that forms five lobes or "fins", which, when cut widthways, make star-shaped slices. These make an excellent garnish for fish or poultry.

Right: Sapodillas have a dull, matt skin, but inside is a wonderfully sweet, flavoursome flesh.

Carambolas are widely available in large supermarkets and Asian stores. When buying, look for shiny-skinned fruits with taut, unmarked skins. They can be stored for 2–3 days in a plastic bag in the refrigerator.

PITAYA

Gaew mungkorn

Also known as dragon fruit, these are very pretty. About 10cm/4in long, they have bright pink or yellow skin, covered with green-tipped scales. The flesh, which is white, and speckled with tiny, edible seeds, tastes rather like melon and the seeds add an interesting crunch. When ripe, pitayas should yield to gentle pressure. They are best eaten chilled. Cut the fruit in half, squeeze over a little lime juice and serve with a teaspoon to scoop out the flesh.

SAPODILLAS

Lamut

About the same size as a kiwi fruit and similar in texture, albeit with a browny orange skin, the sapodilla has sweet flesh with a honey/caramel flavour. Peel the fruit with a knife, then use the knife tip to flick out the inedible seeds from the flesh. The Thais enjoy sapodillas with a squeeze of fresh lime juice as a dessert fruit. When buying, select unbroken fruit that yields slightly when pressed. Sapodillas can be stored in the refrigerator for up to 5 days.

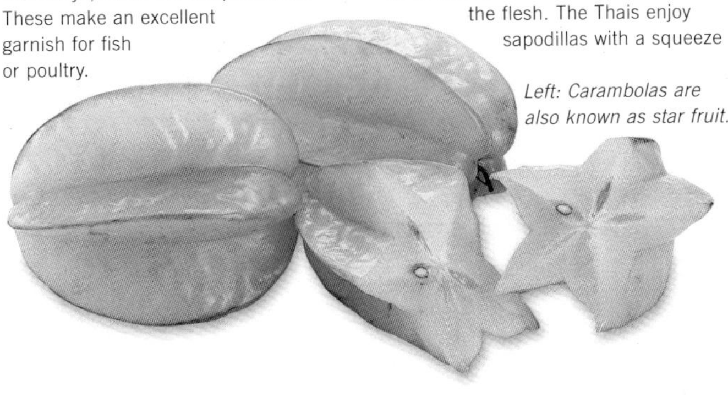

Left: Carambolas are also known as star fruit.

JUJUBES

Phutsa

These fruits are about the same size and shape as plums. They have green, shiny skin, slightly mottled with sienna. Beneath the skin, which is edible, is crisp, white flesh surrounding a single, large stone (pit). The flavour resembles that of an unripe pear: sweet, yet with a hint of sharpness. The firmness of the fruit makes it excellent for carving into elegant garnishes. Buy fruits with smooth unmarked skins. Jujubes will keep for 3–4 days at room temperature.

Below: Jujubes have crisp flesh that is rather like that of an unripe pear.

Above: Limes are a very popular flavouring in Thai cooking.

SWEET TAMARIND

Makman wan

This bean-like fruit, has irregular pods 7.5–15cm/3–6in in length. Inside these, the flesh is white and sweet, with a number of brown seeds. When young, the fruit is frequently eaten in Thailand, usually with a spicy dipping sauce. Fresh tamarind is also used in soups. (*See also* Herbs, Spices and Aromatics.)

LIMES

Manao

These small green and very sour citrus fruits are used extensively throughout Thailand. Thin slices of lime may be used as a counterbalance to very sweet fruits, such as mango and papaya. Fresh lime juice is valued as a drink, served with salt and sugar, and is also used in salad dressings.

KAFFIR LIMES

Makrut

These have almost no juice but their aromatic rind is grated and used in savoury dishes. Kaffir lime leaves are an essential flavouring in Thai cooking. They have a lemony fragrance and are shredded and added to soups, fish and chicken dishes. Buy unblemished, unwrinkled specimens. They will keep in the refrigerator for up to 1 month, or can be frozen. The leaves are sold in bags.

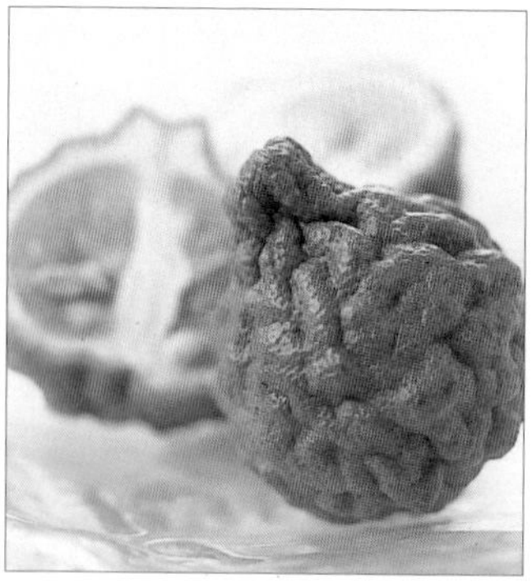

Above: It is the aromatic rind and fragrant leaves of the kaffir lime that are valued in Thai cooking.

ORANGES

Som tra

In Thailand, two main varieties of orange are available: the sweet orange, which has a green/orange skin and sweet, juicy yellow or orange flesh; and the tangerine, with its easily separated segments, sweet flesh and tart flavour. Select fruits with shiny skins and make sure there are no splits or bruises. Oranges should be stored at room temperature and will keep for at least 1 week.

POMELOS

Som-o

The largest member of the citrus family – a single pomelo can weigh as much as 1kg/2¼lb. Several varieties are grown in Thailand, but the most popular, because of their sweetness, are the *khao hom* and the *thongdi*. Both are spherical. The *khao hom* has a greenish-yellow rind and cream-coloured flesh, while the *thongdi* has a dark green rind and sweet and juicy pink flesh. Like papaya, pomelo is a popular breakfast fruit and it is also paired with spicy dishes as a foil to the hot flavours. Choose firm, smooth-skinned fruits with a little give when squeezed. Whole, unpeeled fruits should keep well at room temperature for about 1 month.

Above: Pineapples are an important crop in Thailand.

Below: Jackfruit can weigh up to 40kg/88lb.

PINEAPPLES

Sapparot

In Thailand, there are two main varieties: the *phuket* with its brownish-yellow skin and sweet flesh and the *pattawia*, a larger fruit which is dark green and not quite so sweet. The raw fruit and the juice are very popular but pineapple is also used in cooked sweet and savoury dishes. When buying, sniff the fruit – a ripe pineapple will smell fragrant and sweet – and make sure that the plume of leaves looks green and fresh. Fresh pineapple will keep in a cool place for up to a week. To prepare pineapple, cut off the leaves, then quarter lengthways or cut in slices. Remove the skin and "eyes".

WATERMELONS

Taeng mo

The juicy flesh of this large, round fruit is very refreshing. The thick green rind and pink flesh make it a popular fruit for carving and may be the feature on a banquet table. When buying, choose a firm fruit that reverberates slightly when knocked. To serve, cut it in wedges and remove the shiny black seeds. The flesh can also be diced or sliced and makes a tasty salad. After cutting, leftover melon should be wrapped in clear film (plastic wrap) and then stored in the refrigerator for up to 3 days.

DURIANS

Thurian

These huge fruits can weigh as much as 10kg/22lb. The khaki green skin is covered with fat spikes. Inside is firm yellow flesh surrounding large seeds. Its unpleasant, pungent smell has been likened to that of raw sewage and over-ripe blue cheese. Despite the smell, locals consider the durian to be the king of fruits and it is regarded as an aphrodisiac, much sought after during the season. The variety called *mon tong* is the best and most expensive. The flavour of the flesh is exquisite and most people find that once they start eating the fruit the smell is no longer a problem. When buying durian, look for firm, whole fruits, avoiding any that are split, as the flesh rapidly rots when exposed to the air. They should be kept at room temperature for 3–5 days. Keep durians well away from other foods or, even better, outside the house because of their overpowering odour.

Above:
Watermelon has a high water content, making it very refreshing.

To prepare, the shell must be cut into large segments, following the natural indentations on the side. This will reveal the large seeds each covered with sticky, cream-coloured pulp which can then be spooned out. The seeds can be roasted and eaten.

JACKFRUIT

Khanun

In appearance, jackfruit resemble durians although they are less spiky. When ripe, jackfruit have a greenish-yellow prickly skin, which should be taut. The fruit should give off a mild fragrance; an overpowering odour indicates that the fruit is over-ripe.

The creamy flesh is redolent of pineapple and banana. Succulent and sweet, it tastes rather like banana and is excellent served with ice cream or mixed with other fruits in a fruit salad. It can also be used as a vegetable. The seeds can be roasted and eaten.

To prepare jackfruit, cut it into sections and remove the seeds. Wrap it closely and keep in the refrigerator for 3–5 days if not using immediately, or freeze for 2–3 months.

Coconut and Coconut Products

Coconut palms grow throughout Thailand – and all of South-east Asia. They fringe the golden beaches, surround small villages and soften the silhouettes of palaces and temples.

Coconuts are a very important resource for the Thais. The palm fronds are woven into mats or baskets or used as simple roofing material; the fibrous outer husks that protect the nuts can be used as fuel or made into mats or ropes; the young shoots are a delicious ingredient in curries and the blossoms are a source of sugar. As for the coconut itself, the hard shell can be used as a simple drinking or eating vessel, made into a utensil or carved to make an ornament or piece of jewellery. The nutritious milk can be drunk or used in curries and desserts, and the nut can be eaten as it is, or transformed into oil, and even sunscreens.

Young coconuts contain a jelly-like substance that is the immature flesh. This is delicious eaten straight from a freshly picked green nut. The juice is a refreshing cooling beverage on a hot day. As the nut ripens, the flesh becomes harder and attaches itself to the inside of the shell. The flesh can be used to make coconut cream or milk. It can also be made into sweetmeats such as *kanom bah bin* (coconut cake).

Coconuts are generally sold without their outer husks, as these increase transport costs. When buying, look for nuts that are undamaged and check the three eyes for mould. The nut should feel heavy and when you shake it, you should be able to hear the liquid sloshing around. Older fruits tend to have a little less juice and the flesh may even have become rancid.

Asian stores and supermarkets sell a wide range of coconut products. Most people are familiar with packets of desiccated (dry unsweetened shredded) coconut, but you can also purchase cans and cartons of coconut milk and ready-to-use cream. Some of these may be sweetened with sugar, so do check the labels. Blocks of creamed coconut, if available, can easily be reconstituted with boiling water.

Opening a coconut

The best method involves using the blunt edge of a heavy cleaver. Working over a bowl, which you've placed in the kitchen sink, hold the nut in the palm of one hand, with the "eyes" just above your thumb. The fault line lies between the eyes. Firmly tap the nut all around the fruit line until it splits in two. Pour any remaining liquid into the bowl. Prise out the pieces of fresh coconut. The brown skin can then be removed with a vegetable peeler.

To store the flesh, place it in a container and cover with water or the liquid from the nut. Cover tightly and keep in the refrigerator.

Cooking with coconut milk and cream

Coconut milk tends to be added at the beginning, while coconut cream is usually stirred in towards the end, to avoid it curdling. The single exception to this is when coconut cream is used as a frying medium when cooking a spice paste in preparation for making a Thai curry.

Left: Coconut is amazingly versatile and is a valuable crop.

Making coconut cream or milk

1 Chop the white flesh from a fresh coconut very finely in a food processor or grate it. Place the coconut in a large heatproof bowl and pour over hot but not boiling water. Steep for 10 minutes.

2 Strain the mixture through a fine sieve, lined with muslin (cheesecloth) into another bowl.

3 Squeeze any remaining liquid out of the flesh. This first pressing will produce rich, creamy milk. For pure coconut cream, allow the liquid to settle. As with dairy milk, the cream will rise to the surface and can be skimmed off.

TOFU AND SOYA PRODUCTS

This excellent and inexpensive protein food was invented by the Chinese and is now widely enjoyed throughout the world as a healthy alternative to fish and meat. It is low in sugar and fat.

Tofu – *tow hoo* – is a product of the yellow soya bean. The beans are soaked, husked and pounded with water to produce soya milk. The milk is then filtered, boiled and curdled, using gypsum, to produce the solid cakes of bean curd we know as tofu.

Two types of fresh tofu are now widely available. Silken tofu is very soft and is often used in soups. The firmer white cakes of tofu can stand up to more rigorous handling, although even these need to be handled with care. Both types come packaged in water, either in tubs or vacuum packed. Ideally, tofu should be used straight away, but, if it is kept submerged in water, which is changed daily, it can be stored in the refrigerator for 3–4 days.

There are several other tofu products that are also popular in Thai cooking.

Right: (clockwise from top) Pressed, silken and firm tofu.

PRESSED TOFU

Taohu kao

This is a fresh bean curd cake that has had almost all the moisture squeezed out of it, leaving a solid block with a smooth texture. Brown outside and white inside, it is often seasoned with soy sauce and may also be smoked. You can press your own cakes of tofu by placing the bean curd between two plates. Weigh down the top one. Tilt the plates slightly to allow the liquid to drain off. Pressed tofu can be sliced and stir-fried.

DRIED BEAN CURD SKIN

Fong taohu hang

This can also be purchased at Asian food stores. It consists of thin sheets of curd that are skimmed off simmering soya milk and dried. They are sold flat or rolled to form bean curd sticks. The skins can be used in casseroles, soups or stir-fries, while the sticks are popular in vegetarian dishes. Dried bean curd skins need to be soaked in cold water before they can be used. The sheets require 1–2 hours, but the sticks should be soaked for several hours, preferably overnight.

Left: Pressed tofu has a firm texture and is used in the classic pad Thai *(fried noodles).*

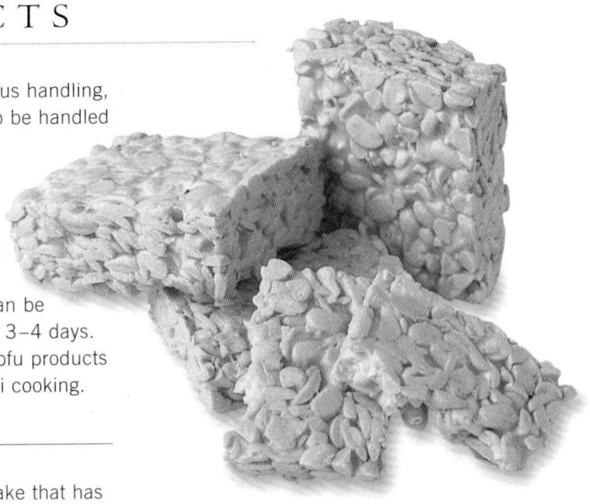

Above: Originally from Indonesia, Tempeh is now popular in Thai cooking.

DEEP-FRIED TOFU

Tau hoo tod

When tofu is deep-fried in hot oil, it puffs up and turns golden brown, the flavour intensifies and the texture becomes chewy. Cubes of deep-fried tofu are sold in Asian markets. Store in the refrigerator and use within 3 days. The cubes absorb other flavours well, and they make a good meat substitute, especially in a stir-fry.

PICKLED TOFU OR BEAN PASTE

Tow hoo yee

This product is made by fermenting fresh tofu, then drying it in the sun before marinating it in an alcohol mixture. The curd can be red or white and the flavour is extremely powerful. The best pickled bean curd comes from China and is sold in bottles or jars.

TEMPEH

This solid bean curd is an Indonesian speciality made by fermenting cooked soya beans with a cultured starter. It resembles firm tofu, but has a slightly nutty, more savoury taste. It benefits from a marinade.

FISH

Thailand is a country blessed with an abundance of fish. In the northern part of the country, most of it comes from freshwater sources – canals, rivers, paddy fields, lakes and ponds. Along the coast, from the border with Cambodia in the south-east to the tip of the narrow southern peninsula flanked by the Indian Ocean and the Gulf of Thailand, seafood of all different kinds is caught in plentiful amounts.

Thai fish is prepared in several ways, depending on the type. Meaty fish is usually fried with lots of pepper and garlic or chilli sauce, sometimes it is wrapped in a banana leaf and either grilled (broiled) or barbecued (grilled), and the more delicate fleshed fish are often steamed with chillies, lime juice and other aromatic ingredients.

FRESHWATER FISH

Several varieties of fish are to be found in the inland waterways in Thailand.

SERPENT HEAD FISH

Pla chorn

This is a fierce-looking fish with a huge mouth full of sharp teeth. During the rainy season farmers catch quite large serpent head fish in their paddy fields, even though the water is only 35–40cm/14–16in deep. The flesh of this fish is rather bland, but it takes on the seasonings of the dish. It is famously used in *pla chorn pae za*, when it is steamed before being served in soup stock, with lime juice and salted plums. It is also used in the soup *tom yam*. The fish can be sun-dried then deep-fried and served with a spicy dip.

Below: Catfish is a fierce-looking fish, which can be cooked in a variety of ways.

CATFISH

Pla doog

The common catfish is about 30cm/12in long. It is very widely distributed throughout the north of Thailand. A favourite way of cooking it is to deep-fry pieces until crisp, then stir-fry them with a spicy chilli paste and other ingredients. Catfish is also used in curries and as the basis of a hot-and-sour salad called *yum pla doong foo*. In addition to the common catfish, there is a slightly smaller version – *pla boo* – which is usually steamed and served whole in soy sauce or lime juice.

TILAPIA

Pla nin

This popular and appetizing fish is farmed throughout Thailand. A mature fish weighs about 500g/1¼lb. One of the most popular restaurant dishes using this fish is *pla nin towd rad prig*, where the fish is deep-fried and then served in a slightly sweet sauce flavoured with mild chillies. Tilapia is also used in the pungent Thai curry called *kaeng som*, and sometimes you will find *haw mok pla nin*, a spicy but flavourful dish where the fish is mixed with condiments and coconut milk and steamed in a banana leaf. Another popular method of eating tilapia is to fry the skin. The scales are first removed and the skin is cut into short narrow strips and then deep-fried. It is served as finger food, often seasoned with lime juice or a slice of onion.

Below: Tilapia has firm white flesh with an extremely good flavour.

GREY FISH

Pla grai

This is a bony grey-coloured fish about 60cm/24in long with pronounced "eye" markings in its soft underbelly. The flesh is of a very soft texture and this is usually removed from the bone and mixed with chillies and other seasonings before being formed into fish cakes. The cakes are deep-fried and served with a sweet, spicy dipping sauce as an appetizer or snack.

TROUT

Pla wan

Although trout is not an indigenous fish of Thailand it is now being farmed as it has become so popular with restaurants all over the country. The delicate and mild-flavoured flesh of this fish is regarded by Thais as a sophisticated alternative to many of the local freshwater varieties. In Thailand, trout is cooked in a variety of different ways but one of the most popular methods is to deep-fry the fish and serve it with a strong chilli sauce – *pla nuea orn*.

SEA FISH

Off the coast of Thailand, in the Indian Ocean to the south-east and the Gulf to the west of the southern peninsula, there are enormous numbers of all kinds of sea fish.

RED SNAPPER

Pla krapong daeng

More than 250 species of snapper are found in the warm seas around the world and the red-skinned variety eaten in Thailand is found in the Indian Ocean. In Thai markets, red snapper is usually sold as fillets, because it is so bony. It is generally either steamed "Chinese-style" with lime juice or soy sauce or deep-fried and covered with chopped mild chillies, or combined with a coconut-based curry paste.

SEA BASS

Pla krapang khan

This versatile fish has a fine-flavoured firm white flesh that is suited to most cooking methods. The soft delicate flesh of this fish makes it ideal for steaming. An excellent way to do this is to marinate the whole fish in spices and wrap it in a banana leaf before cooking it over coals.

Above: White pomfret has tender, fine-flavoured flesh that divides easily into fillets. The soft fin and tail can also be eaten.

Below: Sea bass is an ideal fish for cooking whole, and it is excellent wrapped in a banana leaf and then steamed.

Below: Mackerel are delicious when extremely fresh and they are a popular choice for steaming and frying.

MACKEREL

Pla to

Although it is sometimes wrongly referred to as tuna, this small oily fish is very popular in the markets where it is often displayed on rattan trays. For *nam prig pla tu*, the steamed fish is pounded in a mortar with curry paste and hot chillies to make a chilli sauce. Mackerel is also steamed or fried with a chilli paste flavoured with shrimp paste.

Salted mackerel is dried and packed in oil. It has a very salty taste but a small amount fried, sprinkled with chilli, sliced shallots and lime juice makes a perfect accompaniment to a rice dish.

WHITE POMFRET

Pla jaramed

This is a good, firm-fleshed flat fish with a tasty flavour. These small silvery-skinned fish are shaped like a crescent moon and have curved forked tails not unlike those of a flat fish. The fish are 30–50cm/12–20in in length. They have very few scales and no pelvic fins, making them easy to clean and prepare. The firm texture of the flesh makes these fish ideal for steaming, with aromatic ingredients such as root ginger and spring onions (scallions), which highlight its delicious taste. It can also be prepared like red snapper, or fried and covered with curry sauce or other spicy sauces.

SHELLFISH

The coastal waters that surround Thailand are a wonderful source of shellfish of all types, from prawns (shrimp) to mussels, clams, crayfish, lobsters and scallops. Crabs are eaten with tremendous relish, whether they come from the sea or from fresh water.

PRAWNS/SHRIMP

Gung foi

Prawns are also abundantly used in Thai cooking, whether grilled (broiled), added to a *tom yam* soup, curried, stir-fried with tamarind or served satay-style. Fermented shrimp are used to make a paste and dried shrimp are also an important ingredient.

Deveining and peeling prawns

This is a simple technique. Once mastered, it will speed up your preparation of prawns considerably.

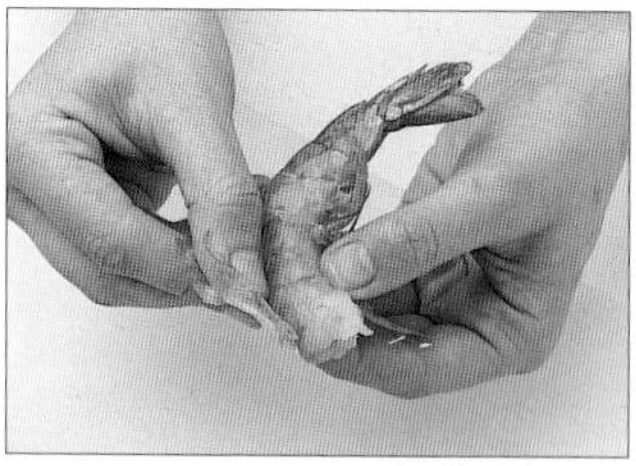

1 Twist off and remove the head, then slice off the tip of the tail. With both thumbs, pull the shell apart from beneath, then discard it, with the legs.

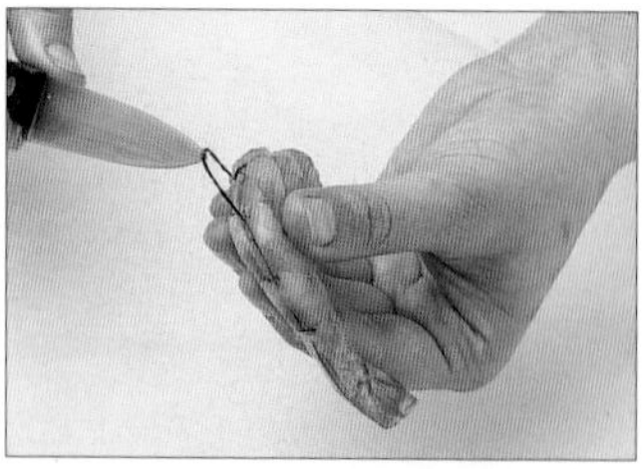

2 With a sharp knife, make a tiny incision down the back of each prawn.

3 Remove the black intestinal cord with the tip of the knife or a pair of tweezers. Rinse the shelled prawn under cold water and pat dry before cooking.

Butterflied prawns

This attractive way to prepare prawns also speeds up the cooking process.

1 Remove the heads and shells of the prawns but leave the tails intact. Slit the backs and devein.

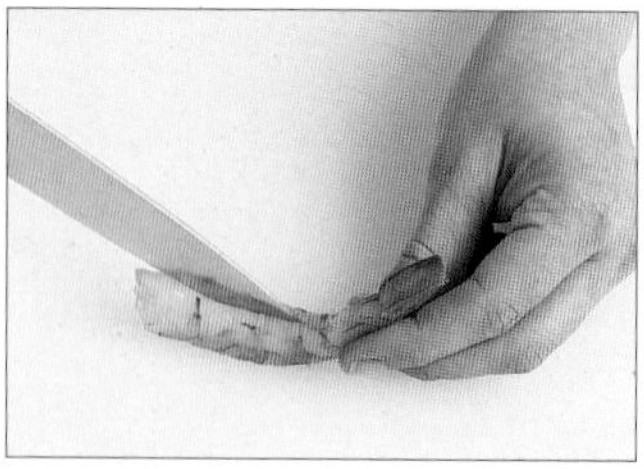

2 Make a cut through the underside of each prawn, then open the two halves of the prawn so they look like wings.

Shrimp balls

Look chin bla

These little shrimp dumplings can be purchased fresh or frozen in Thai markets. They can be used in soups or curries, grilled (broiled), cooked on the barbecue or deep-fried. Shrimp balls are made from puréed shrimps and are usually flavoured with garlic and Thai fish sauce. The mixture is formed into balls and cooked for a few minutes in boiling water. Shrimp balls will keep for about 1 day in a covered container in the refrigerator, or they can be frozen for up to 3 months.

Below: Raw prawns vary in colour.

Below: Prawns turn scarlet on cooking whatever their size, variety and original colour.

Above: Mussels and clams are often combined in a Thai dish.

MUSSELS, CLAMS AND OYSTERS

Hoi malang puu, hoi, hoi naang rom

Mussels and clams frequently feature on the Thai menu. They are served together in a popular dish flavoured with lemon grass and coconut cream. Mussels, steamed with Thai herbs, is another simple but very successful speciality. Oysters are often used with other shellfish to make a seafood salad. They are blanched in boiling water for about 30 seconds, then drained and tossed in a spicy dressing with fresh herbs and served warm.

Preparing mussels

When buying mussels or other bivalves such as clams or oysters, make sure that they come from clean, unpolluted waters. If the mussels have been farmed, it will probably not be necessary to purge them to rid them of sand, but if you have harvested the mussels yourself, clean them thoroughly then soak the mussels for several hours in a bucket of water to which you have added a little flour or oatmeal.

Check the mussels to make sure that the shells are tightly closed. Any that remain open should shut immediately if you tap them. If they don't, throw them away. Scrub the shells thoroughly and pull off the hairy "beards".

To open the shells, place the mussels in a pan with a small amount of boiling liquid. Steam gently for 3–5 minutes. Remove the mussels when the shells open, discarding any that remain resolutely shut. If you prefer, the mussels can be opened in the oven. Place them on a baking sheet and put them in a preheated oven at 150°C/300°F/Gas 2 for a few minutes. When they open, serve on the half shell, or separate the flesh from the shells with a sharp knife.

SQUID

Pla meug

Squid is popular in Thailand and is available both fresh and frozen. The main criteria when cooking squid is to be brief; if cooked for too long it will become rubbery. It only takes about 30 seconds to cook in hot water and 1–2 minutes if stir-fried. Squid can be grilled (broiled), deep-fried, steamed or added to soups and salads.

Below: Squid is ideal for stir-frying, as it requires a very short cooking time.

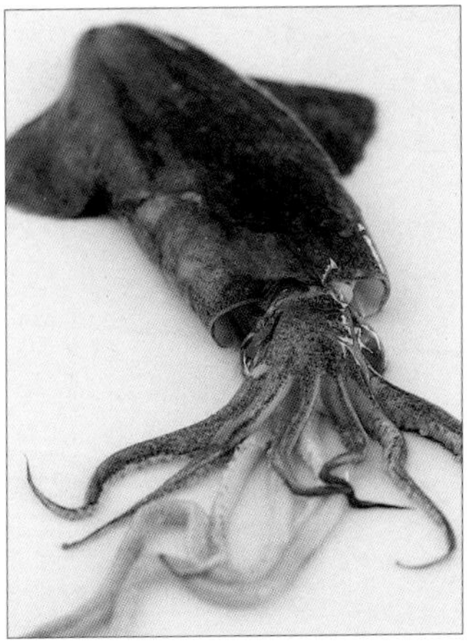

Preparing small squid

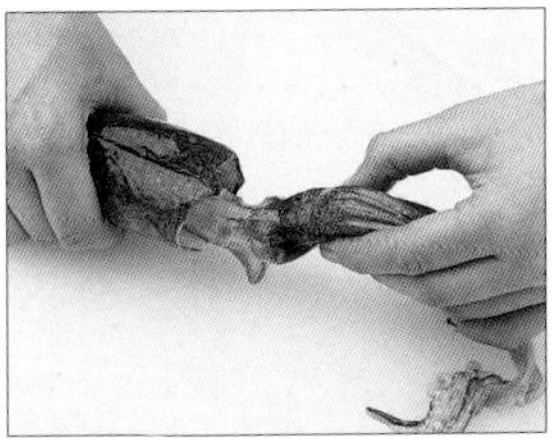

1 Hold the body with one hand and gently pull off the head and the tentacles with the other.

2 Carefully cut between the eyes and tentacles, taking care not to pierce the ink sacs – discard the eyes and ink sacs. Remove and discard the small hard beak between the eyes and tentacles.

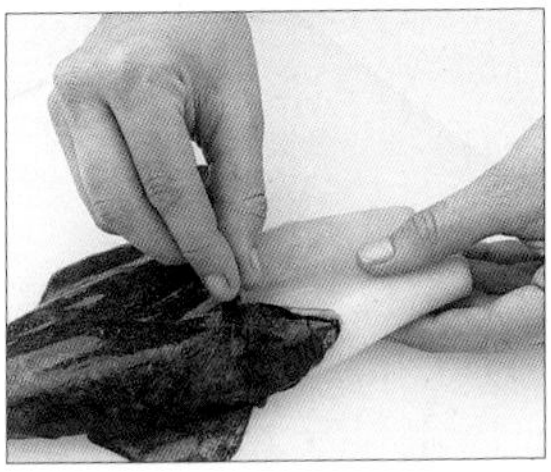

3 Place the body, fin side down, on a board. Use your fingers or an angled knife to scrape off the thin skin. Pull out the guts from inside the sac, then rub the sac inside and out with salt. Set aside for 5 minutes, then rinse off the salt under cold water.

4 Separate the tentacles and cut the longer ones in half.

5 Pat the body and tentacles dry. The body can be stuffed, using the chopped tentacles as part of the filling, or cut into rings. Alternatively, cut it lengthways into four, score the pieces in a criss-cross pattern, then cut into strips.

Poultry

Most Thais purchase their poultry live or freshly killed from the market. While this guarantees freshness, the sight of bamboo cages filled with scrawny chickens, pigeons and ducks can be daunting to the visitor.

CHICKEN

Kai

Chicken is one of the most popular meats in Thailand. Its delicate, versatile flesh suits the pungent Thai spices and simple methods of cooking. It seems that every area of Thailand has its own favourite chicken curry recipe. It also lends itself to other treatments, as when it is teamed with lemon grass or cashew nuts. Frying, cooking on a barbecue or brazier or roasting are also popular methods. Stir-fried chicken with chillies and basil is a speciality, the cool flavour of the holy basil tempering the warmth of the chillies. Chicken is delicious roasted with lime and sweet potatoes, and chicken cooked on a barbecue is a common sight in markets.

Cutting up a chicken

This method produces eight portions. If you need more pieces, say for stir-fries, the portions can be further divided. Accomplished Thai cooks will be able to cut the breast and wing portions into as many as ten pieces, the legs into four pieces and the thighs into six pieces.

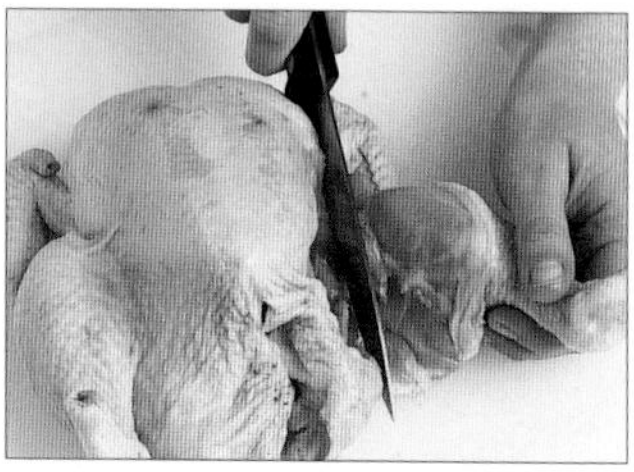

1 Place the chicken breast-side up. Ease one leg away from the body. With a knife, make an incision to reveal the ball of the thigh bone as you pull the leg further away from the body. Once the thigh socket is visible, cut through it to release the drumstick and thigh in one piece. Repeat with the other leg.

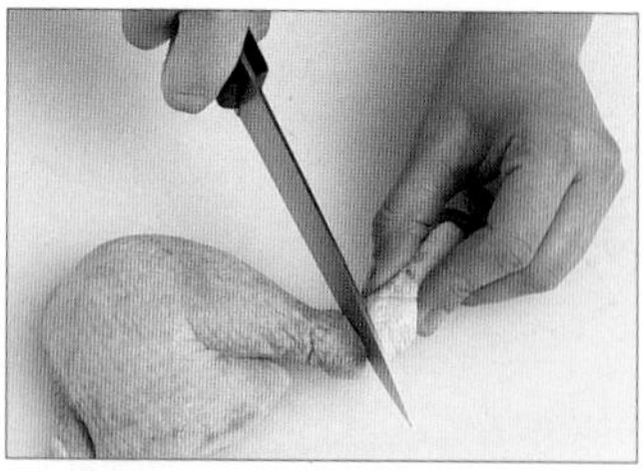

2 Trim off the end of the leg bone using a sharp knife, then turn the leg upside down and locate the knee joint. Cut the leg in half, cutting through the joint to separate the leg and thigh. Repeat with the other leg.

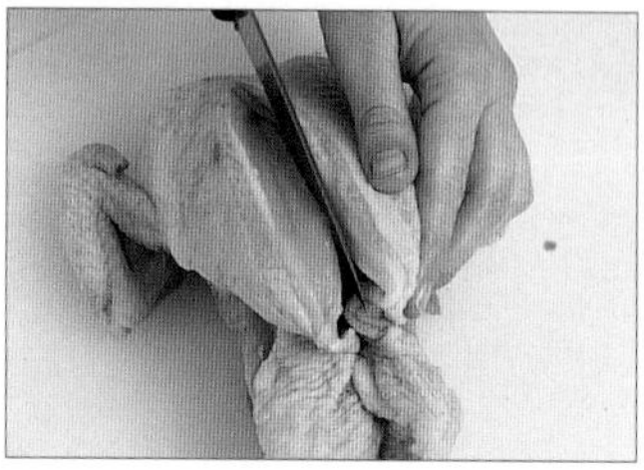

3 Using either a large sharp knife, a pair of poultry shears or strong, sharp scissors, cut through the breastbone, starting at the neck end. Cut and separate each breast and wing portion from the backbone, cutting through the wishbone with a pair of shears or scissors, then trim off any flaps of skin.

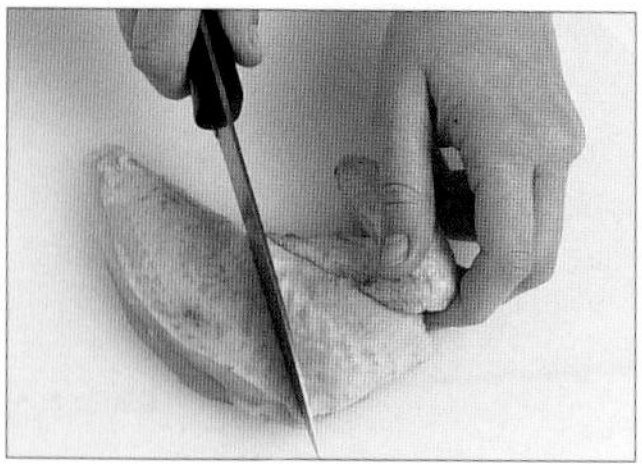

4 Cut both wing and breast pieces into two portions each, slicing through the meat and bone.

COOK'S TIP

Use the leftover bones to make stock, adding onion, celery and a piece of bruised fresh root ginger or crushed lemon grass stalk.

DUCK

Yahng

Thai cuisine owes much to Chinese influences and nowhere is this more apparent than in the Thais' passion for duck. It is often cooked in the same ways as chicken, but some duck dishes are very elaborate. In *bet yahng*, the duck is marinated in a mixture of honey, soy sauce, bean sauce, chilli, garlic and vinegar, then roasted on a spit until the skin is crisp. The skin is then removed and served with rice and the partly cooked meat is used in a stir-fry. Duck meat is also often cut into bitesize pieces and marinated with flavourings such as five-spice powder, sesame oil and orange rind and juice, then cooked with coconut milk to make a hot and spicy curry, or chopped and stir-fried with chilli and Thai fish sauce.

Right: Duck is very popular in Thailand.

MEAT

Although rice, noodles and vegetables form the major part of the Thai diet, Thais are not, in general, vegetarians. Pork is the meat of choice, except for Muslims, who do not eat pork for religious reasons. Where there are large Muslim populations, beef or lamb is usually eaten instead.

PORK

Mu

This meat is enormously popular in Thailand and every part of the pig is eaten, from the tips of the ears, to the end of the tail and everything in between. Pork is very versatile and can be combined with a wide range of ingredients: vegetables, rice, noodles, and the pungent spices and aromatics that are used in Thai cuisine. Many of the pork dishes illustrate the Chinese influence in Thai cuisine, including the ubiquitous barbecue-spiced pork and sweet-and-sour pork. For stir-frying, fillet, lean leg and belly (side) are the preferred cuts, while for stews and braised dishes, belly pork is used.

Above: Pork belly is a popular cut for frying and for snacks.

Pork Belly

Mu sam chan

This is the same cut of pork that is used for making bacon, with a layer of red meat, fat and skin. Pork belly is regarded as one of the tastiest cuts of the animal despite its fatty content and it is a particular favourite, whether fried until crisp or slowly cooked with five-spice powder. The long cooking method makes the pork particularly tender and also helps render much of its excess fat. Cooked this way it is often served with plain boiled rice and vegetables. Pork belly is often used minced as a secret ingredient in other dishes to provide flavour and moistness. It is often combined with prawns (shrimp) in prawn cakes and also with beef to give a certain lightness in Thai meat balls.

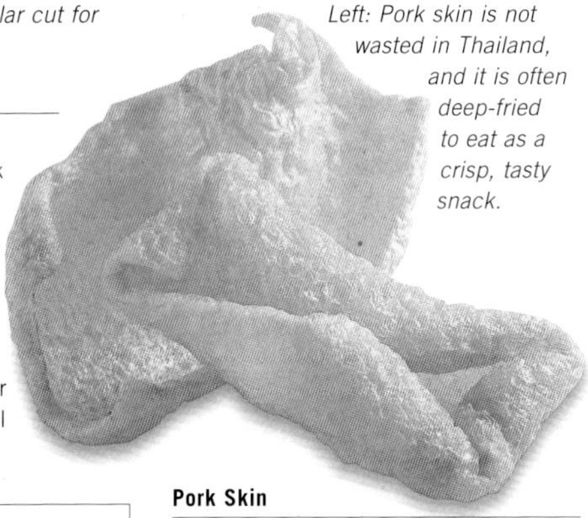

Left: Pork skin is not wasted in Thailand, and it is often deep-fried to eat as a crisp, tasty snack.

Pork Skin

Nang mu

Used as it is or deep-fried, pork skin is a Thai speciality. It is made by removing all the hair and fat from the skin, which is then scraped clean, boiled until tender, then sliced. It can be found in the frozen food section of Asian stores.

Making crispy belly of pork

This is a popular snack food, not unlike pork scratchings.

MAKES ABOUT 675G/1½LB

- 1kg/2¼lb belly (side) of pork
- 120ml/4fl oz/½ cup Thai coconut vinegar
- 60ml/4 tbsp salt
- sunflower oil, for deep-frying

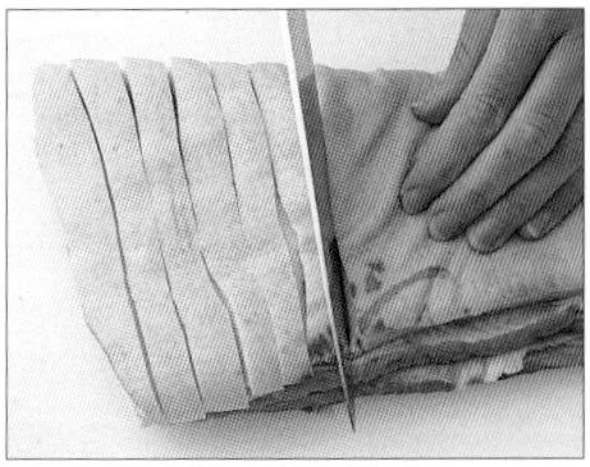

1 Score the skin on the belly of pork crossways with a sharp knife.

2 Brush the skin with the vinegar and leave to dry. Repeat three times, then rub the pork skin with the salt.

3 Cut the pork crossways into thin strips. Spread out the pork on a baking tray and cook in a preheated oven at 120°C/250°F/Gas½ for about 3 hours until completely dry.

4 Heat the oil in a wok, add the pork strips in batches and deep-fry for about 5 minutes, or until the skin has crackled and is golden.

BEEF

Neua

Until fairly recently, beef was rarely eaten in Thailand as cattle were considered beasts of burden and, as such, were highly valued for their work. Today, beef is no longer regarded as such a luxury but it still tends to be expensive, so is used quite sparingly. Beef is generally cut into bitesize pieces. When cutting beef for stir-frying it is first sliced lengthwise along the grain, then crosswise across the grain into paper thin slices. Beef is also grilled (broiled) and served as satay, minced (ground) and stir-fried or made into meatballs, and cut into chunks and cooked slowly in braises or stews.

Dried Fish and Shellfish

Throughout Thailand entire sections of food markets are devoted exclusively to dried and salted fish – *pla haeng* – and both fresh and saltwater varieties are treated in this way. They come in all shapes and sizes and are creatively displayed, although some do look a little gruesome, with their wrinkled bodies and toothy grins. Each type has a different flavour with varying degrees of saltiness.

Small fish are sold whole. The tiniest are frequently deep-fried and served with curries. Where the flavour of the fish is required, but not its obvious presence, the fish is first pounded in a mortar with a pestle before being added to the dish. This is necessary because most types of dried fish remain intact when cooked.

Above: Dried shrimps are used as a flavouring in salads and other dishes.

Larger varieties of dried fish are usually sold in slices. They can either be cut up and used in stir-fries or slow-roasted in the oven.

Some types of fish are cut open and gutted before being dried in the sun. *Pla salit, pla chawn* and *pla nuea* or *pla krob* are considered the best.

Salted fish is also sold preserved in oil in jars. Once a packet or jar has been opened, seal it very tightly in a plastic bag before putting it in the refrigerator, or its strong smell will permeate everything else that is stored in there.

DRIED SHRIMPS

Kung haeng
These should be a natural shrimp pink and have a sharp, but not too salty flavour. Do not buy dried shrimps that even have a tinge of grey in them, as this indicates that they are old. Before being dried in the sun, the shrimps are usually boiled and peeled, but there is one variety, from Songkla, that is dried unpeeled. These are good when deep-fried, as they are very crisp and are the variety to choose if they are available. Dried shrimps come in several sizes, are usually packed in plastic bags and can be found in the chiller cabinets or freezers of Asian stores.

In cooking, dried shrimps are generally used as a seasoning, rather than as a principal ingredient in dishes. They are sometimes reconstituted in water before being used, but if you are adding them to a dish where their crisp texture is a feature, such as a salad, this is not necessary. When you begin to cook with dried shrimp the smell is very strong, but this soon subsides.

Left: Dried ground fish has a strong, pungent flavour and is mixed with other ingredients to make a flavouring.

Above: Dried squid doesn't look very appetizing, but it's prized as a flavouring.

DRIED GROUND FISH

Nahm phrik pla pahn
Grilled (broiled) and pounded dried fish is added as a seasoning to chilli paste and chilli water to make a delicious, spicy dipping sauce.

DRIED SQUID

Pla mouk sang
Pale brown in colour, with a subtle fish aroma, but a very powerful taste. The texture is considerably tougher than that of fresh squid and quite chewy. It is used mainly as a flavouring in meat stews or soups. Before it can be used it must be soaked in warm water for about 30 minutes, then drained and rinsed thoroughly in fresh water. When used for stir-frying, the inside of the flesh is generally scored in a criss-cross pattern, then cut into small pieces. When cooked it opens up into little flowers. Dried squid will keep almost indefinitely if wrapped lightly and kept in a cool, dry place.

Preserved Meat and Eggs

The skilful art of preserving meat and eggs is something that the Thais share with the Chinese.

SALTED DUCK EGGS

Kai khem

To make these, large duck eggs are immersed in salted water in wooden or ceramic bins for up to two weeks. They are then sold, either raw, for cooking at home, or already cooked by the market trader. They can be hard-boiled like regular duck eggs but are usually not shelled. Instead, they are cut in half to reveal the firm yolks and whites surrounded by a brined shell. They are extremely salty and one or two eggs will serve six people as an accompaniment to a rice dish or curry. Uncooked salted eggs will keep in the refrigerator for up to 1 month.

THOUSAND-YEAR-OLD EGGS

Kai yew mah

These eggs are not nearly as old as their name implies, in fact they are really only about a month old. The eggs are covered with a paste of lime, baking soda, rice husks and salt, which is left to ferment and ripen. The egg white turns a gorgeous translucent black, similar in taste to salty gelatine and the yolk becomes a mixture of colours; brown, black and grey and has a creamy soft texture. They can be found in most Asian markets and will keep in the refrigerator for several months. They have a mild, but definite flavour and aroma and are usually served with hot mustard or stir-fried with garlic, chilli and fresh basil.

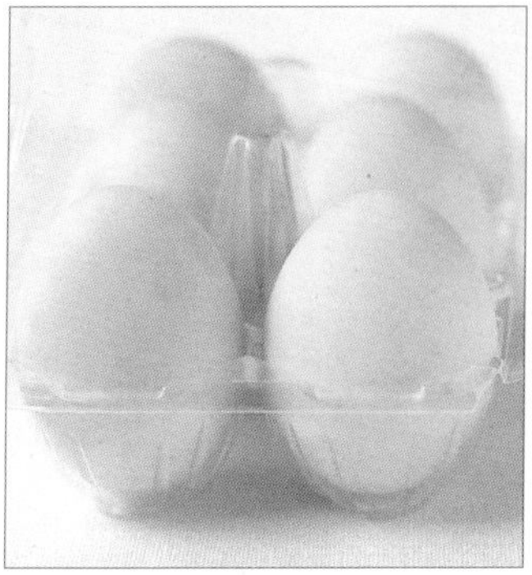

Below: Salted duck eggs are served as an accompaniment.

Above: Fermented I-san sausages are a speciality of northern Thailand and have a strong, distinctive flavour.

SAUSAGES

Moo yaw

Several different types of preserved sausages are enjoyed in Thailand and will often be encountered as street food. They are often strongly flavoured and are cut into pieces and added to dishes.

I-san Sausage

Si grot issan

These sausages from the north of Thailand are a favourite dish throughout the country. The sausage stuffing is left to ferment, giving it a slightly sour taste. Street vendors sell them on sticks, so they can be eaten as the buyers stroll along the street. This type of sausage is also served in slices, with slivers of fresh root ginger, fresh coriander (cilantro) sprigs and a little package of chilli ground peanuts.

Spicy Sausage

Nem

This chilli-laden sausage is made from preserved pork meat and skin, heavily spiced with garlic and black pepper. Traditionally, the sausage filling is wrapped in banana leaves for cooking, but nowadays, commercial sausage casings may be used instead.

Right: Pungent and spicy Thai sausage is flavoured with hot chilli, black pepper and garlic.

Herbs, Spices and Aromatics

One of the distinguishing features of Thai cuisine is the way in which a combination of flavourings is used to achieve precisely the desired taste in a dish. Every herb, spice or aromatic ingredient listed is there for a reason. When cooking, it is important to use the specified item wherever possible to achieve the correct balance. Of course, it isn't always easy to locate specific Asian herbs and spices, but there are some acceptable substitutes.

BASIL

There are three types of basil grown in Thailand, each one with a slightly different appearance, flavour and use.

Above: Thai basil has a more powerful flavour than Western sweet basil.

Below: Holy basil is quite pungent with an almost spicy taste.

Thai Basil

Bai horapa

The most important of the three types, Thai basil has a sweet, anise flavour and, with its shiny green leaves, looks similar to the Western sweet basil. It is used in red curries. Sweet basil can be substituted for it in recipes.

Holy Basil

Bai grapao

This variety tastes rather like cloves, and is just as pungent, which explains its alternative name; hot basil. The leaves release their full flavour only when cooked. Use holy basil as fresh as possible, in fish dishes, and beef and chicken curries. In Thailand it is also sometimes sautéed with frogs' legs.

Lemon Basil

Bai manglaek

This herb does not travel well, so you are not likely to encounter it outside Asia. It looks a little like Italian dwarf basil, and the Thais use it in soups and sprinkle it over salads.

BAY LEAF

Bai grawan

Although the Thai bay leaf is not the same as the Western bay, both plants belong to the family *Lauraceae* and have a similar flavour. Thai bay leaves are used in Mussaman curry and soups.

CARDAMOM

Luk grawan

Cardamoms have a warm, pungent flavour. They consist of small pods – about 1cm/½in – which contain tiny, slightly sticky black seeds. Green cardamoms are the best; the white or straw-coloured pods have been bleached. Cardamoms are used in both savoury and sweet dishes. In Thailand, it is one of the flavourings for Mussaman curry. The pods should be removed and discarded before serving.

Right: Cardamoms add a unique fragrance to food.

Above: Tiny bird's eye chillies are thin-fleshed and fiery hot.

CHILLIES

Prik

These are such an intrinsic part of the Thai cuisine that it's hard to believe they were only introduced to the country by the Portuguese in the 16th century. Before that, black pepper was used to give dishes a hot, spicy flavour. There are hundreds of varieties of chilli. As a rule, the smaller the chilli, the hotter the flavour, but there are exceptions. Much of the heat from chillies is contained in the membrane surrounding the seeds, so if you do not have the Thai predilection for hot dishes, discard the seeds and the membrane to which they are attached before cooking.

Care should be taken when handling and preparing chillies. They contain a volatile oil – capsaicin – which can irritate the skin severely. Avoid touching your lips and eyes, and wash your hands thoroughly with hot, soapy water immediately after handling these hot peppers. Better still, wear rubber gloves. Likewise, clean chopping boards and knives in hot, soapy water.

Thailand is one of the world's major producers of chillies. Many of the varieties on sale would be unfamiliar to anyone from outside the country, but the fiery bird's eye chillies and the slender, tapering long chillies are sold the world over.

Bird's Eye Chillies

Prik kee noo
Small and very hot, these popular chillies are used in curries as well as pickles, soups and sauces.

Long Chillies

Prik chee fa
Also known as cayenne chillies and used for the eponymous spice powder, these may be red, yellow or green. In Thailand long chillies are often used as a garnish for curries and salads. The dried form are used in red curries. Long chillies are not quite as hot as bird's eye chillies.

Right: Long red chillies have masses of seeds and thin skins.

Dried Red Chillies

Prig hang
A huge range of dried chillies are used in Thai cooking and they are available from Asian stores either in packages or strung together. Dry-roasting the chillies in a heavy pan heightens their flavour. They can also be crushed in a mortar with a pestle before adding to dishes. Whole or crushed dried chillies will keep for several months if stored in a sealed container.

Chilli Powder

Prig kee nu bonn
This is made from ground dried red chillies, sometimes with additional spices. The strength varies but Thai chilli powder is invariably very hot.

PREPARING CHILLIES

Always wash your hands with soap and water immediately after handling chillies. The volatile oils can cause extreme stinging if placed near your eyes or face and other sensitive parts of your body. Another option is to use rubber gloves when preparing chillies.

Preparing fresh chillies

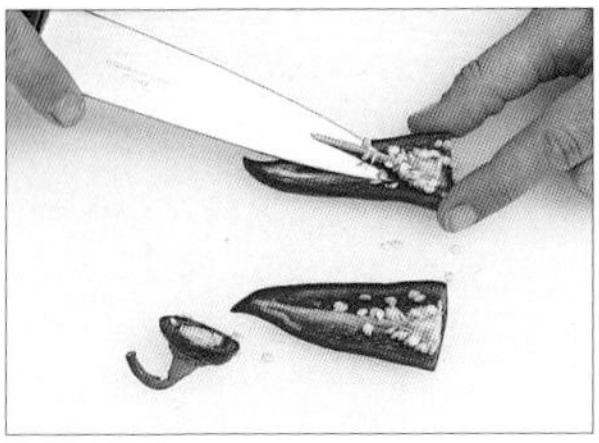

Remove the stalks and halve lengthways. Scrape out the pith and seeds, then slice, shred or chop the flesh as required. The seeds can be either discarded or added to the dish, depending on the amount of heat that is required.

Preparing dried chillies

1 Remove the stems and seeds with a knife, then leave the dried flesh whole or cut into 2–3 pieces.

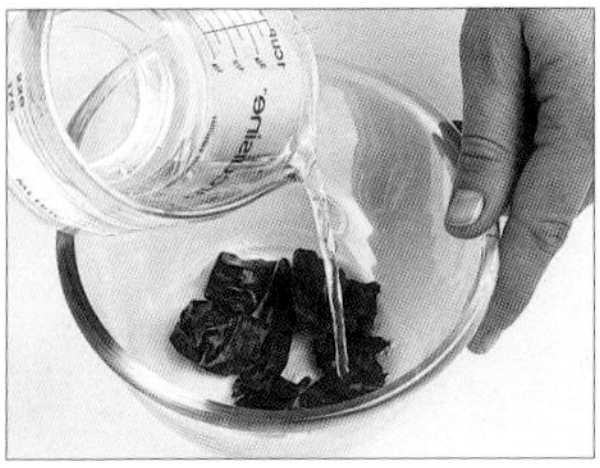

2 Put the dried flesh in a small bowl, pour over hot water to cover and leave the chillies to soak for about 30 minutes. Drain, reserving the soaking water if it can usefully be added to the dish. Use the pieces of chilli as they are, or chop them more finely.

Making chilli flowers

Thai cooks are famous for their beautiful presentation, and often garnish platters with chilli flowers.

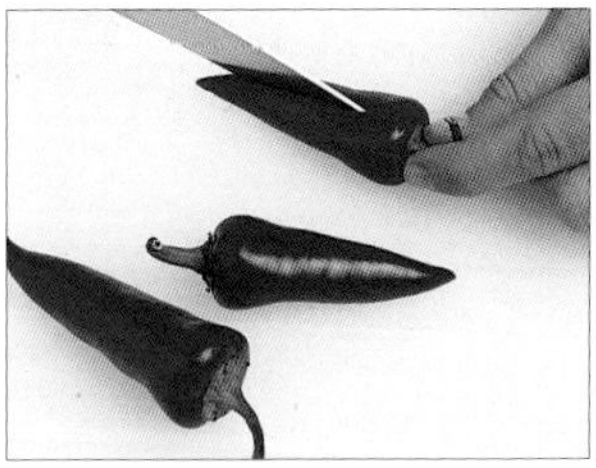

1 Holding each chilli by the stem, slit it in half lengthways.

2 Keeping the stem end of the chilli intact, carefully cut it lengthways into fine strips.

3 Put the chillies in a large bowl of iced water, cover and chill for several hours. The cut chilli strips will curl back to resemble the petals of a flower. Drain the flowers well then use as a garnish. Small chillies may be very hot, so don't be tempted to eat the flowers.

CORIANDER/CILANTRO

Pak chee

The entire coriander plant is used in Thai cooking. Each part, whether roots, stems, leaves or seeds, has its own unique flavour and specific use. The fresh, delicate leaves are used in sauces, curries and for garnishes, the roots and stems are crushed and used for marinades, and the seeds are ground to add flavour to various curry pastes. The seeds may be toasted before they are ground.

Below: Coriander is a versatile herb, and Thai cooks use every part from the leaves and seeds to the roots.

Although fresh coriander is now sold in most supermarkets, it is better to buy it from an Asian food store, when the roots are far more likely to remain attached. Use the stems and leaves as soon as possible after purchase. The roots will keep for several days if washed, dried and stored in a sealed container in the refrigerator.

Coriander seeds are small, round and brown in colour. They are widely available. They have a long shelf life and can easily be ground in a mortar or spice grinder. It is preferable to do this when a recipe calls for ground coriander, as the ready ground powder available in jars soon loses its warm, but subtle flavour.

SAW LEAF HERB

Pak chii farang

Also known as the sawtooth herb, this takes its name from the appearance of the leaves, which are long, slender and serrated. The herb has a similar but rather more pungent flavour than the coriander leaf. Saw leaf herb is used as a flavouring for meat dishes.

CUMIN

Mellet yira

The whole seeds of this aromatic spice are not used in Thai cooking, but ground cumin is an important ingredient in curry pastes such as *krung gaeng*.

Left: Cumin seeds are always ground before they are added to other ingredients in Thai cooking.

GALANGAL

Kah or *laos*

This rhizome is a member of the ginger family and it has a similar appearance. It is slightly harder than ginger, but is used in much the same way. When young, the skin is creamy white with pink sprouts. At this stage the flavour is almost lemony, and is best used in soups. As galangal matures, the skin thickens and the flesh changes colour to a light gold. The flavour intensifies and becomes more peppery and is used in curry pastes. Fresh galangal will keep for about 1 week if sealed in a plastic bag and kept in the refrigerator. It can also be frozen. If fresh galangal is unobtainable, both dried and bottled galangal are available in Thai stores.

LESSER GALANGAL

Kra-chai

Also referred to as lesser ginger, this unusual rhizome is not well known in the West. The flavour is a cross between ginger and black pepper and the fresh spice is most often used in jungle curries and with fish. Lesser galangal is available both dried and pickled, but neither of these options make a good substitute for the fresh rhizome. It is seldom available outside Asia, but if you do obtain it, peel and prepare it in the same way as ginger.

Below: Galangal, which comes in both dried and fresh forms, is similar in flavour and appearance to ginger.

GARLIC

Kratiem

With coriander (cilantro) root and black pepper, garlic makes up the famous Thai seasoning trio. The Thais use huge amounts of garlic in their cooking. Thai garlic tends to be smaller and more pungent than most garlic sold in the West. It typically has a thin pink skin, which is seldom removed before use.

GINGER

Khing

In Thailand there are several different types of ginger. The roots are used medicinally and for flavouring food. Common – or King – ginger is the best-known variety. It is picked during the rainy season, when the young roots are pale yellow and pink. They are used to flavour drinks, to make pickles and for crystallizing (candying). Young fresh roots are also pounded for use in marinades for meat. Later in the year, the ginger is called "old" ginger, but is still perfectly juicy. Well-wrapped, it will keep for up to 2 weeks in the refrigerator. It also freezes well and can be grated from frozen. Fresh root ginger is widely available from supermarkets.

Deep-fried garlic

This is delicious sprinkled on top of soups and salads. Peel garlic cloves, if necessary, slice them lengthways and deep-fry them in safflower oil over a medium heat, stirring constantly to make sure that they cook evenly. After 2–3 minutes, when they are light golden, remove them with a slotted spoon and transfer to kitchen paper. Do not have the heat too high or try to rush the cooking process, or they will burn and become unpleasantly bitter.

Left: Fresh root ginger is valued as an aromatic.

JASMINE

Malee horm

Also known as Arabian Jasmine, and is the basis of jasmine essence – *yod nam malee.* The buds are soaked in water overnight, and the water is then used to flavour cakes and desserts, such as perfumed rice. Rose petals are sometimes used instead. Jasmine essence can be bought in bottles, but the commercial product lacks the subtlety of fresh jasmine water.

LEMON GRASS

Takrai

Widely available fresh in Asian stores and supermarkets, this is an essential ingredient in Thai cooking. Lemon grass stalks are sold in bundles of 6–8 and are 12–23cm/5–9in long. The citrus flavoured plant is used in curries and hot-and-sour soups. To prepare, peel away and discard the fibrous layers surrounding the stalk. Only the bottom 10–15cm/4–6in end of the stalk is used in recipes, although whole stalks and the upper portions of cut stalks are sometimes used for flavouring stock. The edible portion of the stem is either sliced or pounded to a paste. Sliced lemon grass can be frozen and used directly from the freezer. Chopped lemon grass is sold in jars and it is also available dried but these make a poor substitute.

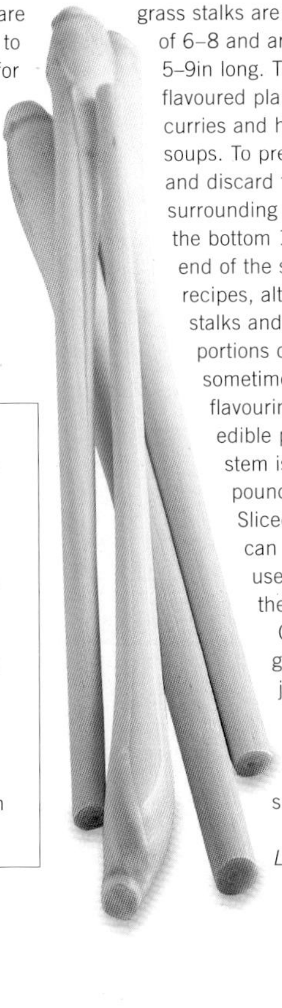

Left: Lemon grass

Preparing fresh root ginger

Fresh root ginger is generally peeled before being used for cooking. The dry thin skin is easy to either scrape or peel away using a sharp small knife. You can then either slice the flesh thinly, cut it into fine slithers, chop it or grate it. If it is to be discarded after cooking and used purely as a flavouring it should be bruised, using a cleaver or flat knife.

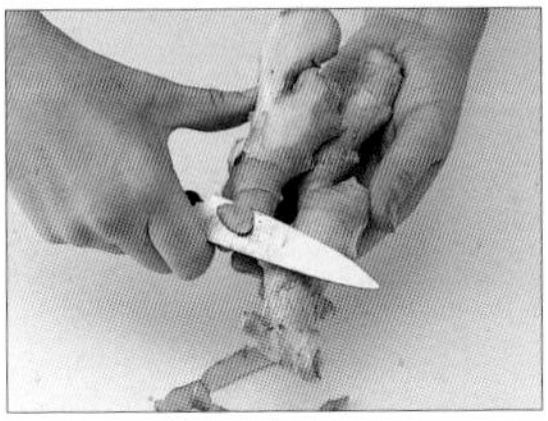

1 Thinly peel the skin using a vegetable peeler or sharp knife.

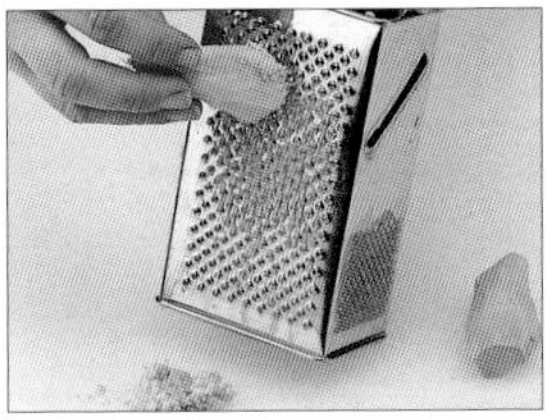

2 Hold the root firmly and grate it.

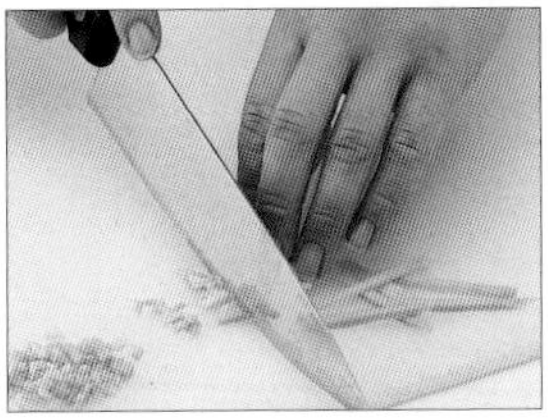

3 Alternatively, cut into thin slices, then cut again into matchstick strips, or coarsely chop the strips. Bruise the flesh for use in dishes where the ginger is to be removed.

Right: Mint is often used in Thai cooking, especially in salads.

MINT

Bai saranee
Mint is a popular herb in Thailand. The leaves are often used fresh in salad.

PANDAN LEAF

Bai toey hom
Leaves from this fragrant member of the Pandanus or screwpine family are long and slender, and look a bit like a whisk broom. They are used as a wrapping for seasoned pieces of chicken or pork and also as a flavouring for cakes and desserts. Pandan leaves have a slightly woody, nutty taste. They are available fresh from Asian food stores. Frozen leaves are also available, and although they are not so fragrant as the fresh ones, they impart a better flavour than the essence sold in bottles.

Below: Green peppercorns are used as a garnish.

Left: White peppercorns

PEPPERCORNS

Prik Thai
Before chillies arrived in Thailand, pepper was the major spice to provide the heat for Thai food. Thai cooks use only two types of peppercorns: white for seasoning and green as a garnish for jungle curries and stir-fries. A widely used, traditional Thai seasoning consists of a mixture of pounded white pepper, coriander (cilantro) root and garlic.

TAMARIND

Mak-kaam
Tamarind juice is one of the main souring agents in Thai cooking. It is both fruity and refreshing and has a tart and sour flavour without being bitter. It is an essential ingredient of Thai hot-and-sour soups. In Thailand fresh tamarind – the fruit pods of a semi evergreen, tropical tree – are widely available, but in the West you are more likely to encounter tamarind in a compressed block. This looks similar to a block of compressed dates and the pulp tastes a little like sour dates. (The word tamarind means "date of India".)

Tamarind juice can be kept in the refrigerator for up to 1 week. Tamarind is also available in dried slices, as a concentrate and as a paste. If you are unable to find tamarind, you can use lemon juice instead, but you'll need twice as much as the flavour won't be quite the same.

TURMERIC

Kamin
Related to ginger and arrowroot, this tuberous rhizome is a bright orange yellow inside and until fairly recently was used to colour the robes of Buddhist monks. It can also stain the skin, so some people wear gloves when preparing the fresh root. When cut it has a peppery aroma and it imparts a slightly musky flavour to any food with which it is cooked. In Thailand it often forms part of curry pastes, especially those of Indian origin, and is used to give rice a golden colour.

Fresh turmeric will keep for two or three weeks if stored in a cool, dark and dry place. It can also be kept in the refrigerator, but must be well wrapped to keep it from drying out.

FENNEL SEEDS

Yira
When ground, these warm, aromatic seeds are one of the ingredients of five-spice powder, a Chinese ingredient that is popular in Thailand.

Below: Turmeric is most often sold ready ground in the West, but the fresh root is sometimes available.

CURRY PASTES AND POWDERS

Thai curries, almost without exception, are based on "wet" spice mixtures, pastes that are produced by grinding spices and aromatics in a heavy mortar with a rough surface. Only curries of Indian or Burmese origin are made using curry powder. In Thailand, it is possible to buy freshly made pastes from the market, but outside the country they are only available in jars.

RED CURRY PASTE

Krung gaeng ped
This paste gets its colour from the large number of fresh red chillies that are the prime ingredient. It is a complex paste, and classically includes cumin seeds, shallots, garlic, galangal and lemon grass, as well as fresh coriander (cilantro) roots, peppercorns, cinnamon, ground turmeric and shrimp paste. Red curry paste is most often used in beef curries and robust chicken dishes.

GREEN CURRY PASTE

Krung gaeng keo wan
This curry paste is made from herbs and fresh green chillies. It is most often used to make chicken curries.

Below: Green and red curry pastes – the first step to many Thai curries.

Above: Yellow curry paste is very spicy and ideal for using with beef.

ORANGE CURRY PASTE

Krung gaeng som
Made from pounded red chillies and flavoured with shrimp paste, this tangy paste is often used in seafood curries, including sour shrimp curry soup.

YELLOW CURRY PASTE

Krung gaeng karee
This is very similar to Mussaman curry paste. A quick version can be made by adding a generous amount of ground turmeric to red curry paste. Yellow curry paste is very spicy and is used for chicken and beef curries.

MUSSAMAN CURRY PASTE

Nam prig gang mussaman
Milder in flavour than any of the pastes defined by their colour, this curry paste owes its origins to India. It is usually based on dried chillies and contains coriander and cumin.

PENANG CURRY PASTE

Nam prig gang panang
This sweet curry paste is made with ground roasted peanuts and is relatively mild. It originated in Penang, in Malaysia, hence the name. This paste can be used equally well with chicken or beef and is ideal for dishes that are cooked in coconut milk.

Above: Mussaman curry paste is based on dried chillies and aromatic spices.

CURRY POWDER

Pong gka-ree
This dry spice mixture is not much used in Thai cooking, except in recipes of Indian or Burmese origin. When curry powder is used, it tends to be in a stir-fry, marinades or a peanut sauce.

Making a curry paste

Preparing curry paste in the traditional Thai way needs time and patience, but it is certainly worth the effort. By using a mortar and pestle the spices are pounded in a way that releases the oils that hold the flavours and aromas. It also makes sure that all the flavours are integrated in a complex fashion so that no single one dominates. When spices are ground in a food processor, you inevitably end up with a coarsely ground mixture rather than a harmonious paste.

There's a technique to using a pestle. Most uninitiates assume that a great deal of force is needed to grind the spices. Thai cooks, however, let the pestle do most of the work, letting it drop on to the ingredients, so that its weight breaks down items like ginger and garlic. This action is repeated until the larger ingredients are pulverized, and only then is the pestle used to work the mixture to a paste.

Any extra paste that isn't used immediately can be kept in a jar with a screw-top lid in the refrigerator for at least a week, or frozen.

Store-cupboard Ingredients

OILS

Naam man
Lard used to be the popular medium for cooking traditional Thai dishes but nowadays various light vegetable oils tend to be used instead.

Groundnut/Peanut Oil

The advantage of using groundnut oil for stir-frying and deep-frying is that it can be heated to a high temperature without smoking. This mild oil is also excellent for dressing salads.

Corn Oil

This is also very good for frying at high temperatures, but it is less suitable for salad dressings, where its stronger flavour might dominate.

Safflower and Sunflower Oil

Both these oils are lighter in colour and taste than groundnut or corn oil, but they are slightly less suitable for stir-frying.

Soya Oil

This is used for general cooking, but is not appropriate for salad dressings.

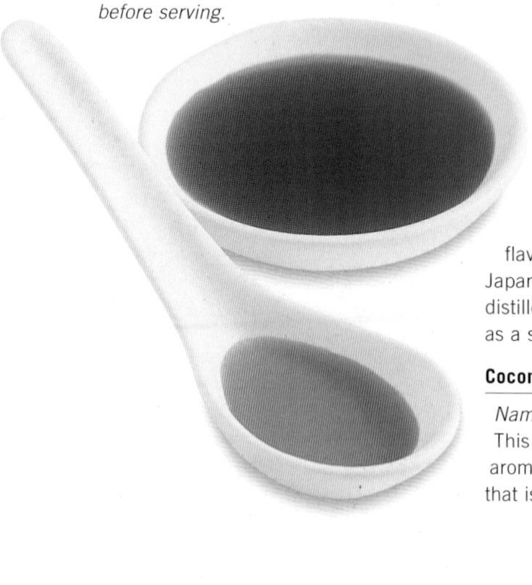

Below: Sesame oil and chilli oil are used for seasoning rather than for cooking and are generally added to dishes just before serving.

Sesame Oil

Seldom used for frying as it burns easily, sesame oil has a strong, nutty flavour and rich brown colour. It is often used as a seasoning oil, sprinkled over food before serving.

Chilli Oil

This spicy oil is never used in cooking, but is used as a dipping sauce. It is often added to stir-fried prawns (shrimp) just before serving.

VINEGARS

Rice Vinegar

Nam som sai chu
This white vinegar is made from fermented rice grain and has a sharp clean taste. The Thai variety has a milder flavour than the Chinese or Japanese equivalent. White distilled vinegar may be used as a substitute.

Below: Amber and white rice vinegars have a distinctive sharpness.

Coconut Vinegar

Nam som maplow
This opaque liquid has a fruity aroma and a sweet and sour flavour that is typically Thai. As the name suggests, it is made from coconut juice and is used as a seasoning, particularly for seafood, and a dressing for salads. It must be stored in the refrigerator once it has been opened.

Left: Coconut vinegar has a sweet, sour flavour.

SAUCES AND PASTES

Chilli Bean Paste

Naam prik pao
This is made from soya beans, chillies and other seasoning. The paste is very hot. It is usually sold in airtight jars that should be kept tightly closed in the refrigerator after opening.

Below: Chilli bean paste should be used with caution, as it is very hot.

Chilli Sauce

Saus prik
Made from chillies, water, vinegar, sugar and salt, this is mainly used as a dipping sauce for seafood. It comes in several intensities as regards heat, and the sweetness also varies. The sweeter varieties go well with chicken or seafood.

Shrimp Paste

Kapee
One of the most widely used ingredients in the Thai kitchen, this paste has a very powerful flavour. It is

Above: Chilli sauces vary in heat.

Right: Oyster sauce is widely used in Thailand.

made from tiny shrimp which have been salted and dried, then pulverized and left to ferment. It is then compressed and sold in blocks or small cans, tubs or jars. There are many types of *kapee*, varying in colour from pink to dark brown. The pink one is good for curry paste, the darker one for making dipping sauces. *Kapee* should always be cooked before eating. It can be used as it is in a cooked dish, but many recipes suggest warming the paste first, by wrapping it in foil and heating it in a dry frying pan. When cooked, the flavour mellows somewhat.

Below: Shrimp paste is salty and very strongly flavoured.

Thai Fish Sauce

Nam pla

One of the most important ingredients in Thai cuisine, fish sauce is made from salted fish, usually anchovies, which are fermented to create the thin liquid that is the basis of the sauce. The strong flavour become less pronounced with cooking.

Oyster Sauce

Hoy nangrom

This sauce originated in China, but is frequently used in Thailand. Thick and dark brown, its principal ingredients are soy sauce and oyster extract. It has a distinctive taste which, strangely, is not at all fishy. Oyster sauce is available from most supermarkets and Asian stores.

Sriracha Sauce

Nam jim sriracha

Named after the seaside town in Thailand where it originated, this sweet-tart, hot or mild bottled table sauce is made from red chillies and resembles light-coloured ketchup.

Chilli Paste

Nam prik

This is the most popular condiment in Thailand. It is on the table at every meal. There are many different versions of the sauce but the main ingredients are chopped red chillies – with the seeds – fresh lime juice, shrimp paste, Thai fish sauce, garlic and a little sugar. Chopped dried shrimp are often added, as are pea aubergines (eggplant). For *nam prik pao* or roasted *nam prik*, the garlic cloves are first dry-fried with shallots in a heavy iron pan. Peanuts can be roasted and included as well.

Soy Sauce

Namm see ewe and *namm see ewe sai*

Two basic types of soy sauce are used in Thai cooking: salty and sweet. There are two versions of the saltier sauce. One is light coloured while the other is darker and thicker. The sweeter sauce comes in two strengths. One is thin and the other, which has been processed with molasses, is slightly thicker. Both are used with the salty soy sauce in noodle dishes or stir-fries. All soy sauces vary considerably in taste. Opened bottles should be stored in the refrigerator.

Left: Thai fish sauce is a ubiquitous ingredient.

Magic Paste

Prig gang nam ya
This commercial product is sold in Asian stores. It is a blend of garlic, coriander (cilantro) root and white pepper and is used a great deal in Thai cooking.

DRY INGREDIENTS

Agar Agar

Sarai talay
This setting agent, made from seaweed, is used instead of gelatine in Thailand.

Palm Sugar

Nam taan peep
Made from the sap of the coconut palm or the sugar palm tree, palm sugar varies in colour from golden to light brown. It has a distinctive flavour and is not so sweet as cane sugar. It is often sold as a solid cake. If this is the case, grate it before use. If it is not available, use soft brown sugar instead.

Tapioca

Meun
This is made from the tubers of the cassava plant. Pearl shaped pieces of tapioca are used in Thai desserts, giving them a slightly gelatinous consistency. Tapioca flour is used to thicken sauces and desserts as well as for making batters and coating foods for frying. It is lighter than cornflour (cornstarch).

Toasted Rice Powder

Khao kua pon
Also known as roasted rice powder, this seasoning and binding agent is sold commercially in Thai stores. It is pale brown with a nutty flavour and is used with minced (ground) shrimp or meat for kebabs, sprinkled on soups and tossed with meat, poultry or seafood for salads. To prepare the powder, dry-fry raw white rice over a medium heat for 3–5 minutes, stirring until golden brown, then grind in a spice mill.

Above: Palm sugar, sometimes called jaggery, is dark brown, moist and unrefined. It has a distinctive, but extremely delicate flavour.

NUTS AND SEEDS

Lotus Seeds

Med bua
Fresh lotus seeds are eaten as a snack food, and puréed and mixed with sugar to make a filling for cakes. The dried seeds must be soaked in water before use. Remove the young green shoot in the centre of each seed before use. The seeds are prized for their texture and ability to absorb other flavours. They are often added to soups. Look for dried lotus seeds in Asian stores. They keep well stored in sealed bags in a cool place.

Below: Skinned, raw and whole peanuts, and white and black sesame seeds.

Peanuts

Tua lii song
Peanuts are used extensively as a garnish and to add texture to salads. Chopped, they form the base for satay sauce and thick red curries and they are also the main ingredient of Penang curry paste.

Left: Lotus roots and both fresh and dried seeds are popular.

Sesame Seeds

Ngaa
These tiny seeds are flat and pear shaped. They are usually white, but can be cream to brown, red or black. Raw sesame seeds have very little aroma and they are almost tasteless until they are roasted or dry-fried, which brings out their distinctive nutty flavour and aroma. Toasted sesame seeds are used in many Chinese-influenced dishes and are often sprinkled over salads and other dishes just before serving.

BEVERAGES

BEER

Bia

Without a doubt, beer is the best alcoholic beverage to drink with a Thai meal, especially in the heat of Thailand itself. There are two major brands of beer brewed in Thailand, Singha and Amarit. Singha is the most popular brand, its flavour having been compared to that of San Miguel or Kirin. Amarit is a lighter beer and is likened to a good German brew.

RICE WHISKY

Wisakee

The best known brand of Thai rice whisky is Mekon and this word is often used as a catch-all term for all whisky produced in that country. The flavour of Thai rice whisky is closer to that of bourbon than Scotch whisky and it is relatively cheap. It makes a very palatable drink mixed with cola, ice and lemon, but be warned, it is notorious for producing severe hangovers.

WINE

A very acceptable wine is produced by Chaijudh Karnasuta, the Chairman of the Oriental Hotel, at his Chateau de Loei vineyard. Most other wine sold in the country is prohibitively expensive.

Below: Beer is the perfect partner to a spicy Thai meal.

Above: Singha beer is Thailand's best-known and most popular brand.

FRUIT DRINKS

The sheer variety of fruits available in Thailand means there is a good choice of fruit drinks to be had. Fruit drinks are generally served with both salt and sugar and popular ones are pomegranate, mango and orange. Sugar cane juice and the liquid from young coconuts are also delicious thirst quenchers although sugar cane is very sweet and to some is an acquired taste.

Thailand's smoothies are elaborate. From watermelon smoothies served into its own watermelon bowl to a freshly blended combination of carrots, dragon fruit, orange and pomegranate many smoothies are made with specific health benefits in mind.

Below: Mango juice is one of many fresh fruit juices found in Thailand.

Above: Coconut juice is a refreshing drink that is widely enjoyed.

Below: Sugar cane juice makes a sweet cooler on a hot day.

EQUIPMENT

You can produce authentic Thai food at home with just a few simple pieces of kitchen equipment.

MORTAR AND PESTLE

Krok and *saak*

The most important piece of equipment in any Thai kitchen is without a doubt the mortar and pestle. Ideally, it would be good to have a selection of different sizes or at least two, one for grinding spices and the other for making salads. They are made of granite, earthenware or wood. Buy one that has a capacity of at least 450ml/¾ pint/scant 2 cups and is about 18cm/7in in diameter. The granite mortar and pestle are ideal for grinding spices and herbs whereas the earthenware and wooden ones are usually used for the less robust method of making salads.

Some people use a coffee grinder (kept specially for the purpose), or a blender or food processor for grinding their spices and herbs, but none of these produces the authentic texture or flavour that the traditional method of grinding achieves.

To remove any pungent odour or staining from your equipment, soak in a mixture of distilled vinegar and water for about an hour, and then rinse out. If, as is likely, chillies have been ground, a mixture of salt and lime juice can be used to clean the equipment.

Below: A granite mortar and pestle is useful for making the traditional Thai wet spice pastes.

Above: Woks may have flat or rounded bases and one or two handles.

WOK

Kata

Following closely on the heels of the mortar and pestle's prime position on the kitchen shelf is the wok. It can be used for stir-frying, deep-frying, roasting or steaming. The wide, sloping shape of the wok makes it efficient to cook in and easy to use.

Woks are available in different materials, spun carbon steel, stainless steel or aluminium. The best material is spun carbon steel. There are non-stick versions made with a special coating, but they do not conduct the heat so efficiently as the traditional ones and they also cannot be heated to such high temperatures.

If you have a gas stove, a round-based wok is best. If your stove is electric, then you will have to use a flat-based wok. A wok stand is used to help keep the wok steady on the hob (stovetop). It is very helpful if you want to use the wok for steaming, deep-frying or braising.

The light, domed wok lid, which is used for steaming, is available from Asian stores. If you are unable to find one, any pot lid that fits tightly will do.

Seasoning a wok

All woks that are not non-stick need to be seasoned before you can use them. When new, they should be thoroughly washed and scrubbed to remove the machine oil that protects them during their transportation. Scrub the inside first with a cream cleaner, then rinse and dry. Place the wok over a very low heat and add 30ml/2 tbsp cooking oil rubbing it all over the inside with kitchen paper, making sure that the inside surface is coated. Continue heating the wok gently for a further 10–15 minutes, then wipe it again with a thick pad of kitchen paper, protecting your fingers. Repeat the process until the paper comes away clean.

FINE KNIFE

Miit

This thin knife is used for peeling and carving fruit and vegetables.

UTILITY KNIFE

Li-toh

This hardy, hatchet-like utility knife can be used for splitting coconut shells and chopping wood for kindling.

Above: A Chinese cleaver is finely balanced.

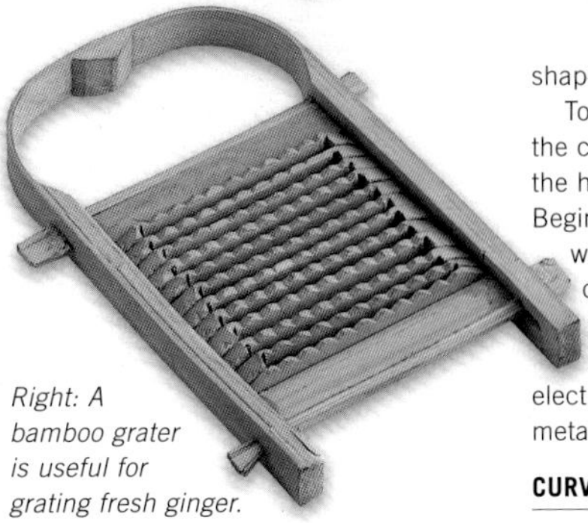

Right: A bamboo grater is useful for grating fresh ginger.

CHINESE CLEAVER

Miit muu

This is an extremely versatile piece of equipment. A cleaver is used for chopping through bones and also for cutting delicate slices for stir-frying. It must always be kept razor sharp. Alternatively, a large heavy chef's knife can be used.

SOUP SERVER

Tao fai

A rather odd-shaped utensil, a soup server can be made of aluminium, tin-lined copper or brass. They are sometimes referred to as Mongolian hot pots. Whichever variety you buy, always make sure that it has a non-corrodible lining such as tin.

GRATER

Tsota-drap

Bamboo graters are ideal for grating ginger, while a stainless steel box grater is useful for shredding vegetables and grating coconut flesh for milk.

Traditionally coconut was prepared using a special coconut grater – *maew khuut ma-phroat*. These are now more collectors' items rather than everyday kitchen utensils. What were once plain, small stools with sharp metal graters set into one end have evolved into elaborate pieces of equipment and were often carved into the shape of a rabbit or other animal.

To use the traditional coconut grater, the chef sits astride the seat, holding the halved coconut against the grater. Beginning at the outside rim and working towards the centre, the coconut is grated to different thicknesses, depending on what it is to be used for. Today both electric graters and small hand-held metal graters are used.

CURVED SPATULA

Phai

This long-handled, curved wooden spatula is an essential tool for stir-frying in a wok.

STEAMERS

The traditional Thai steamer – *huat* – is a set of bamboo trays, which are stacked over a wok of boiling water with a cover on top. Chinese merchants introduced perforated metal pans which are used in the same way (and are more hygienic). Electric steamers are also widely used today.

To prevent the food from sticking to the steamer while cooking, banana leaves, damp muslin (cheesecloth) or greaseproof (waxed) paper may be placed under the food. Before using a bamboo steamer for the first time, wash and rinse it and then steam empty for at least 5 minutes.

A special round, flat steamer – *rang theung* – made of steel or bamboo is used for steaming delicate fish, dumplings, desserts or other dishes.

CHOPPING BOARD

Khiang

A traditional Thai chopping board is round, about 5cm/2in thick and made from tamarind wood. Any hard wood or acrylic board would be suitable, as they are easy to clean, hygienic and will last for a long time. Never place cooked meat on a board where raw meat or poultry has been cut. Dedicate a separate board for the preparation of raw meat and wash thoroughly each time you use it.

SIEVE

Kra-chawn

You will need a selection of different size sieves for straining different items, from rice to juices and oils.

METAL BATTER MOULDS

Krasthongs

These shell-shaped brass moulds are set on the end of a long wooden handle. The mould is dipped first into hot oil, then batter, and then back into the oil where it cooks to form crisp little cups. These cups are filled with savoury mixtures and are served as snacks called *krathon*.

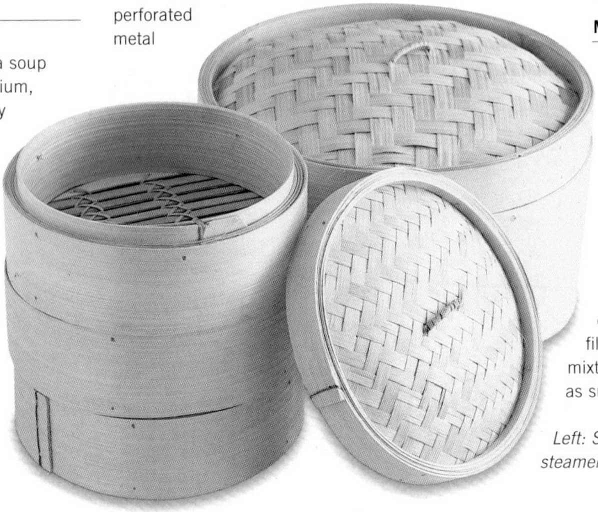

Left: Stacking bamboo steamers are used in a wok.

Classic Cooking Techniques

Careful preparation is the foundation of all Thai cooking, from preparing and chopping ingredients to grinding spices and washing and trimming garnishes. Once the ingredients are prepared, then the cooking, which is often relatively quick, can commence.

There are a few classic preparation and cooking techniques upon which the whole Thai cuisine relies. The most important, without a doubt, is the preparation of spices and herbs, which give Thai dishes their unique flavour and character. Traditional Thai cooks prepare almost everything from scratch (although in the West, there are a number of very good ready-made ingredients such as curry pastes that can be great time-savers).

Spices are roasted and ground into pastes, which form the basis of most dishes. Once the flavouring is prepared, the cooking is usually simple: stewing, steaming, boiling, stir-frying, deep-frying and grilling over hot coals. A few Chinese-influenced dishes such as roast duck and pork, are "roasted" but this is not a traditional Thai cooking method.

GRINDING SPICES

The ideal method for grinding spices is to use a large, rough, Asian-style mortar. The rough sides tend to "grip" the spices, preventing them flying out of the mortar as you pound them. Dry spices are usually dry-roasted (*pow*) in a heavy frying pan before grinding.

1 Spread the dry spices in a single layer and cook over a very high heat for about 1 minute, shaking the pan. Lower the heat and cook for a few more minutes, until they start to colour and emit their aroma.

2 Transfer the toasted spices to the mortar and pound to a fine powder. This releases the essential oils that are vital to the authentic flavour of Thai food.

POUNDING AND PURÉEING

Dry and wet spices, aromatics and herbs are often pounded together to form spice pastes. Other flavouring ingredients such as strong-tasting shrimp paste may also be added.

1 Place the spices, herbs and any other flavouring ingredients in a mortar and pound with a pestle for several minutes to form a smooth paste.

SLOW-COOKING

Stewing (*keang*) is the typical method for preparing soups and curries, and the lengthy cooking time makes sure that meats become very tender. Traditionally, a heavy clay pot, placed over a fire of medium intensity, would have been used.

1 Put all the ingredients in a clay pot and place in an oven preheated to the required temperature. (A heavy, flameproof casserole makes a good alternative if you do not have a clay pot. It can also be placed over a medium heat on the stovetop if you prefer.)

STEAMING

This is an excellent way of preparing delicate foods such as fish and vegetables. Steaming (*neung*) helps to retain the flavour of ingredients and keeps them intact.

1 Place the food in a bamboo steamer. (Some recipes require the steamer to be lined with banana leaves.) Put the steamer on a wok rack over a wok half-filled with boiling water. Steam the food, replenishing the water constantly to prevent it boiling dry.

2 Parcels of food wrapped in banana leaves can also produce steamed results. Place a well-sealed parcel over a barbecue or in a preheated oven. The moisture is trapped within the parcel and steams the food inside.

STIR-FRYING

This is a very quick cooking method and it is usually the preparation of the ingredients that takes time. It is important to prepare all the ingredients before you start to stir-fry (*pad*). The order in which ingredients are added to the pan is very important.

1 Pour a little oil into a wok and place over a high heat for a few minutes.

2 Add spices and aromatics to the wok and stir-fry for a few moments.

3 Add evenly chopped pieces of meat, poultry, fish or shellfish to the wok and stir-fry for 1 or 2 minutes more, shaking the pan constantly.

4 Add any hardy vegetables such as carrots, green beans or (bell) peppers and stir-fry for 1 minute.

5 Add any delicate vegetables and leaves such as beansprouts, spinach or morning glory and stir-fry for about 1 minute more.

6 Finally add more seasoning and add any fresh herbs such as basil or coriander (cilantro) that should not be cooked for long. Toss to combine and serve immediately.

DEEP-FRYING

This method (*tord*) is used for many dishes such as wontons, spring rolls and prawn crackers. Use an oil that can be heated to a high temperature, such as groundnut (peanut) oil.

1 Pour the oil into a pan or wok (filling it no more than two-thirds full) and heat to about 180°C/350°F. To test the temperature, add a drop of batter or a piece of onion. If it sinks, the oil is not hot enough; if it burns, it is too hot. If it sizzles and rises to the surface, the temperature is perfect.

2 Cook the food in small batches until crisp and lift out with a slotted spoon or wire mesh skimmer when cooked. Drain on a wire rack lined with kitchen paper and serve immediately, or keep warm in the oven until ready to serve.

BOILING

This method (*dom*) is often used to cook delicate meat such as chicken breast portions or duck.

1 Place the meat and any flavourings in a pan and add just enough water to cover. Bring to the boil, then remove from the heat and leave to stand, covered, for 10 minutes, then drain.

COOKING ON THE BARBECUE

Grilling (*yarng*) food over glowing coals is very popular. It is widely used by street vendors who cook skewered snacks such as satay or barbecue-cooked chicken (*kai yang*) or seafood over small open braziers.

1 When using charcoal, light the coals and wait until they are covered with a thin layer of white or pale grey ash before starting to cook. Place the skewers, meat, poultry, fish or shellfish on a rack over the coals and grill, turning occasionally, until browned on all sides and cooked through.

2 If you do not have time to set up a barbecue, cook the food under a preheated grill (broiler).

Wooden and Bamboo Skewers
If you are using wooden or bamboo skewers, soak them in water for about 30 minutes before using to prevent them from burning.

APPETIZERS AND SNACKS

Wander around the streets in any Thai city or town and you will see vendors standing behind portable cooking carts or squatting beside burners with battered woks ready to receive garlic, ginger, chillies and vegetables. The smells are enticing and those who are tempted to taste are seldom disappointed. The good news is that you don't have to travel to try these treats. Follow these simple recipes for delicious appetizers such as Roasted Coconut Cashew Nuts, Corn Fritters and Firecrackers.

Prawn and Sesame Toasts

These attractive little toast triangles are ideal for serving with pre-dinner drinks and are always a favourite hot snack at parties. They are surprisingly easy to prepare and you can cook them in just a few minutes.

SERVES FOUR

INGREDIENTS
- 225g/8oz peeled raw prawns (shrimp)
- 15ml/1 tbsp sherry
- 15ml/1 tbsp soy sauce
- 30ml/2 tbsp cornflour (cornstarch)
- 2 egg whites
- 4 slices white bread
- 115g/4oz/½ cup sesame seeds
- oil, for deep-frying
- sweet chilli sauce, to serve

1 Process the prawns, sherry, soy sauce and cornflour in a food processor.

2 In a grease-free bowl, whisk the egg whites until stiff. Fold them into the prawn and cornflour mixture.

3 Cut each slice of bread into four triangular quarters. Spread out the sesame seeds on a large plate. Spread the prawn paste over one side of each bread triangle, then press the coated sides into the sesame seeds so that they stick and cover the prawn paste.

4 Heat the oil in a wok or deep-fryer, to 190°C/375°F or until a cube of bread, added to the oil, browns in about 45 seconds. Add the toasts, a few at a time, prawn side down, and deep-fry for 2–3 minutes, then turn and fry on the other side until golden.

5 Drain on kitchen paper and serve hot with sweet chilli sauce.

RICE CAKES WITH SPICY DIPPING SAUCE

A CLASSIC THAI APPETIZER, THESE RICE CAKES ARE EASY TO MAKE AND WILL KEEP ALMOST INDEFINITELY IN AN AIRTIGHT CONTAINER. START MAKING THEM AT LEAST A DAY BEFORE YOU PLAN TO SERVE THEM, AS THE RICE NEEDS TO DRY OUT OVERNIGHT.

SERVES FOUR TO SIX

INGREDIENTS
- 175g/6oz/1 cup Thai jasmine rice
- 350ml/12fl oz/1½ cups water
- oil, for deep-frying and greasing

For the spicy dipping sauce
- 6–8 dried chillies
- 2.5ml/½ tsp salt
- 2 shallots, chopped
- 2 garlic cloves, chopped
- 4 coriander (cilantro) roots
- 10 white peppercorns
- 250ml/8fl oz/1 cup coconut milk
- 5ml/1 tsp shrimp paste
- 115g/4oz minced (ground) pork
- 115g/4oz cherry tomatoes, chopped
- 15ml/1 tbsp Thai fish sauce
- 15ml/1 tbsp palm sugar or light muscovado (brown) sugar
- 30ml/2 tbsp tamarind juice (tamarind paste mixed with warm water)
- 30ml/2 tbsp coarsely chopped roasted peanuts
- 2 spring onions (scallions), chopped

1 Make the sauce. Snap off the stems of the chillies, shake out the seeds and soak the chillies in warm water for 20 minutes. Drain and put in a mortar. Sprinkle over the salt and crush. Add the shallots, garlic, coriander and peppercorns. Pound to a coarse paste.

2 Pour the coconut milk into a pan and bring to the boil. When it begins to separate, stir in the pounded chilli paste. Cook for 2–3 minutes, until the mixture is fragrant. Stir in the shrimp paste and cook for 1 minute more.

3 Add the pork, stirring to break up any lumps. Cook for 5–10 minutes, then stir in the tomatoes, fish sauce, palm sugar and tamarind juice. Simmer, stirring occasionally, until the sauce thickens, then stir in the chopped peanuts and spring onions. Remove the sauce from the heat and leave to cool.

4 Preheat the oven to the lowest setting. Grease a baking sheet. Wash the rice in several changes of water. Put it in a pan, add the water and cover tightly. Bring to the boil, reduce the heat and simmer gently for about 15 minutes.

5 Remove the lid and fluff up the rice. Spoon it on to the baking sheet and press it down with the back of a spoon. Leave in the oven to dry out overnight.

6 Break the rice into bitesize pieces. Heat the oil in a wok or deep-fryer. Deep-fry the rice cakes, in batches, for about 1 minute, until they puff up but are not browned. Remove and drain well. Serve with the dipping sauce.

Roasted Coconut Cashew Nuts

Serve these hot and sweet cashew nuts in paper or cellophane cones at parties. Not only do they look enticing and taste terrific, but the cones help to keep clothes and hands clean and can simply be thrown away afterwards.

SERVES SIX TO EIGHT

INGREDIENTS

- 15ml/1 tbsp groundnut (peanut) oil
- 30ml/2 tbsp clear honey
- 250g/9oz/2 cups cashew nuts
- 115g/4oz/1⅓ cups desiccated (dry unsweetened shredded) coconut
- 2 small fresh red chillies, seeded and finely chopped
- salt and ground black pepper

VARIATIONS

Almonds also work well, or choose peanuts for a more economical snack.

1 Heat the oil in a wok or large frying pan and then stir in the honey. After a few seconds add the nuts and coconut and stir-fry until both are golden brown.

2 Add the chillies, with salt and pepper to taste. Toss until all the ingredients are well mixed. Serve warm or cooled in paper cones or saucers.

CHICKEN SATAY WITH PEANUT SAUCE

THESE MINIATURE KEBABS ARE POPULAR ALL OVER SOUTH-EAST ASIA, AND THEY ARE ESPECIALLY DELICIOUS WHEN COOKED ON A BARBECUE. THE PEANUT DIPPING SAUCE IS A PERFECT PARTNER FOR THE MARINATED CHICKEN.

SERVES FOUR

INGREDIENTS
- 4 skinless, boneless chicken breast portions

For the marinade
- 2 garlic cloves, crushed
- 2.5cm/1in piece fresh root ginger, finely grated
- 10ml/2 tsp Thai fish sauce
- 30ml/2 tbsp light soy sauce
- 15ml/1 tbsp clear honey

For the satay sauce
- 90ml/6 tbsp crunchy peanut butter
- 1 fresh red chilli, seeded and finely chopped
- juice of 1 lime
- 60ml/4 tbsp coconut milk
- salt

1 First, make the satay sauce. Put all the ingredients in a food processor or blender. Process until smooth, then check the seasoning and add more salt or lime juice if necessary. Spoon the sauce into a bowl, cover with clear film (plastic wrap) and set aside.

2 Using a sharp knife, slice each chicken breast portion into four long strips. Put all the marinade ingredients in a large bowl and mix well, then add the chicken strips and toss together until thoroughly coated. Cover and leave for at least 30 minutes in the refrigerator to marinate. Meanwhile, soak 16 wooden satay sticks or kebab skewers in water, to prevent them from burning during cooking.

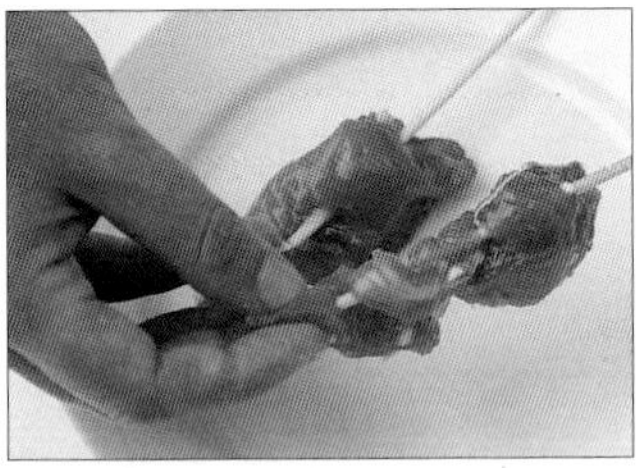

3 Preheat the grill (broiler) to high or prepare the barbecue. Drain the satay sticks or skewers. Drain the chicken strips. Thread one strip on to each satay stick or skewer. Grill (broil) for 3 minutes on each side, or until the chicken is golden brown and cooked through. Serve immediately with the satay sauce.

CORN FRITTERS

SOMETIMES IT IS THE SIMPLEST DISHES THAT TASTE THE BEST. THESE FRITTERS, PACKED WITH CRUNCHY CORN, ARE VERY EASY TO PREPARE AND UNDERSTANDABLY POPULAR.

MAKES TWELVE

INGREDIENTS

3 corn cobs, total weight about 250g/9oz
1 garlic clove, crushed
small bunch fresh coriander (cilantro), chopped
1 small fresh red or green chilli, seeded and finely chopped
1 spring onion (scallion), finely chopped
15ml/1 tbsp soy sauce
75g/3oz/¾ cup rice flour or plain (all-purpose) flour
2 eggs, lightly beaten
60ml/4 tbsp water
oil, for shallow frying
salt and ground black pepper
sweet chilli sauce, to serve

1 Using a sharp knife, slice the kernels from the cobs and place them in a large bowl. Add the garlic, chopped coriander, red or green chilli, spring onion, soy sauce, flour, beaten eggs and water and mix well. Season with salt and pepper to taste and mix again. The mixture should be firm enough to hold its shape, but not stiff.

2 Heat the oil in a large frying pan. Add spoonfuls of the corn mixture, gently spreading each one out with the back of the spoon to make a roundish fritter. Cook for 1–2 minutes on each side.

3 Drain on kitchen paper and keep hot while frying more fritters in the same way. Serve hot with sweet chilli sauce.

TUNG TONG

POPULARLY CALLED "GOLD BAGS", THESE CRISP PASTRY PURSES HAVE A CORIANDER-FLAVOURED FILLING BASED ON WATER CHESTNUTS AND CORN. THEY ARE THE PERFECT VEGETARIAN SNACK.

MAKES EIGHTEEN

INGREDIENTS
- 18 spring roll wrappers, about 8cm/3¼in square, thawed if frozen
- oil, for deep-frying
- plum sauce, to serve

For the filling
- 4 baby corn cobs
- 130g/4½oz can water chestnuts, drained and chopped
- 1 shallot, coarsely chopped
- 1 egg, separated
- 30ml/2 tbsp cornflour (cornstarch)
- 60ml/4 tbsp water
- small bunch fresh coriander (cilantro), chopped
- salt and ground black pepper

1 Make the filling. Place the baby corn, water chestnuts, shallot and egg yolk in a food processor or blender. Process to a coarse paste. Place the egg white in a cup and whisk it lightly with a fork.

2 Put the cornflour in a small pan and stir in the water until smooth. Add the corn mixture and chopped coriander and season with salt and pepper to taste. Cook over a low heat, stirring constantly, until thickened.

3 Leave the filling to cool slightly, then place 5ml/1 tsp in the centre of a spring roll wrapper. Brush the edges with the beaten egg white, then gather up the points and press them firmly together to make a pouch or bag.

4 Repeat with remaining wrappers and filling. Heat the oil in a deep-fryer or wok to 190°C/375°F or until a cube of bread, added to the oil, browns in about 45 seconds. Fry the bags, in batches, for about 5 minutes, until golden brown. Drain on kitchen paper and serve hot, with the plum sauce.

FIRECRACKERS

IT'S EASY TO SEE HOW THESE PASTRY-WRAPPED PRAWN SNACKS GOT THEIR NAME (KRATHAK IN THAI) – AS WELL AS RESEMBLING FIREWORKS, THEIR CONTENTS EXPLODE WITH FLAVOUR.

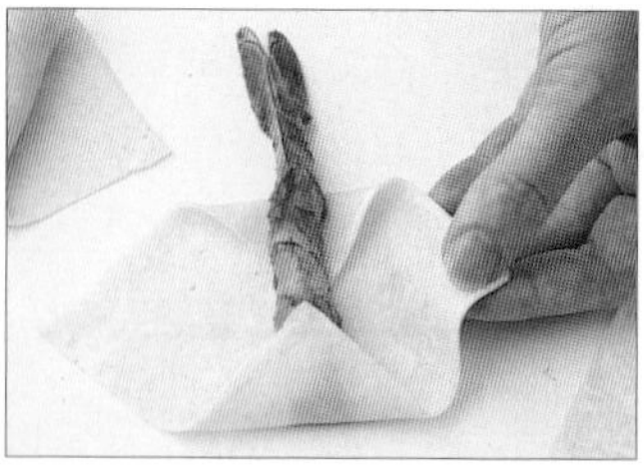

MAKES SIXTEEN

INGREDIENTS

- 16 large, raw king prawns (jumbo shrimp), heads and shells removed but tails left on
- 5ml/1 tsp red curry paste
- 15ml/1 tbsp Thai fish sauce
- 16 small wonton wrappers, about 8cm/3¼in square, thawed if frozen
- 16 fine egg noodles, soaked (see Cook's Tip)
- oil, for deep-frying

1 Place the prawns on their sides and cut two slits through the underbelly of each, one about 1cm/½in from the head end and the other about 1cm/½in from the first cut, cutting across the prawn. This will prevent the prawns from curling when they are cooked.

2 Mix the curry paste with the fish sauce in a shallow dish. Add the prawns and turn them in the mixture until they are well coated. Cover and leave to marinate for 10 minutes.

3 Place a wonton wrapper on the work surface at an angle so that it forms a diamond shape, then fold the top corner over so that the point is in the centre. Place a prawn, slits down, on the wrapper, with the tail projecting from the folded end, then fold the bottom corner over the other end of the prawn.

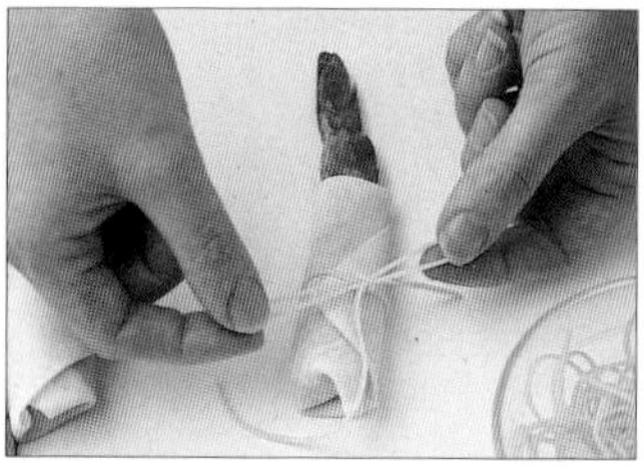

4 Fold each side of the wrapper over in turn to make a tightly folded roll. Tie a noodle in a bow around the roll and set it aside. Repeat with the remaining prawns and wrappers.

5 Heat the oil in a deep-fryer or wok to 190°C/375°F or until a cube of bread, added to the oil, browns in 45 seconds. Fry the prawns, a few at a time, for 5–8 minutes, until golden brown and cooked through. Drain well on kitchen paper and keep hot while you cook the remaining batches.

COOK'S TIP

Soak the fine egg noodles used as ties for the prawn rolls in a bowl of boiling water for 2–3 minutes, until softened, then drain, refresh under cold running water and drain well again.

Green Curry Puffs

Shrimp paste and green curry sauce, used judiciously, give these puffs their distinctive, spicy, savoury flavour, and the addition of chilli steps up the heat.

MAKES TWENTY-FOUR

INGREDIENTS

24 small wonton wrappers, about 8cm/3¼in square, thawed if frozen
15ml/1 tbsp cornflour (cornstarch), mixed to a paste with 30ml/2 tbsp water
oil, for deep-frying

For the filling

1 small potato, about 115g/4oz, boiled and mashed
25g/1oz/3 tbsp cooked petits pois (baby peas)
25g/1oz/3 tbsp cooked corn
few sprigs fresh coriander (cilantro), chopped
1 small fresh red chilli, seeded and finely chopped
½ lemon grass stalk, finely chopped
15ml/1 tbsp soy sauce
5ml/1 tsp shrimp paste or fish sauce
5ml/1 tsp Thai green curry paste

1 Combine the filling ingredients. Lay out one wonton wrapper and place a teaspoon of the filling in the centre.

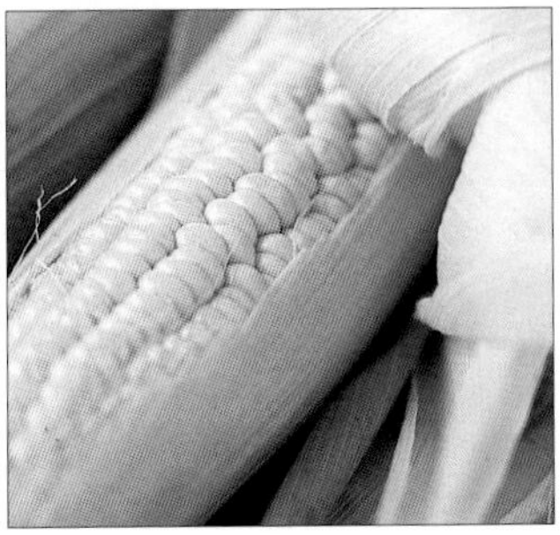

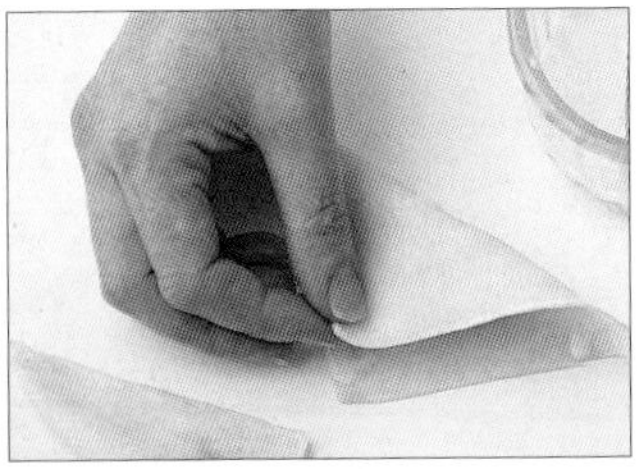

2 Brush a little of the cornflour paste along two sides of the square. Fold the other two sides over to meet them, then press together to make a triangular pastry and seal in the filling. Make more pastries in the same way.

3 Heat the oil in a deep-fryer or wok to 190°C/375°F or until a cube of bread, added to the oil, browns in about 45 seconds. Add the pastries to the oil, a few at a time, and fry them for about 5 minutes, until golden brown.

4 Remove from the fryer or wok and drain on kitchen paper. If you intend serving the puffs hot, place them in a low oven while cooking successive batches. The puffs also taste good cold.

COOK'S TIP

Wonton wrappers dry out quickly, so keep them covered, using clear film (plastic wrap), until you are ready to use them.

FISH CAKES WITH CUCUMBER RELISH

THESE WONDERFUL SMALL FISH CAKES ARE A VERY FAMILIAR AND POPULAR APPETIZER IN THAILAND AND INCREASINGLY THROUGHOUT SOUTH-EAST ASIA. THEY ARE USUALLY SERVED WITH THAI BEER.

MAKES ABOUT TWELVE

INGREDIENTS

- 8 kaffir lime leaves
- 300g/11oz cod fillet, cut into chunks
- 30ml/2 tbsp red curry paste
- 1 egg
- 30ml/2 tbsp Thai fish sauce
- 5ml/1 tsp granulated sugar
- 30ml/2 tbsp cornflour (cornstarch)
- 15ml/1 tbsp chopped fresh coriander (cilantro)
- 50g/2oz/½ cup green beans, thinly sliced
- vegetable oil, for deep-frying

For the cucumber relish

- 60ml/4 tbsp coconut or rice vinegar
- 50g/2oz/¼ cup granulated sugar
- 60ml/4 tbsp water
- 1 head pickled garlic
- 1cm/½in piece fresh root ginger, peeled
- 1 cucumber, cut into thin batons
- 4 shallots, thinly sliced

1 Make the cucumber relish. Mix the coconut or rice vinegar, sugar and water in a small pan. Heat gently, stirring constantly until the sugar has completely dissolved. Remove the pan from the heat and leave to cool.

2 Separate the pickled garlic into cloves. Chop the cloves finely, along with the ginger, and place in a bowl. Add the cucumber batons and shallots, pour over the vinegar mixture and mix lightly. Cover and set aside.

3 Reserve five kaffir lime leaves for the garnish and thinly slice the remainder. Put the chunks of fish, curry paste and egg in a food processor and process to a smooth paste. Transfer the mixture to a bowl and stir in the fish sauce, sugar, cornflour, sliced kaffir lime leaves, coriander and green beans. Mix well, then shape the mixture into about twelve 5mm/¼in thick cakes, each measuring about 5cm/2in in diameter.

4 Heat the oil in a deep-frying pan or wok to 190°C/375°F or until a cube of bread, added to the oil, browns in about 45 seconds. Fry the fish cakes, a few at a time, for about 4–5 minutes, until cooked and evenly brown.

5 Lift out the fish cakes and drain them on kitchen paper. Keep each batch hot while frying successive batches. Garnish with the reserved kaffir lime leaves and serve with the cucumber relish.

CRISP-FRIED CRAB CLAWS

CRAB CLAWS ARE READILY AVAILABLE FROM THE FREEZER CABINET OF MANY ASIAN STORES AND SUPERMARKETS. THAW THEM THOROUGHLY AND DRY ON KITCHEN PAPER BEFORE COATING THEM.

SERVES FOUR

INGREDIENTS

- 50g/2oz/⅓ cup rice flour
- 15ml/1 tbsp cornflour (cornstarch)
- 2.5ml/½ tsp granulated sugar
- 1 egg
- 60ml/4 tbsp cold water
- 1 lemon grass stalk, root trimmed
- 2 garlic cloves, finely chopped
- 15ml/1 tbsp chopped fresh coriander (cilantro)
- 1–2 fresh red chillies, seeded and finely chopped
- 5ml/1 tsp Thai fish sauce
- vegetable oil, for deep-frying
- 12 half-shelled crab claws, thawed if frozen
- ground black pepper

For the chilli vinegar dip

- 45ml/3 tbsp granulated sugar
- 120ml/4fl oz/½ cup water
- 120ml/4fl oz/½ cup red wine vinegar
- 15ml/1 tbsp Thai fish sauce
- 2–4 fresh red chillies, seeded and chopped

1 First make the chilli vinegar dip. Mix the sugar and water in a pan. Heat gently, stirring until the sugar has dissolved, then bring to the boil. Lower the heat and simmer for 5–7 minutes. Stir in the rest of the ingredients, pour into a serving bowl and set aside.

2 Combine the rice flour, cornflour and sugar in a bowl. Beat the egg with the cold water, then stir the egg and water mixture into the flour mixture and beat well until it forms a light batter.

3 Cut off the lower 5cm/2in of the lemon grass stalk and chop it finely. Add the lemon grass to the batter, with the garlic, coriander, red chillies and fish sauce. Stir in pepper to taste.

4 Heat the oil in a deep-fryer or wok to 190°C/375°F or until a cube of bread browns in 45 seconds. Dip the crab claws into the batter, then fry, in batches, until golden. Serve with the dip.

THAI TEMPEH CAKES WITH SWEET CHILLI DIPPING SAUCE

MADE FROM SOYA BEANS, TEMPEH IS SIMILAR TO TOFU BUT HAS A NUTTIER TASTE. HERE, IT IS COMBINED WITH A FRAGRANT BLEND OF LEMON GRASS, CORIANDER AND GINGER.

MAKES EIGHT

INGREDIENTS

- 1 lemon grass stalk, outer leaves removed and inside finely chopped
- 2 garlic cloves, chopped
- 2 spring onions (scallions), finely chopped
- 2 shallots, finely chopped
- 2 fresh red chillies, seeded and finely chopped
- 2.5cm/1in piece fresh root ginger, finely chopped
- 60ml/4 tbsp chopped fresh coriander (cilantro), plus extra to garnish
- 250g/9oz/2¼ cups tempeh, thawed if frozen, sliced
- 15ml/1 tbsp fresh lime juice
- 5ml/1 tsp granulated sugar
- 45ml/3 tbsp plain (all-purpose) flour
- 1 large (US extra large) egg, lightly beaten
- salt and freshly ground black pepper
- vegetable oil, for frying

For the dipping sauce

- 45ml/3 tbsp mirin (see Cook's Tip)
- 45ml/3 tbsp white wine vinegar
- 2 spring onions (scallions), thinly sliced
- 15ml/1 tbsp granulated sugar
- 2 fresh red chillies, seeded and finely chopped
- 30ml/2 tbsp chopped fresh coriander (cilantro)
- large pinch of salt

1 Make the dipping sauce. Mix together the mirin, vinegar, spring onions, sugar, chillies, coriander and salt in a small bowl. Cover with clear film (plastic wrap) and set aside until ready to serve.

COOK'S TIP

Mirin is a sweet rice wine from Japan. It has quite a delicate flavour and is used for cooking. Rice wine for drinking, called sake, is rather more expensive. Both are available from Asian food stores. If you cannot locate mirin, dry sherry can be used instead, although the results will not be quite the same.

2 Place the lemon grass, garlic, spring onions, shallots, chillies, ginger and coriander in a food processor or blender, then process to a coarse paste. Add the tempeh, lime juice and sugar and process until combined. Add the flour and egg, with salt and pepper to taste. Process again until the mixture forms a coarse, sticky paste.

3 Scrape the paste into a bowl. Take one-eighth of the mixture at a time and form it into rounds with your hands.

4 Heat a little oil in a large frying pan. Fry the tempeh cakes for 5–6 minutes, turning once, until golden. Drain on kitchen paper. Transfer to a platter, garnish and serve with the sauce.

POTATO, SHALLOT AND GARLIC SAMOSAS WITH GREEN PEAS

MOST SAMOSAS ARE DEEP-FRIED. THESE ARE BAKED, MAKING THEM A HEALTHIER OPTION. THEY ARE ALSO PERFECT FOR PARTIES, SINCE THE PASTRIES NEED NO LAST-MINUTE ATTENTION.

MAKES TWENTY-FIVE

INGREDIENTS
- 1 large potato, about 250g/9oz, diced
- 15ml/1 tbsp groundnut (peanut) oil
- 2 shallots, finely chopped
- 1 garlic clove, finely chopped
- 60ml/4 tbsp coconut milk
- 5ml/1 tsp Thai red or green curry paste
- 75g/3oz/¾ cup peas
- juice of ½ lime
- 25 samosa wrappers or 10 x 5cm/4 x 2in strips of filo pastry
- salt and ground black pepper
- oil, for brushing

1 Preheat the oven to 220°C/425°F/Gas 7. Bring a small pan of water to the boil, add the diced potato, cover and cook for 10–15 minutes, until tender. Drain and set aside.

2 Meanwhile, heat the groundnut oil in a large frying pan and cook the shallots and garlic over a medium heat, stirring occasionally, for 4–5 minutes, until softened and golden.

3 Add the drained diced potato, coconut milk, red or green curry paste, peas and lime juice to the frying pan. Mash together coarsely with a wooden spoon. Season to taste with salt and pepper and cook over a low heat for 2–3 minutes, then remove the pan from the heat and set aside until the mixture has cooled a little.

4 Lay a samosa wrapper or filo strip flat on the work surface. Brush with a little oil, then place a generous teaspoonful of the mixture in the middle of one end. Turn one corner diagonally over the filling to meet the long edge.

5 Continue folding over the filling, keeping the triangular shape as you work down the strip. Brush with a little more oil if necessary and place on a baking sheet. Prepare all the other samosas in the same way.

6 Bake for 15 minutes, or until the pastry is golden and crisp. Leave to cool slightly before serving.

COOK'S TIP

Many Asian food stores sell what is described as a samosa pad. This is a packet, usually frozen, containing about 50 oblong pieces of samosa pastry. Filo pastry, cut to size, can be used instead.

THAI SPRING ROLLS

CRUNCHY SPRING ROLLS ARE AS POPULAR IN THAILAND AS THEY ARE IN CHINA. THAIS FILL THEIR VERSION WITH A DELICIOUS GARLIC, PORK AND NOODLE MIXTURE.

MAKES TWENTY-FOUR

INGREDIENTS

- 24 × 15cm/6in square spring roll wrappers, thawed if frozen
- 30ml/2 tbsp plain (all-purpose) flour
- vegetable oil, for deep-frying
- sweet chilli dipping sauce, to serve

For the filling

- 4–6 Chinese dried mushrooms, soaked for 30 minutes in warm water to cover
- 50g/2oz cellophane noodles
- 30ml/2 tbsp vegetable oil
- 2 garlic cloves, chopped
- 2 fresh red chillies, seeded and chopped
- 225g/8oz minced (ground) pork
- 50g/2oz peeled cooked prawns (shrimp), thawed if frozen
- 30ml/2 tbsp Thai fish sauce
- 5ml/1 tsp granulated sugar
- 1 carrot, grated
- 50g/2oz piece of canned bamboo shoot, drained and chopped
- 50g/2oz/⅔ cup beansprouts
- 2 spring onions (scallions), finely chopped
- 15ml/1 tbsp chopped fresh coriander (cilantro)
- ground black pepper

1 Make the filling. Drain the soaked mushrooms. Cut off and discard the stems, then chop the caps finely.

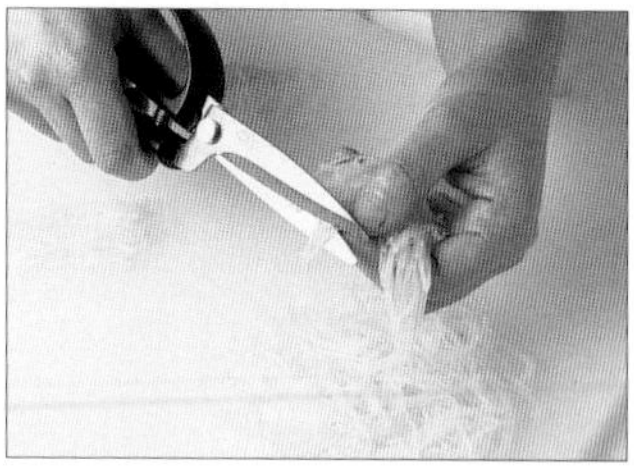

2 Place the noodles in a large bowl, cover with boiling water and soak for 10 minutes. Drain the noodles and snip them into 5cm/2in lengths.

3 Heat the oil in a wok, add the garlic and chillies and stir-fry for 30 seconds. Transfer to a plate. Add the pork to the wok and stir-fry until it has browned.

4 Add the mushrooms, noodles and prawns. Stir in the fish sauce and sugar, then add pepper to taste.

5 Tip the mixture into a bowl. Stir in the grated carrot, chopped bamboo shoot, beansprouts, spring onions and chopped coriander. Add the reserved chilli mixture and mix well.

6 Unwrap the spring roll wrappers. Cover them with a dampened dishtowel while you are making the rolls, so that they do not dry out, and work on them one at a time. Put the flour in a small bowl and stir in a little water to make a paste. Place a spoonful of the filling in the centre of a spring roll wrapper.

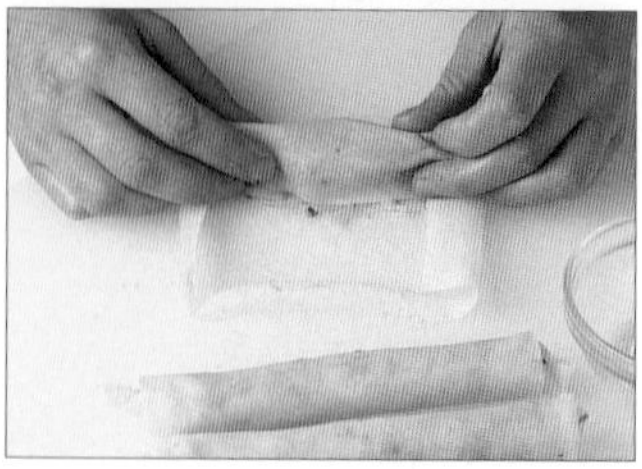

7 Turn the bottom edge over to cover the filling, then fold in the sides. Roll up the wrapper almost to the top, then brush the top edge with the flour paste and seal. Fill the remaining wrappers.

8 Heat the oil in a deep-fryer or wok to 190°C/375°F or until a cube of bread browns in about 45 seconds. Fry the spring rolls, in batches, until crisp and golden. Drain on kitchen paper and serve hot with sweet chilli sauce.

STUFFED THAI OMELETTES

THAI FOOD OFTEN CLEVERLY COMBINES HOT CHILLI WITH SWEET FLAVOURS, AS IN THE FILLING FOR THE OMELETTES. IT MAKES AN INTERESTING CONTRAST TO THE DELICATE FLAVOUR OF THE EGG.

SERVES FOUR

INGREDIENTS

- 30ml/2 tbsp groundnut (peanut) oil
- 2 garlic cloves, finely chopped
- 1 small onion, finely chopped
- 225g/8oz minced (ground) pork
- 30ml/2 tbsp Thai fish sauce
- 5ml/1 tsp granulated sugar
- 2 tomatoes, peeled and chopped
- 15ml/1 tbsp chopped fresh coriander (cilantro)
- ground black pepper
- fresh coriander (cilantro) sprigs and sliced fresh red chillies, to garnish

For the omelettes

- 5 eggs
- 15ml/1 tbsp Thai fish sauce
- 30ml/2 tbsp groundnut (peanut) oil

1 Heat the oil in a wok or frying pan, add the garlic and onion, and cook over a medium heat, stirring occasionally, for 3–4 minutes, until soft. Add the pork and cook for about 8 minutes, stirring frequently, until lightly browned.

2 Stir in the Thai fish sauce, sugar and tomatoes, season to taste with pepper and simmer over a low heat until slightly thickened. Mix in the fresh coriander. Remove the wok or frying pan from the heat, cover to keep warm and set aside while you make the omelettes.

3 To make the omelettes, put the eggs and Thai fish sauce in a bowl and beat together lightly with a fork.

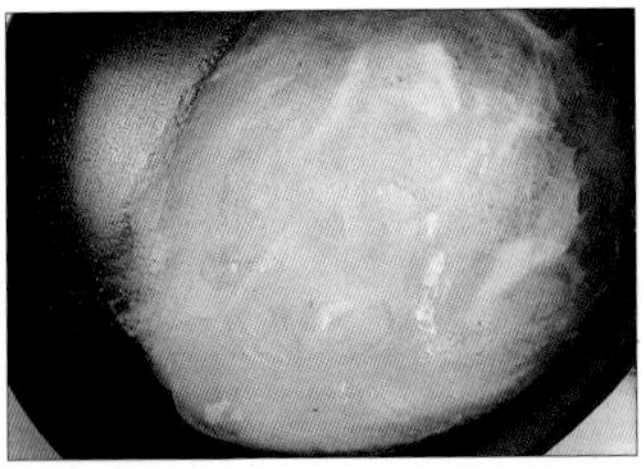

4 Heat 15ml/1 tbsp of the oil in an omelette pan or wok over a medium heat. When the oil is very hot, but not smoking, add half the beaten egg mixture and immediately tilt the pan or wok to spread the egg into a thin, even layer over the base. Cook over a medium heat until the omelette is just set and the underside is golden.

5 Spoon half the filling into the centre of the omelette. Fold into a neat square parcel by bringing the opposite sides of the omelette towards each other. Slide the parcel on to a serving dish, folded side down. Make another omelette parcel in the same way. Garnish with the coriander sprigs and chillies. Cut each omelette in half to serve.

Egg Rolls

The title of this recipe could lead to some confusion, especially in the United States, where egg rolls are the same as spring rolls. These egg rolls, however, are wedges of a rolled Thai-flavoured omelette. They are frequently served as finger food.

SERVES TWO

INGREDIENTS

- 3 eggs, beaten
- 15ml/1 tbsp soy sauce
- 1 bunch garlic chives, thinly sliced
- 1–2 small fresh red or green chillies, seeded and finely chopped
- small bunch fresh coriander (cilantro), chopped
- pinch of granulated sugar
- salt and ground black pepper
- 15ml/1 tbsp groundnut (peanut) oil

For the dipping sauce

- 60ml/4 tbsp light soy sauce
- fresh lime juice, to taste

COOK'S TIP

Wear gloves while preparing chillies or cut them up with a knife and fork. Wash your hands after in warm, soapy water.

1 Make the dipping sauce. Pour the soy sauce into a bowl. Add a generous squeeze of lime juice. Taste and add more lime juice if needed.

2 Mix the eggs, soy sauce, chives, chillies and coriander. Add the sugar and season to taste. Heat the oil in a large frying pan, pour in the egg mixture and swirl the pan to make an omelette.

3 Cook for 1–2 minutes, until the omelette is just firm and the underside is golden. Slide it out on to a plate and roll up as though it were a pancake. Leave to cool completely.

4 When the omelette is cool, slice it diagonally in 1cm/½in pieces. Arrange the slices on a serving platter and serve with the bowl of dipping sauce.

SON-IN-LAW EGGS

THE FASCINATING NAME FOR THIS DISH COMES FROM A STORY ABOUT A PROSPECTIVE BRIDEGROOM WHO VERY MUCH WANTED TO IMPRESS HIS FUTURE MOTHER-IN-LAW AND DEVISED A NEW RECIPE BASED ON THE ONLY DISH HE KNEW HOW TO MAKE – BOILED EGGS.

SERVES FOUR TO SIX

INGREDIENTS
- 30ml/2 tbsp vegetable oil
- 6 shallots, thinly sliced
- 6 garlic cloves, thinly sliced
- 6 fresh red chillies, sliced
- oil, for deep-frying
- 6 hard-boiled eggs, shelled
- salad leaves, to serve
- sprigs of fresh coriander (cilantro), to garnish

For the sauce
- 75g/3oz/6 tbsp palm sugar or light muscovado (brown) sugar
- 75ml/5 tbsp Thai fish sauce
- 90ml/6 tbsp tamarind juice

COOK'S TIP
The level of heat varies, depending on which type of chillies are used and whether you include the seeds.

1 Make the sauce. Put the sugar, fish sauce and tamarind juice in a pan. Bring to the boil, stirring until the sugar dissolves, lower the heat and simmer for 5 minutes. Taste and add more sugar, fish sauce or tamarind juice, if needed. Transfer the sauce to a bowl.

2 Heat the vegetable oil in a frying pan and cook the shallots, garlic and chillies for 5 minutes. Transfer to a bowl.

3 Heat the oil in a deep-fryer or wok to 190°C/375°F or until a cube of bread, added to the oil, browns in about 45 seconds. Deep-fry the eggs in the hot oil for 3–5 minutes, until golden brown. Remove and drain well on kitchen paper. Cut the eggs in quarters and arrange them on a bed of leaves. Drizzle with the sauce and sprinkle over the shallot mixture. Garnish with coriander sprigs and serve immediately.

Soups

In Thailand, soups are not seen as curtain-raisers, but are served throughout the meal, providing the palate with tastes and textures that complement or contrast with those in more dominant dishes. You may choose to serve any of these soups solo, as a light lunch or supper dish, or as a prelude to a dinner party, but however and whenever you place them before your guests, treats like Cellophane Noodle Soup and Northern Squash Soup are certain to prove popular.

HOT AND SWEET VEGETABLE AND TOFU SOUP

AN INTERESTING COMBINATION OF HOT, SWEET AND SOUR FLAVOURS THAT MAKES FOR A SOOTHING, NUTRITIOUS SOUP. IT TAKES ONLY MINUTES TO MAKE AS THE SPINACH AND SILKEN TOFU ARE SIMPLY PLACED IN BOWLS AND COVERED WITH THE FLAVOURED HOT STOCK.

SERVES FOUR

INGREDIENTS
- 1.2 litres/2 pints/5 cups vegetable stock
- 5–10ml/1–2 tsp Thai red curry paste
- 2 kaffir lime leaves, torn
- 40g/1½oz/3 tbsp palm sugar or light muscovado (brown) sugar
- 30ml/2 tbsp soy sauce
- juice of 1 lime
- 1 carrot, cut into thin batons
- 50g/2oz baby spinach leaves, any coarse stalks removed
- 225g/8oz block silken tofu, diced

1 Heat the stock in a large pan, then add the red curry paste. Stir constantly over a medium heat until the paste has dissolved. Add the lime leaves, sugar and soy sauce and bring to the boil.

2 Add the lime juice and carrot to the pan. Reduce the heat and simmer for 5–10 minutes. Place the spinach and tofu in four individual serving bowls and pour the hot stock on top to serve.

MIXED VEGETABLE SOUP

In Thailand, this type of soup is usually made in large quantities and then reheated for consumption over several days. If you would like to do the same, double or treble the quantities. Chill leftover soup rapidly and reheat thoroughly before serving.

SERVES FOUR

INGREDIENTS

- 30ml/2 tbsp groundnut (peanut) oil
- 15ml/1 tbsp magic paste (see Cook's Tip)
- 90g/3½oz Savoy cabbage or Chinese leaves (Chinese cabbage), finely shredded
- 90g/3½oz mooli (daikon), finely diced
- 1 medium cauliflower, coarsely chopped
- 4 celery sticks, coarsely chopped
- 1.2 litres/2 pints/5 cups vegetable stock
- 130g/4½oz fried tofu, cut into 2.5cm/1in cubes
- 5ml/1 tsp palm sugar or light muscovado (brown) sugar
- 45ml/3 tbsp light soy sauce

1 Heat the groundnut oil in a large, heavy pan or wok. Add the magic paste and cook over a low heat, stirring frequently, until it gives off its aroma. Add the shredded Savoy cabbage or Chinese leaves, mooli, cauliflower and celery. Pour in the vegetable stock, increase the heat to medium and bring to the boil, stirring occasionally. Gently stir in the tofu cubes.

2 Add the sugar and soy sauce. Reduce the heat and simmer for 15 minutes, until the vegetables are cooked and tender. Taste and add a little more soy sauce if needed. Serve hot.

COOK'S TIP

Magic paste is a mixture of crushed garlic, white pepper and coriander (cilantro). Look for it at Thai markets.

Omelette Soup

A very satisfying soup that is quick and easy to prepare. It is versatile, too, in that you can vary the vegetables according to what is available.

SERVES FOUR

INGREDIENTS

- 1 egg
- 15ml/1 tbsp groundnut (peanut) oil
- 900ml/1½ pints/3¾ cups vegetable stock
- 2 large carrots, finely diced
- 4 outer leaves Savoy cabbage, shredded
- 30ml/2 tbsp soy sauce
- 2.5ml/½ tsp granulated sugar
- 2.5ml/½ tsp ground black pepper
- fresh coriander (cilantro) leaves, to garnish

VARIATION

Use pak choi (bok choy) instead of Savoy cabbage. In Thailand there are about forty different types of pak choi, including miniature versions.

1 Put the egg in a bowl and beat lightly with a fork. Heat the oil in a small frying pan until it is hot, but not smoking. Pour in the egg and swirl the pan so that it coats the base evenly. Cook over a medium heat until the omelette has set and the underside is golden. Slide it out of the pan and roll it up like a pancake. Slice into 5mm/¼in rounds and set aside for the garnish.

2 Put the stock into a large pan. Add the carrots and cabbage and bring to the boil. Reduce the heat and simmer for 5 minutes, then add the soy sauce, granulated sugar and pepper.

3 Stir well, then pour into warmed bowls. Lay a few omelette rounds on the surface of each portion and complete the garnish with the coriander leaves.

CELLOPHANE NOODLE SOUP

THE NOODLES USED IN THIS SOUP GO BY VARIOUS NAMES: GLASS NOODLES, CELLOPHANE NOODLES, BEAN THREAD OR TRANSPARENT NOODLES. THEY ARE ESPECIALLY VALUED FOR THEIR BRITTLE TEXTURE.

SERVES FOUR

INGREDIENTS

- 4 large dried shiitake mushrooms
- 15g/½oz dried lily buds
- ½ cucumber, coarsely chopped
- 2 garlic cloves, halved
- 90g/3½oz white cabbage, chopped
- 1.2 litres/2 pints/5 cups boiling water
- 115g/4oz cellophane noodles
- 30ml/2 tbsp soy sauce
- 15ml/1 tbsp palm sugar or light muscovado (brown) sugar
- 90g/3½oz block silken tofu, diced
- fresh coriander (cilantro) leaves, to garnish

1 Soak the shiitake mushrooms in warm water for 30 minutes. In a separate bowl, soak the dried lily buds in warm water, also for 30 minutes.

2 Meanwhile, put the cucumber, garlic and cabbage in a food processor and process to a smooth paste. Scrape the mixture into a large pan and add the measured boiling water.

3 Bring to the boil, then reduce the heat and cook for 2 minutes, stirring occasionally. Strain this stock into another pan, return to a low heat and bring to simmering point.

4 Drain the lily buds, rinse under cold running water, then drain again. Cut off any hard ends. Add the lily buds to the stock with the noodles, soy sauce and sugar and cook for 5 minutes more.

5 Strain the mushroom soaking liquid into the soup. Discard the mushroom stems, then slice the caps. Divide them and the tofu among four bowls. Pour the soup over, garnish and serve.

Northern Squash Soup

As the title of the recipe suggests, this comes from northern Thailand. It is quite hearty, something of a cross between a soup and a stew. The banana flower isn't essential, but it does add a unique and authentic flavour.

SERVES FOUR

INGREDIENTS
- 1 butternut squash, about 300g/11oz
- 1 litre/1¾ pints/4 cups vegetable stock
- 90g/3½ oz/scant 1 cup green beans, cut into 2.5cm/1in pieces
- 45g/1¾ oz dried banana flower (optional)
- 15ml/1 tbsp Thai fish sauce
- 225g/8oz raw prawns (shrimp)
- small bunch fresh basil
- cooked rice, to serve

For the chilli paste
- 115g/4oz shallots, sliced
- 10 drained bottled green peppercorns
- 1 small fresh green chilli, seeded and finely chopped
- 2.5ml/½ tsp shrimp paste

1 Peel the butternut squash and cut it in half. Scoop out the seeds with a teaspoon and discard, then cut the flesh into neat cubes. Set aside.

2 Make the chilli paste by pounding the shallots, peppercorns, chilli and shrimp paste together using a mortar and pestle or puréeing them in a spice blender.

3 Heat the stock gently in a large pan, then stir in the chilli paste. Add the squash, beans and banana flower, if using. Bring to the boil and cook for 15 minutes.

4 Add the fish sauce, prawns and basil. Bring to simmering point, then simmer for 3 minutes. Serve in warmed bowls, accompanied by rice.

SMOKED MACKEREL AND TOMATO SOUP

ALL THE INGREDIENTS FOR THIS UNUSUAL SOUP ARE COOKED IN A SINGLE PAN, SO IT IS NOT ONLY QUICK AND EASY TO PREPARE, BUT REDUCES THE CLEARING UP. SMOKED MACKEREL GIVES THE SOUP A ROBUST FLAVOUR, BUT THIS IS TEMPERED BY THE CITRUS TONES IN THE LEMON GRASS AND TAMARIND.

SERVES FOUR

INGREDIENTS

- 200g/7oz smoked mackerel fillets
- 4 tomatoes
- 1 litre/1¾ pints/4 cups vegetable stock
- 1 lemon grass stalk, finely chopped
- 5cm/2in piece fresh galangal, finely diced
- 4 shallots, finely chopped
- 2 garlic cloves, finely chopped
- 2.5ml/½ tsp dried chilli flakes
- 15ml/1 tbsp Thai fish sauce
- 5ml/1 tsp palm sugar or light muscovado (brown) sugar
- 45ml/3 tbsp thick tamarind juice, made by mixing tamarind paste with warm water
- small bunch fresh chives or spring onions (scallions), to garnish

1 Prepare the smoked mackerel fillets. Remove and discard the skin, if necessary, then chop the flesh into large pieces. Remove any stray bones with your fingers or a pair of tweezers.

2 Cut the tomatoes in half, squeeze out most of the seeds with your fingers, then finely dice the flesh with a sharp knife. Set aside.

3 Pour the stock into a large pan and add the lemon grass, galangal, shallots and garlic. Bring to the boil, reduce the heat and simmer for 15 minutes.

4 Add the fish, tomatoes, chilli flakes, fish sauce, sugar and tamarind juice. Simmer for 4–5 minutes, until the fish and tomatoes are heated through. Serve garnished with chives or spring onions.

GALANGAL, CHICKEN AND COCONUT SOUP

This aromatic soup is rich with coconut milk and intensely flavoured with galangal, lemon grass and kaffir lime leaves.

SERVES FOUR TO SIX

INGREDIENTS

- 4 lemon grass stalks, roots trimmed
- 2 x 400ml/14fl oz cans coconut milk
- 475ml/16fl oz/2 cups chicken stock
- 2.5cm/1in piece fresh galangal, peeled and thinly sliced
- 10 black peppercorns, crushed
- 10 kaffir lime leaves, torn
- 300g/11oz skinless, boneless chicken breast portions, cut into thin strips
- 115g/4oz/1 cup button (white) mushrooms, halved if large
- 50g/2oz/½ cup baby corn cobs, quartered lengthways
- 60ml/4 tbsp fresh lime juice
- 45ml/3 tbsp Thai fish sauce
- chopped fresh red chillies, spring onions (scallions) and fresh coriander (cilantro) leaves, to garnish

1 Cut off the lower 5cm/2in from each lemon grass stalk and chop it finely. Bruise the remaining pieces of stalk. Bring the coconut milk and chicken stock to the boil in a large pan over a medium heat. Add the chopped and bruised lemon grass, the galangal, peppercorns and half the kaffir lime leaves, reduce the heat to low and simmer gently for 10 minutes. Strain the soup into a clean pan.

2 Return the soup to a low heat, then stir in the chicken strips, mushrooms and corn. Simmer gently, stirring occasionally, for 5–7 minutes, or until the chicken is cooked.

3 Stir in the lime juice and fish sauce, then add the remaining lime leaves. Ladle into warm bowls and serve, garnished with chopped chillies, spring onions and coriander leaves.

HOT-AND-SOUR PRAWN SOUP

This is a classic Thai seafood soup – Tom Yam Kung – and it is one of the most popular and best-known Thai soups.

SERVES FOUR TO SIX

INGREDIENTS

- 450g/1lb raw king prawns (jumbo shrimp), thawed if frozen
- 1 litre/1¾ pints/4 cups chicken stock or water
- 3 lemon grass stalks, roots trimmed
- 10 kaffir lime leaves, torn in half
- 225g/8oz can straw mushrooms, drained
- 45ml/3 tbsp Thai fish sauce
- 60ml/4 tbsp fresh lime juice
- 30ml/2 tbsp chopped spring onion (scallion)
- 15ml/1 tbsp fresh coriander (cilantro) leaves
- 4 fresh red chillies, seeded and thinly sliced
- salt and ground black pepper

1 Peel the prawns, reserving the shells. Devein the prawns and set aside.

2 Rinse the shells under cold water, then put them in a large pan with the stock or water. Bring to the boil.

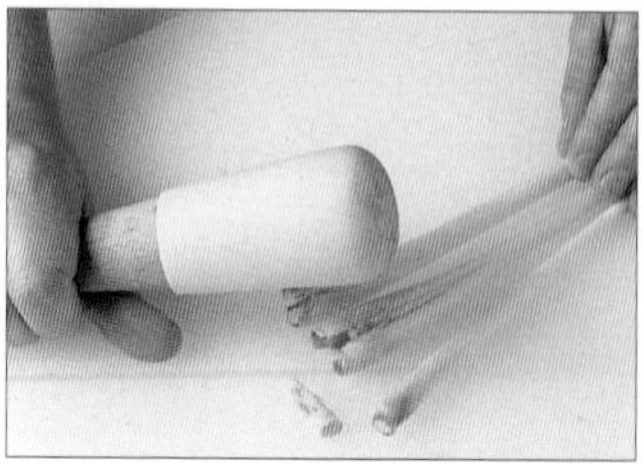

3 Bruise the lemon grass stalks and add them to the stock with half the lime leaves. Simmer gently for 5–6 minutes, until the stock is fragrant.

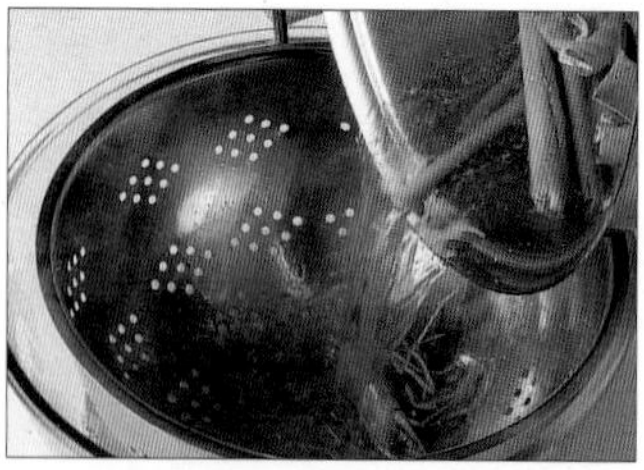

4 Strain the stock, return it to the clean pan and reheat. Add the drained mushrooms and the prawns, then cook until the prawns turn pink.

5 Stir the fish sauce, lime juice, spring onion, coriander, chillies and the remaining lime leaves into the soup. Taste and adjust the seasoning if necessary. The soup should be sour, salty, spicy and hot.

PUMPKIN AND COCONUT SOUP

THE NATURAL SWEETNESS OF THE PUMPKIN IS HEIGHTENED BY THE ADDITION OF A LITTLE SUGAR IN THIS LOVELY LOOKING SOUP, BUT THIS IS BALANCED BY THE CHILLIES, SHRIMP PASTE AND DRIED SHRIMP. COCONUT CREAM BLURS THE BOUNDARIES BEAUTIFULLY.

SERVES FOUR TO SIX

INGREDIENTS
- 450g/1lb pumpkin
- 2 garlic cloves, crushed
- 4 shallots, finely chopped
- 2.5ml/½ tsp shrimp paste
- 1 lemon grass stalk, chopped
- 2 fresh green chillies, seeded
- 15ml/1 tbsp dried shrimp soaked for 10 minutes in warm water to cover
- 600ml/1 pint/2½ cups chicken stock
- 600ml/1 pint/2½ cups coconut cream
- 30ml/2 tbsp Thai fish sauce
- 5ml/1 tsp granulated sugar
- 115g/4oz small cooked shelled prawns (shrimp)
- salt and ground black pepper

To garnish
- 2 fresh red chillies, seeded and thinly sliced
- 10–12 fresh basil leaves

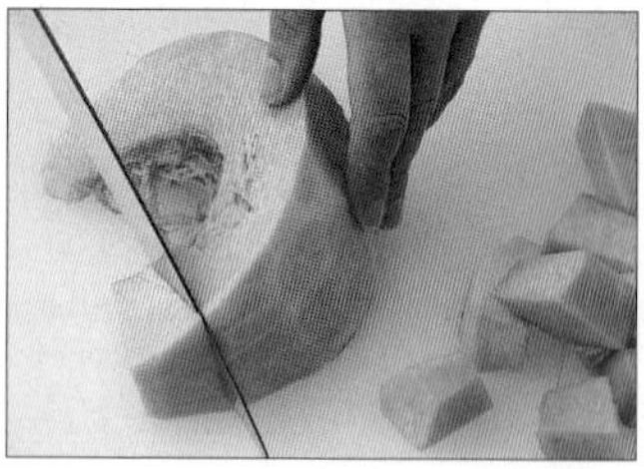

1 Peel the pumpkin and cut it into quarters with a sharp knife. Scoop out the seeds with a teaspoon and discard. Cut the flesh into chunks about 2cm/¾in thick and set aside.

2 Put the garlic, shallots, shrimp paste, lemon grass, green chillies and salt to taste in a mortar. Drain the dried shrimp, discarding the soaking liquid, and add them, then use a pestle to grind the mixture into a paste. Alternatively, place all the ingredients in a food processor and process to a paste.

3 Bring the chicken stock to the boil in a large pan. Add the ground paste and stir well to dissolve.

4 Add the pumpkin chunks and bring to a simmer. Simmer for 10–15 minutes, or until the pumpkin is tender.

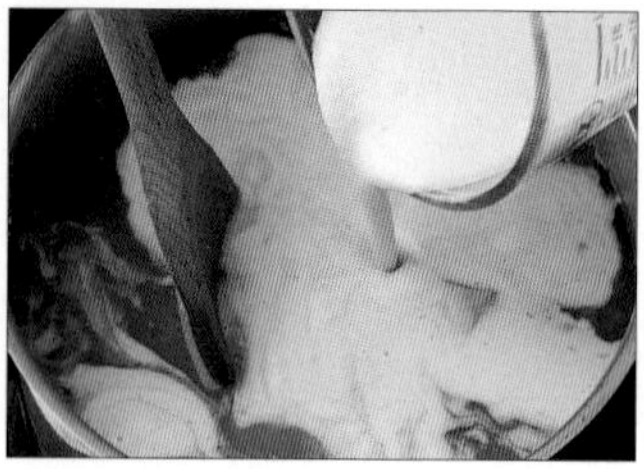

5 Stir in the coconut cream, then bring the soup back to simmering point. Do not let it boil. Add the fish sauce, sugar and ground black pepper to taste.

6 Add the prawns and cook for a further 2–3 minutes, until they are heated through. Serve in warm soup bowls, garnished with chillies and basil leaves.

COOK'S TIP

Shrimp paste is made from ground shrimp fermented in brine.

CHIANG MAI NOODLE SOUP

NOWADAYS A SIGNATURE DISH OF THE CITY OF CHIANG MAI, THIS DELICIOUS NOODLE SOUP ORIGINATED IN BURMA, NOW CALLED MYANMAR, WHICH LIES ONLY A LITTLE TO THE NORTH. IT IS ALSO THE THAI EQUIVALENT OF THE FAMOUS MALAYSIAN "LAKSA".

SERVES FOUR TO SIX

INGREDIENTS

- 600ml/1 pint/2½ cups coconut milk
- 30ml/2 tbsp Thai red curry paste
- 5ml/1 tsp ground turmeric
- 450g/1lb chicken thighs, boned and cut into bitesize chunks
- 600ml/1 pint/2½ cups chicken stock
- 60ml/4 tbsp Thai fish sauce
- 15ml/1 tbsp dark soy sauce
- juice of ½–1 lime
- 450g/1lb fresh egg noodles, blanched briefly in boiling water
- salt and ground black pepper

To garnish

- 3 spring onions (scallions), chopped
- 4 fresh red chillies, chopped
- 4 shallots, chopped
- 60ml/4 tbsp sliced pickled mustard leaves, rinsed
- 30ml/2 tbsp fried sliced garlic
- coriander (cilantro) leaves
- 4–6 fried noodle nests (optional)

1 Pour about one-third of the coconut milk into a large, heavy pan or wok. Bring to the boil over a medium heat, stirring frequently with a wooden spoon until the milk separates.

2 Add the curry paste and ground turmeric, stir to mix completely and cook until the mixture is fragrant.

3 Add the chunks of chicken and toss over the heat for about 2 minutes, making sure that all the chunks are thoroughly coated with the paste.

4 Add the remaining coconut milk, the chicken stock, fish sauce and soy sauce. Season with salt and pepper to taste. Bring to simmering point, stirring frequently, then lower the heat and cook gently for 7–10 minutes. Remove from the heat and stir in lime juice to taste.

5 Reheat the fresh egg noodles in boiling water, drain and divide among four to six warmed bowls. Divide the chunks of chicken among the bowls and ladle in the hot soup. Top each serving with spring onions, chillies, shallots, pickled mustard leaves, fried garlic, coriander leaves and a fried noodle nest, if using. Serve immediately.

RICE PORRIDGE

Originating in China, this dish has now spread throughout the whole of South-East Asia and is loved for its comforting blandness. It is invariably served with a few strongly flavoured accompaniments.

SERVES TWO

INGREDIENTS
- 900ml/1½ pints/3¾ cups vegetable stock
- 200g/7oz/1¾ cups cooked rice
- 225g/8oz minced (ground) pork
- 15ml/1 tbsp Thai fish sauce
- 2 heads pickled garlic, finely chopped
- 1 celery stick, finely diced
- salt and ground black pepper

To garnish
- 30ml/2 tbsp groundnut (peanut) oil
- 4 garlic cloves, thinly sliced
- 4 small red shallots, finely sliced

1 Make the garnishes by heating the groundnut oil in a frying pan and cooking the garlic and shallots over a low heat until brown. Drain on kitchen paper and reserve for the soup.

2 Pour the stock into a large pan. Bring to the boil and add the rice. Season the minced pork. Add it by taking small teaspoons and tapping the spoon on the side of the pan so that the meat falls into the soup in small lumps.

3 Stir in the fish sauce and pickled garlic and simmer for 10 minutes, until the pork is cooked. Stir in the celery.

4 Serve the rice porridge in individual warmed bowls. Sprinkle the prepared garlic and shallots on top and season with plenty of ground pepper.

COOK'S TIP
Pickled garlic has a distinctive flavour and is available from Asian food stores.

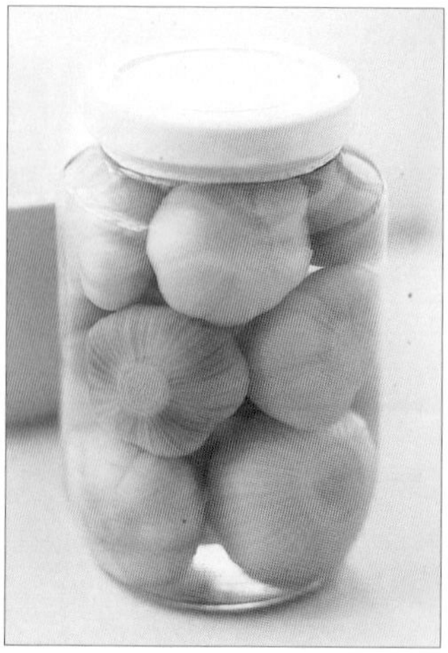

COCONUT AND SEAFOOD SOUP

THE LONG LIST OF INGREDIENTS COULD MISLEAD YOU INTO THINKING THAT THIS SOUP IS COMPLICATED AND VERY TIME-CONSUMING TO PREPARE. IN FACT, IT IS EXTREMELY EASY TO PUT TOGETHER AND THE MARRIAGE OF FLAVOURS WORKS BEAUTIFULLY.

SERVES FOUR

INGREDIENTS

- 600ml/1 pint/2½ cups fish stock
- 5 thin slices fresh galangal or fresh root ginger
- 2 lemon grass stalks, chopped
- 3 kaffir lime leaves, shredded
- bunch garlic chives, about 25g/1oz
- small bunch fresh coriander (cilantro), about 15g/½oz
- 15ml/1 tbsp vegetable oil
- 4 shallots, chopped
- 400ml/14fl oz can coconut milk
- 30–45ml/2–3 tbsp Thai fish sauce
- 45–60ml/3–4 tbsp Thai green curry paste
- 450g/1lb raw large prawns (shrimp), peeled and deveined
- 450g/1lb prepared squid
- a little fresh lime juice (optional)
- salt and ground black pepper
- 60ml/4 tbsp crisp fried shallot slices, to serve

1 Pour the fish stock into a large pan and add the slices of galangal or ginger, the lemon grass and half the shredded kaffir lime leaves.

VARIATIONS

- Instead of squid, you could add 400g/14oz firm white fish, such as monkfish, cut into small pieces.
- You could also replace the squid with mussels. Steam 675g/1½lb live mussels in a tightly covered pan for 3–4 minutes, or until they have opened. Discard any that remain shut, then remove them from their shells and add to the soup.

2 Reserve a few garlic chives for the garnish, then chop the remainder. Add half the chopped garlic chives to the pan. Strip the coriander leaves from the stalks and set the leaves aside. Add the stalks to the pan. Bring to the boil, reduce the heat to low and cover the pan, then simmer gently for 20 minutes. Strain the stock into a bowl.

3 Rinse and dry the pan. Add the oil and shallots. Cook over a medium heat for 5–10 minutes, until the shallots are just beginning to brown.

4 Stir in the strained stock, coconut milk, the remaining kaffir lime leaves and 30ml/2 tbsp of the fish sauce. Heat gently until simmering and cook over a low heat for 5–10 minutes.

5 Stir in the curry paste and prawns, then cook for 3 minutes. Add the squid and cook for a further 2 minutes. Add the lime juice, if using, and season, adding more fish sauce to taste. Stir in the remaining chives and the reserved coriander leaves. Serve in bowls and sprinkle each portion with fried shallots and whole garlic chives.

SALADS

Like all hot countries, Thailand has a fine repertoire of salads and cold dishes. These aren't salads in the Western sense, but rather combinations of fresh and cooked vegetables, often with a little chicken, beef or seafood. Dressings are seldom oil-based. Instead, they tend to be tart and spicy mixtures, made by adding Thai fish sauce to lime juice, tamarind juice or a little rice vinegar. Noodles often feature and it is not uncommon for fruit, such as papaya or mango, to be included.

Pomelo Salad

Typically, a Thai meal includes a selection of about five dishes, one of which is often a refreshing and palate-cleansing salad that features tropical fruit.

SERVES FOUR TO SIX

INGREDIENTS
- 30ml/2 tbsp vegetable oil
- 4 shallots, finely sliced
- 2 garlic cloves, finely sliced
- 1 large pomelo
- 15ml/1 tbsp roasted peanuts
- 115g/4oz cooked peeled prawns (shrimp)
- 115g/4oz cooked crab meat
- 10–12 small fresh mint leaves

For the dressing
- 30ml/2 tbsp Thai fish sauce
- 15ml/1 tbsp palm sugar or light muscovado (brown) sugar
- 30ml/2 tbsp fresh lime juice

For the garnish
- 2 spring onions (scallions), thinly sliced
- 2 fresh red chillies, seeded and thinly sliced
- fresh coriander (cilantro) leaves
- shredded fresh coconut (optional)

1 Make the dressing. Mix the fish sauce, sugar and lime juice in a bowl. Whisk well, then cover with clear film (plastic wrap) and set aside.

2 Heat the oil in a small frying pan, add the shallots and garlic and cook over a medium heat until they are golden. Remove from the pan and set aside.

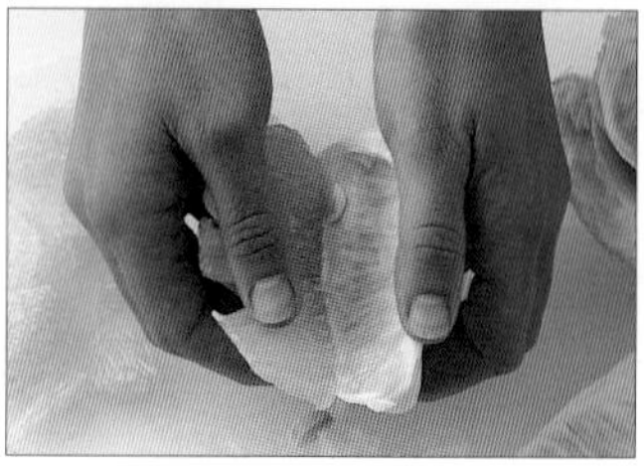

3 Peel the pomelo and break the flesh into small pieces, taking care to remove any membranes.

4 Grind the peanuts coarsely and put them in a salad bowl. Add the pomelo flesh, prawns, crab meat, mint leaves and the shallot mixture. Pour over the dressing, toss lightly and sprinkle with the spring onions, chillies and coriander leaves. Add the shredded coconut, if using. Serve immediately.

COOK'S TIP

The pomelo is a large citrus fruit that looks rather like a grapefruit, although it is not, as is sometimes thought, a hybrid. It is slightly pear-shaped with thick, yellow, dimpled skin and pinkish-yellow flesh that is both sturdier and drier than that of a grapefruit. It also has a sharper taste. Pomelos are sometimes known as "shaddocks" after the sea captain who brought them from their native Polynesia to the Caribbean.

RICE SALAD

THE SKY'S THE LIMIT WITH THIS RECIPE. USE WHATEVER FRUIT, VEGETABLES AND EVEN LEFTOVER MEAT THAT YOU MIGHT HAVE, MIX WITH COOKED RICE AND POUR OVER THE FRAGRANT DRESSING.

SERVES FOUR TO SIX

INGREDIENTS
- 350g/12oz/3 cups cooked rice
- 1 Asian pear, cored and diced
- 50g/2oz dried shrimp, chopped
- 1 avocado, peeled, stoned (pitted) and diced
- ½ medium cucumber, finely diced
- 2 lemon grass stalks, finely chopped
- 30ml/2 tbsp sweet chilli sauce
- 1 fresh green or red chilli, seeded and finely sliced
- 115g/4oz/1 cup flaked (sliced) almonds, toasted
- small bunch fresh coriander (cilantro), chopped
- fresh Thai sweet basil leaves, to garnish

For the dressing
- 300ml/½ pint/1¼ cups water
- 10ml/2 tsp shrimp paste
- 15ml/1 tbsp palm sugar or light muscovado (brown) sugar
- 2 kaffir lime leaves, torn into small pieces
- ½ lemon grass stalk, sliced

1 Make the dressing. Put the measured water in a small pan with the shrimp paste, sugar, kaffir lime leaves and lemon grass. Heat gently, stirring, until the sugar dissolves, then bring to boiling point and simmer for 5 minutes. Strain into a bowl and set aside until cold.

2 Put the cooked rice in a large salad bowl and fluff up the grains with a fork. Add the Asian pear, dried shrimp, avocado, cucumber, lemon grass and sweet chilli sauce. Mix well.

3 Add the diced chilli, almonds and coriander to the bowl and toss well. Garnish with Thai basil leaves and serve with the bowl of dressing to spoon over the top of individual portions.

Hot and Sour Noodle Salad

Noodles make the perfect basis for a salad, absorbing the dressing and providing a contrast in texture to the crisp vegetables.

SERVES TWO

INGREDIENTS

- 200g/7oz thin rice noodles
- small bunch fresh coriander (cilantro)
- 2 tomatoes, seeded and sliced
- 130g/4½oz baby corn cobs, sliced
- 4 spring onions (scallions), thinly sliced
- 1 red (bell) pepper, seeded and finely chopped
- juice of 2 limes
- 2 small fresh green chillies, seeded and finely chopped
- 10ml/2 tsp granulated sugar
- 115g/4oz/1 cup peanuts, toasted and chopped
- 30ml/2 tbsp soy sauce
- salt

1 Bring a large pan of lightly salted water to the boil. Snap the noodles into short lengths, add to the pan and cook for 3–4 minutes. Drain, then rinse under cold water and drain again.

2 Set aside a few coriander leaves for the garnish. Chop the remaining leaves and place them in a large serving bowl.

3 Add the noodles to the bowl, with the tomato slices, corn cobs, spring onions, red pepper, lime juice, chillies, sugar and toasted peanuts. Season with the soy sauce, then taste and add a little salt if you think the mixture needs it. Toss the salad lightly but thoroughly, then garnish with the reserved coriander leaves and serve immediately.

Fried Egg Salad

Chillies and eggs may seem unlikely partners, but actually work very well together. The peppery flavour of the watercress makes it the perfect foundation for this tasty salad.

SERVES TWO

INGREDIENTS
- 15ml/1 tbsp groundnut (peanut) oil
- 1 garlic clove, thinly sliced
- 4 eggs
- 2 shallots, thinly sliced
- 2 small fresh red chillies, seeded and thinly sliced
- ½ small cucumber, finely diced
- 1cm/½in piece fresh root ginger, peeled and grated
- juice of 2 limes
- 30ml/2 tbsp soy sauce
- 5ml/1 tsp caster (superfine) sugar
- small bunch coriander (cilantro)
- bunch watercress, coarsely chopped

1 Heat the oil in a frying pan. Add the garlic and cook over a low heat until it starts to turn golden. Crack in the eggs. Break the yolks with a wooden spatula, then fry until the eggs are almost firm. Remove from the pan and set aside.

2 Mix the shallots, chillies, cucumber and ginger in a bowl. In a separate bowl, whisk the lime juice with the soy sauce and sugar. Pour this dressing over the vegetables and toss lightly.

3 Set aside a few coriander sprigs for the garnish. Chop the rest and add them to the salad. Toss it again.

4 Reserve a few watercress sprigs and arrange the remainder on two serving plates. Cut the fried eggs into slices and divide them between the watercress mounds. Spoon the shallot mixture over them and serve, garnished with the reserved coriander and watercress.

AUBERGINE SALAD WITH SHRIMP AND EGG

AN APPETIZING AND UNUSUAL SALAD THAT YOU WILL FIND YOURSELF MAKING OVER AND OVER AGAIN. ROASTING THE AUBERGINES REALLY BRINGS OUT THEIR FLAVOUR.

SERVES FOUR TO SIX

INGREDIENTS

- 2 aubergines (eggplant)
- 15ml/1 tbsp vegetable oil
- 30ml/2 tbsp dried shrimp, soaked in warm water for 10 minutes
- 15ml/1 tbsp coarsely chopped garlic
- 1 hard-boiled egg, chopped
- 4 shallots, thinly sliced into rings
- fresh coriander (cilantro) leaves and 2 fresh red chillies, seeded and sliced, to garnish

For the dressing

- 30ml/2 tbsp fresh lime juice
- 5ml/1 tsp palm sugar or light muscovado (brown) sugar
- 30ml/2 tbsp Thai fish sauce

1 Preheat the grill (broiler) to medium or preheat the oven to 180°C/350°F/Gas 4. Prick the aubergines several times with a skewer, then arrange on a baking sheet. Cook them under the grill for 30–40 minutes, or until they are charred and tender. Alternatively, roast them by placing them directly on the shelf of the oven for about 1 hour, turning them at least twice. Remove the aubergines and set aside until they are cool enough to handle.

2 Meanwhile, make the dressing. Put the lime juice, palm or muscovado sugar and fish sauce into a small bowl. Whisk well with a fork or balloon whisk. Cover with clear film (plastic wrap) and set aside until required.

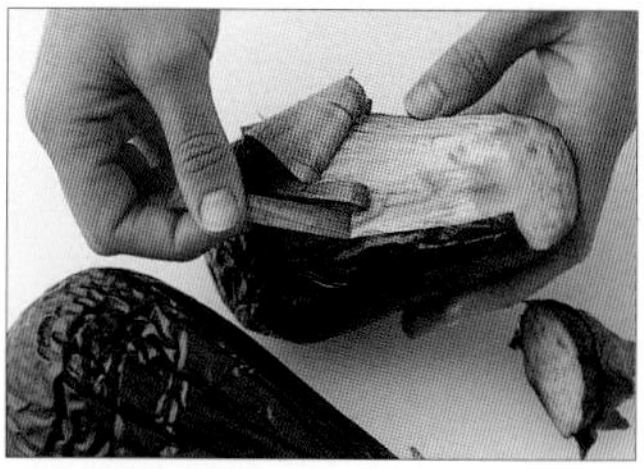

3 When the aubergines are cool enough to handle, peel off the skin and cut the flesh into medium slices.

4 Heat the oil in a small frying pan. Drain the dried shrimp thoroughly and add them to the pan with the garlic. Cook over a medium heat for about 3 minutes, until golden. Remove from the pan and set aside.

5 Arrange the aubergine slices on a serving dish. Top with the hard-boiled egg, shallots and dried shrimp mixture. Drizzle over the dressing and garnish with the coriander and red chillies.

VARIATION

For a special occasion, use salted duck's or quail's eggs, cut in half, instead of chopped hen's eggs.

Seafood Salad with Fragrant Herbs

This is a spectacular salad. The luscious combination of prawns, scallops and squid makes it the ideal choice for a special celebration.

SERVES FOUR TO SIX

INGREDIENTS

- 250ml/8fl oz/1 cup fish stock or water
- 350g/12oz squid, cleaned and cut into rings
- 12 raw king prawns (jumbo shrimp), peeled, with tails intact
- 12 scallops
- 50g/2oz cellophane noodles, soaked in warm water for 30 minutes
- ½ cucumber, cut into thin batons
- 1 lemon grass stalk, finely chopped
- 2 kaffir lime leaves, finely shredded
- 2 shallots, thinly sliced
- 30ml/2 tbsp chopped spring onions (scallions)
- 30ml/2 tbsp fresh coriander (cilantro) leaves
- 12–15 fresh mint leaves, coarsely torn
- 4 fresh red chillies, seeded and cut into slivers
- juice of 1–2 limes
- 30ml/2 tbsp Thai fish sauce
- fresh coriander sprigs, to garnish

1 Pour the fish stock or water into a medium pan, set over a high heat and bring to the boil. Cook each type of seafood separately in the stock for 3–4 minutes. Remove with a slotted spoon and set aside to cool.

2 Drain the noodles. Using scissors, cut them into short lengths, about 5cm/2in long. Place them in a serving bowl and add the cucumber, lemon grass, kaffir lime leaves, shallots, spring onions, coriander, mint and chillies.

3 Pour over the lime juice and fish sauce. Mix well, then add the seafood. Toss lightly. Garnish with the fresh coriander sprigs and serve.

THAI PRAWN SALAD WITH GARLIC DRESSING AND FRIZZLED SHALLOTS

In this intensely flavoured salad, sweet prawns and mango are partnered with a sweet-sour garlic dressing heightened with the hot taste of chilli. The crisp frizzled shallots are a traditional addition to Thai salads.

SERVES FOUR TO SIX

INGREDIENTS

- 675g/1½lb medium raw prawns (shrimp), peeled and deveined, with tails intact
- finely shredded rind of 1 lime
- ½ fresh red chilli, seeded and finely chopped
- 30ml/2 tbsp olive oil, plus extra for brushing
- 1 ripe but firm mango
- 2 carrots, cut into long thin shreds
- 10cm/4in piece cucumber, sliced
- 1 small red onion, halved and thinly sliced
- a few fresh mint sprigs
- a few fresh coriander (cilantro) sprigs
- 45ml/3 tbsp roasted peanuts, coarsely chopped
- 4 large shallots, thinly sliced and fried until crisp in 30ml/2 tbsp groundnut (peanut) oil
- salt and ground black pepper

For the dressing

- 1 large garlic clove, chopped
- 10–15ml/2–3 tsp caster (superfine) sugar
- juice of 2 limes
- 15–30ml/1–2 tbsp Thai fish sauce
- 1 fresh red chilli, seeded and finely chopped
- 5–10ml/1–2 tsp light rice vinegar

1 Place the prawns in a glass dish with the lime rind, chilli, oil and seasoning. Toss to mix and leave to marinate at room temperature for 30–40 minutes.

2 Make the dressing. Place the garlic in a mortar with 10ml/2 tsp of the caster sugar. Pound with a pestle until smooth, then work in about three-quarters of the lime juice, followed by 15ml/1 tbsp of the Thai fish sauce.

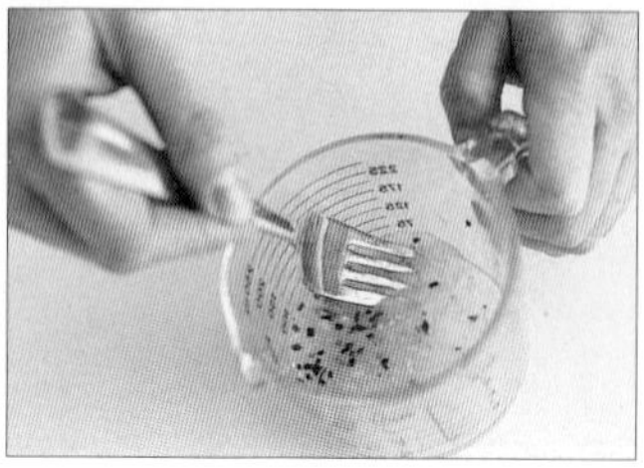

3 Transfer the dressing to a jug (pitcher). Stir in half the chopped red chilli. Taste the dressing and add more sugar, lime juice and/or fish sauce, if you think they are necessary, and stir in light rice vinegar to taste.

4 Peel and stone (pit) the mango. The best way to do this is to cut either side of the large central stone (pit), as close to it as possible, with a sharp knife. Cut the flesh into very fine strips and cut off any flesh still adhering to the stone.

5 Place the strips of mango in a bowl and add the carrots, cucumber slices and red onion. Pour over about half the dressing and toss thoroughly. Arrange the salad on four to six individual serving plates or in bowls.

6 Heat a ridged, cast-iron griddle pan or heavy frying pan until very hot. Brush with a little oil, then sear the marinated prawns for 2–3 minutes on each side, until they turn pink and are patched with brown on the outside. Arrange the prawns on the salads.

7 Sprinkle the remaining dressing over the salads and garnish with the mint and coriander sprigs. Sprinkle over the remaining chilli with the peanuts and crisp-fried shallots. Serve immediately.

COOK'S TIP

To devein the prawns (shrimp), make a shallow cut down the back of each prawn, using a small, sharp knife. Using the tip of the knife, lift out the thin, black vein, then rinse the prawn thoroughly under cold, running water, drain it and pat it dry with kitchen paper.

Scented Fish Salad

For a tropical taste of the Far East, try this delicious fish salad scented with coconut, fruit and warm Thai spices. Do try to locate the pitaya or dragon fruit. The flesh of these fuchsia-pink or yellow exotics is sweet and refreshing, with a slightly acidic melon-like flavour that goes particularly well with fish.

SERVES FOUR

INGREDIENTS

- 350g/12oz fillet of red mullet, sea bream or snapper
- 1 cos or romaine lettuce
- 1 papaya or mango, peeled and sliced
- 1 pitaya, peeled and sliced
- 1 large ripe tomato, cut into wedges
- ½ cucumber, peeled and cut into batons
- 3 spring onions (scallions), sliced
- salt

For the marinade

- 5ml/1 tsp coriander seeds
- 5ml/1 tsp fennel seeds
- 2.5ml/½ tsp cumin seeds
- 5ml/1 tsp caster (superfine) sugar
- 2.5ml/½ tsp hot chilli sauce
- 30ml/2 tbsp garlic oil

For the dressing

- 15ml/1 tbsp creamed coconut (coconut cream)
- 45ml/3 tbsp boiling water
- 60ml/4 tbsp groundnut (peanut) oil
- finely grated rind and juice of 1 lime
- 1 fresh red chilli, seeded and finely chopped
- 5ml/1 tsp granulated sugar
- 45ml/3 tbsp chopped fresh coriander (cilantro)

1 Cut the fish into even strips, removing any stray bones. Place it on a plate.

2 Make the marinade. Put the coriander, fennel and cumin seeds in a mortar. Add the sugar and crush with a pestle. Stir in the chilli sauce, garlic oil, and salt to taste and mix to a paste.

3 Spread the paste over the fish, cover and leave to marinate in a cool place for at least 20 minutes.

4 Make the dressing. Place the coconut and salt in a screw-top jar. Stir in the water. Add the oil, lime rind and juice, chilli, sugar and coriander. Shake well.

5 Wash and dry the lettuce leaves. Place in a bowl and add the papaya or mango, pitaya, tomato, cucumber and spring onions. Pour in the dressing and toss well to coat.

6 Heat a large non-stick frying-pan, add the fish and cook for 5 minutes, turning once. Add the cooked fish to the salad, toss lightly and serve immediately.

COOK'S TIPS

- If planning ahead, you can leave the fish in its marinade for up to 8 hours in the refrigerator. The dressing can also be made in advance, but do not add the fresh coriander (cilantro) until the last minute and shake vigorously again before pouring it over the salad.
- To make garlic oil, heat 120ml/4fl oz/½ cup bland-flavoured oil, such as sunflower, in a small pan. Add 30ml/2 tbsp crushed garlic and cook gently for 5 minutes, until the garlic is pale gold. Do not let it burn or the oil will taste bitter. Cool, strain into a clean screw-top jar and use as required.

PIQUANT PRAWN SALAD

THE FISH SAUCE DRESSING ADDS A SUPERB FLAVOUR TO THE NOODLES AND PRAWNS. THIS DELICIOUS SALAD CAN BE ENJOYED WARM OR COLD, AND WILL SERVE SIX AS AN APPETIZER.

SERVES FOUR

INGREDIENTS
- 200g/7oz rice vermicelli
- 8 baby corn cobs, halved
- 150g/5oz mangetouts (snow peas)
- 15ml/1 tbsp vegetable oil
- 2 garlic cloves, finely chopped
- 2.5cm/1in piece fresh root ginger, peeled and finely chopped
- 1 fresh red or green chilli, seeded and finely chopped
- 450g/1lb raw peeled tiger prawns (jumbo shrimp)
- 4 spring onions (scallions), very thinly sliced
- 15ml/1 tbsp sesame seeds, toasted
- 1 lemon grass stalk, thinly shredded

For the dressing
- 15ml/1 tbsp chopped fresh chives
- 15ml/1 tbsp Thai fish sauce
- 5ml/1 tsp soy sauce
- 45ml/3 tbsp groundnut (peanut) oil
- 5ml/1 tsp sesame oil
- 30ml/2 tbsp rice vinegar

1 Put the rice vermicelli in a wide heatproof bowl, pour over boiling water and leave to soak for 10 minutes. Drain, refresh under cold water and drain well again. Tip into a large serving bowl and set aside until required.

2 Boil or steam the corn cobs and mangetouts for about 3 minutes, until tender but still crunchy. Refresh under cold running water and drain. Make the dressing by mixing all the ingredients in a screw-top jar. Close tightly and shake vigorously to combine.

3 Heat the oil in a large frying pan or wok. Add the garlic, ginger and red or green chilli and cook for 1 minute. Add the tiger prawns and toss over the heat for about 3 minutes, until they have just turned pink. Stir in the spring onions, corn cobs, mangetouts and sesame seeds, and toss lightly to mix.

4 Tip the contents of the pan or wok over the rice vermicelli. Pour the dressing on top and toss well. Sprinkle with lemon grass and serve, or chill for 1 hour before serving.

TANGY CHICKEN SALAD

THIS FRESH AND LIVELY DISH TYPIFIES THE CHARACTER OF THAI CUISINE. IT IS IDEAL FOR A LIGHT LUNCH ON A HOT AND LAZY SUMMER'S DAY.

SERVES FOUR TO SIX

INGREDIENTS

- 4 skinless, boneless chicken breast portions
- 2 garlic cloves, crushed
- 30ml/2 tbsp soy sauce
- 30ml/2 tbsp vegetable oil
- 120ml/4fl oz/½ cup coconut cream
- 30ml/2 tbsp Thai fish sauce
- juice of 1 lime
- 30ml/2 tbsp palm sugar or light muscovado (brown) sugar
- 115g/4oz/½ cup water chestnuts, sliced
- 50g/2oz/½ cup cashew nuts, roasted and coarsely chopped
- 4 shallots, thinly sliced
- 4 kaffir lime leaves, thinly sliced
- 1 lemon grass stalk, thinly sliced
- 5ml/1 tsp chopped fresh galangal
- 1 large fresh red chilli, seeded and finely chopped
- 2 spring onions (scallions), thinly sliced
- 10–12 fresh mint leaves, torn
- 1 lettuce, separated into leaves, to serve
- 2 fresh red chillies, seeded and sliced, to garnish

1 Place the chicken in a large dish. Rub with the garlic, soy sauce and 15ml/1 tbsp of the oil. Cover and leave to marinate for 1–2 hours.

2 Heat the remaining oil in a wok or frying pan and stir-fry the chicken for 3–4 minutes on each side, or until cooked. Remove and set aside to cool.

3 In a pan, heat the coconut cream, fish sauce, lime juice and sugar. Stir until the sugar has dissolved; set aside.

4 Tear the cooked chicken into strips and put it in a bowl. Add the water chestnuts, cashew nuts, shallots, kaffir lime leaves, lemon grass, galangal, red chilli, spring onions and mint leaves.

5 Pour the coconut dressing over the mixture and toss well. Serve the chicken on a bed of lettuce leaves and garnish with sliced red chillies.

SAENG WA OF GRILLED PORK

PORK FILLET IS CUT IN STRIPS BEFORE BEING GRILLED. SHREDDED AND THEN TOSSED WITH A DELICIOUS SWEET-SOUR SAUCE, IT MAKES A MARVELLOUS WARM SALAD.

SERVES FOUR

INGREDIENTS
- 30ml/2 tbsp dark soy sauce
- 15ml/1 tbsp clear honey
- 400g/14oz pork fillet (tenderloin)
- 6 shallots, very thinly sliced lengthways
- 1 lemon grass stalk, thinly sliced
- 5 kaffir lime leaves, thinly sliced
- 5cm/2in piece fresh root ginger, peeled and sliced into fine shreds
- ½ fresh long red chilli, seeded and sliced into fine shreds
- small bunch fresh coriander (cilantro), chopped

For the dressing
- 30ml/2 tbsp palm sugar or light muscovado (brown) sugar
- 30ml/2 tbsp Thai fish sauce
- juice of 2 limes
- 20ml/4 tsp thick tamarind juice, made by mixing tamarind paste with warm water

1 Preheat the grill (broiler) to medium. Mix the soy sauce with the honey in a small bowl or jug (pitcher) and stir until the honey has completely dissolved.

2 Using a sharp knife, cut the pork fillet lengthways into quarters to make four long, thick strips. Place the pork strips in a grill pan. Brush generously with the soy sauce and honey mixture, then grill (broil) for about 10–15 minutes, until cooked through and tender. Turn the strips over frequently and baste with the soy sauce and honey mixture.

3 Transfer the cooked pork strips to a board. Slice the meat across the grain, then shred it with a fork. Place in a large bowl and add the shallot slices, lemon grass, kaffir lime leaves, ginger, chilli and chopped coriander.

4 Make the dressing. Place the sugar, fish sauce, lime juice and tamarind juice in a bowl. Whisk until the sugar has completely dissolved. Pour the dressing over the pork mixture and toss well to mix, then serve.

VARIATION

If you want to extend this dish a little, add cooked rice or noodles. Thin strips of red or yellow (bell) pepper could also be added. For a colour contrast, add lightly cooked green beans, sugar snap peas or mangetouts (snow peas).

BEEF AND MUSHROOM SALAD

ALL THE INGREDIENTS FOR THIS TRADITIONAL THAI DISH – KNOWN AS YAM NUA YANG *– ARE WIDELY AVAILABLE IN LARGER SUPERMARKETS.*

SERVES FOUR

INGREDIENTS

- 675g/1½lb fillet (tenderloin) or rump (round) steak
- 30ml/2 tbsp olive oil
- 2 small mild red chillies, seeded and sliced
- 225g/8oz/3¼ cups fresh shiitake mushrooms, stems removed and caps sliced

For the dressing

- 3 spring onions (scallions), finely chopped
- 2 garlic cloves, finely chopped
- juice of 1 lime
- 15–30ml/1–2 tbsp Thai fish sauce
- 5ml/1 tsp soft light brown sugar
- 30ml/2 tbsp chopped fresh coriander (cilantro)

To serve

- 1 cos or romaine lettuce, torn into strips
- 175g/6oz cherry tomatoes, halved
- 5cm/2in piece cucumber, peeled, halved and thinly sliced
- 45ml/3 tbsp toasted sesame seeds

VARIATION

If you can find them, yellow chillies make a colourful addition to this dish.

1 Preheat the grill (broiler) to medium, then cook the steak for 2–4 minutes on each side, depending on how well done you like it. (In Thailand, the beef is traditionally served quite rare.) Leave to cool for at least 15 minutes.

2 Slice the meat as thinly as possible and place the slices in a bowl.

3 Heat the olive oil in a small frying pan. Add the seeded and sliced red chillies and the sliced shiitake mushroom caps. Cook for 5 minutes, stirring occasionally. Turn off the heat and add the steak slices to the pan. Stir well to coat the beef slices in the chilli and mushroom mixture.

4 Make the dressing by mixing all the ingredients in a bowl, then pour it over the meat mixture and toss gently.

5 Arrange the lettuce, tomatoes and cucumber on a serving plate. Spoon the steak mixture in the centre and sprinkle the sesame seeds over. Serve at once.

Larp of Chiang Mai

Chiang Mai is a city in the north-east of Thailand. The city is culturally very close to Laos. It is famous for its chicken salad, which was originally called "Laap" or "Larp". Duck, beef or pork can be used instead of chicken.

SERVES FOUR TO SIX

INGREDIENTS

- 450g/1lb minced (ground) chicken
- 1 lemon grass stalk, root trimmed
- 3 kaffir lime leaves, finely chopped
- 4 fresh red chillies, seeded and chopped
- 60ml/4 tbsp fresh lime juice
- 30ml/2 tbsp Thai fish sauce
- 15ml/1 tbsp roasted ground rice (see Cook's Tip)
- 2 spring onions (scallions), finely chopped
- 30ml/2 tbsp fresh coriander (cilantro) leaves
- thinly sliced kaffir lime leaves, mixed salad leaves and fresh mint sprigs, to garnish

1 Heat a large, non-stick frying pan. Add the minced chicken and moisten with a little water. Stir constantly over a medium heat for 7–10 minutes, until it is cooked through. Remove the pan from the heat and drain off any excess fat. Cut off the lower 5cm/2in of the lemon grass stalk and chop it finely.

2 Transfer the cooked chicken to a bowl and add the chopped lemon grass, lime leaves, chillies, lime juice, fish sauce, roasted ground rice, spring onions and coriander. Mix thoroughly.

3 Spoon the chicken mixture into a salad bowl. Sprinkle sliced lime leaves over the top and garnish with salad leaves and sprigs of mint.

COOK'S TIP

Use glutinous rice for the roasted ground rice. Put the rice in a frying pan and dry-roast it until golden brown. Remove and grind to a powder, using a mortar and pestle or a food processor. When the rice is cold, store it in a glass jar in a cool and dry place.

Thai Beef Salad

A hearty main meal salad, this combines tender strips of sirloin steak with thinly shredded cucumber and a wonderfully piquant chilli and lime dressing.

SERVES FOUR

INGREDIENTS

- 2 sirloin steaks, each about 225g/8oz
- 1 lemon grass stalk, root trimmed
- 1 red onion or 4 Thai shallots, thinly sliced
- ½ cucumber, cut into strips
- 30ml/2 tbsp chopped spring onion (scallion)
- juice of 2 limes
- 15–30ml/1–2 tbsp Thai fish sauce
- 2–4 fresh red chillies, seeded and finely chopped
- Chinese mustard cress, salad cress or fresh coriander (cilantro), to garnish

COOK'S TIP

Look for gui chai leaves in Thai and Chinese groceries. These look like very thin spring onions (scallions) and are often used as a substitute for the more familiar vegetable.

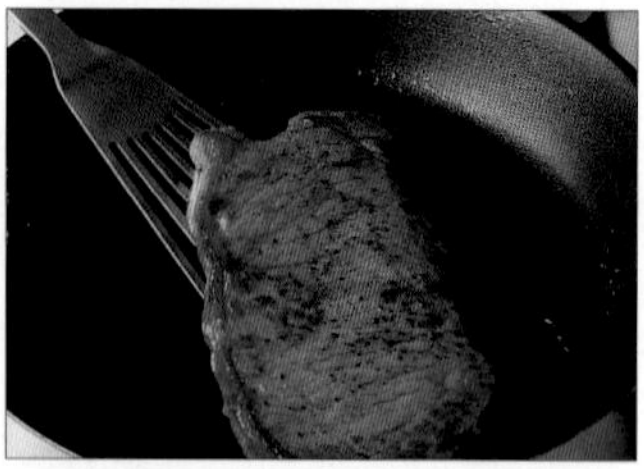

1 Pan-fry the steaks in a large, heavy frying pan over a medium heat. Cook them for 4–6 minutes for rare, 6–8 minutes for medium-rare and about 10 minutes for well done, depending on their thickness. (In Thailand the beef is traditionally served quite rare.) Alternatively, cook them under a preheated grill (broiler). Remove the steaks from the pan and leave to rest for 10–15 minutes. Meanwhile, cut off the lower 5cm/2in from the lemon grass stalk and chop it finely.

2 When the meat is cool, slice it thinly and put the slices in a large bowl. Add the sliced onion or shallots, cucumber, lemon grass and chopped spring onion to the meat slices.

3 Toss the salad and add lime juice and fish sauce to taste. Add the red chillies and toss again. Transfer to a serving bowl or plate. Serve the salad at room temperature or chilled, garnished with the Chinese mustard cress, salad cress or coriander leaves.

Poultry Dishes

One of the remarkable attributes of Thai meat dishes is the speed with which they are prepared. Even curries, which elsewhere tend to require slow cooking, can often be cooked in less than half an hour. Of course, short cooking times depend upon using tender, good quality meat, so many recipes call for chicken breast portions. In central and northern Thailand, wild fowl are sometimes used instead of domestic birds, and the delicious duck recipes are largely a Chinese legacy.

GREEN CHICKEN CURRY

USE ONE OR TWO FRESH GREEN CHILLIES IN THIS DISH, DEPENDING ON HOW HOT YOU LIKE YOUR CURRY. THE MILD AROMATIC FLAVOUR OF THE RICE IS A GOOD FOIL FOR THE SPICY CHICKEN.

SERVES THREE TO FOUR

INGREDIENTS
- 4 spring onions (scallions), trimmed and coarsely chopped
- 1–2 fresh green chillies, seeded and coarsely chopped
- 2cm/¾ in piece fresh root ginger, peeled
- 2 garlic cloves
- 5ml/1 tsp Thai fish sauce
- large bunch fresh coriander (cilantro)
- small handful of fresh parsley
- 30–45ml/2–3 tbsp water
- 30ml/2 tbsp sunflower oil
- 4 skinless, boneless chicken breast portions, diced
- 1 green (bell) pepper, seeded and thinly sliced
- 600ml/1 pint/2½ cups coconut milk or 75g/3oz piece of creamed coconut dissolved in 400ml/14fl oz/ 1⅔ cups boiling water
- salt and ground black pepper
- hot coconut rice, to serve

1 Put the spring onions, green chillies, ginger, garlic, fish sauce, coriander and parsley in a food processor or blender. Pour in 30ml/2 tbsp of the water and process to a smooth paste, adding a further 15ml/1 tbsp water if required.

COOK'S TIP

Virtually every Thai cook has their own recipe for curry pastes, which are traditionally made by pounding the ingredients in a mortar with a pestle. Using a food processor or blender simply makes the task less laborious.

2 Heat half the oil in a large frying pan. Cook the diced chicken until evenly browned. Transfer to a plate.

3 Heat the remaining oil in the pan. Add the green pepper and stir-fry for 3–4 minutes, then add the chilli and ginger paste. Stir-fry for 3–4 minutes, until the mixture becomes fairly thick.

4 Return the chicken to the pan and add the coconut liquid. Season with salt and pepper and bring to the boil, then reduce the heat, half cover the pan and simmer for 8–10 minutes.

5 When the chicken is cooked, transfer it, with the green pepper, to a plate. Boil the cooking liquid remaining in the pan for 10–12 minutes, until it is well reduced and fairly thick.

6 Return the chicken and pepper to the green curry sauce, stir well and cook gently for 2–3 minutes to heat through. Spoon the curry over the coconut rice, and serve immediately.

FRAGRANT CHICKEN CURRY

THIS DISH IS PERFECT FOR A PARTY AS THE CHICKEN AND SAUCE CAN BE PREPARED IN ADVANCE AND COMBINED AND HEATED AT THE LAST MINUTE.

SERVES FOUR

INGREDIENTS
- 45ml/3 tbsp oil
- 1 onion, coarsely chopped
- 2 garlic cloves, crushed
- 15ml/1 tbsp Thai red curry paste
- 115g/4oz creamed coconut dissolved in 900ml/1½ pints/3¾ cups boiling water, or 1 litre/1¾ pints/4 cups coconut milk
- 2 lemon grass stalks, coarsely chopped
- 6 kaffir lime leaves, chopped
- 150ml/¼ pint/⅔ cup Greek (US strained plain) yogurt
- 30ml/2 tbsp apricot jam
- 1 cooked chicken, about 1.5kg/3–3½ lb
- 30ml/2 tbsp chopped fresh coriander (cilantro)
- salt and ground black pepper
- kaffir lime leaves, shredded, toasted coconut and fresh coriander (cilantro), to garnish
- boiled rice, to serve

COOK'S TIP
If you prefer the sauce to be thicker, stir in a little more creamed coconut after adding the chicken.

1 Heat the oil in a large pan. Add the onion and garlic and cook over a low heat for 5–10 minutes until soft. Stir in the red curry paste. Cook, stirring constantly, for 2–3 minutes. Stir in the diluted creamed coconut or coconut milk, then add the lemon grass, lime leaves, yogurt and apricot jam. Stir well. Cover and simmer for 30 minutes.

2 Remove the pan from the heat and leave to cool slightly. Transfer the sauce to a food processor or blender and process to a smooth purée, then strain it back into the rinsed-out pan, pressing as much of the puréed mixture as possible through the sieve with the back of a wooden spoon. Set aside while you prepare the chicken.

3 Remove the skin from the chicken, slice the meat off the bones and cut it into bitesize pieces. Add to the sauce.

4 Bring the sauce back to simmering point. Stir in the fresh coriander and season with salt and pepper. Garnish with extra lime leaves, shredded coconut and coriander. Serve with rice.

RED CHICKEN CURRY WITH BAMBOO SHOOTS

BAMBOO SHOOTS HAVE A LOVELY CRUNCHY TEXTURE. IT IS QUITE ACCEPTABLE TO USE CANNED ONES, AS FRESH BAMBOO IS NOT READILY AVAILABLE IN THE WEST. BUY CANNED WHOLE BAMBOO SHOOTS, WHICH ARE CRISPER AND OF BETTER QUALITY THAN SLICED SHOOTS.

SERVES FOUR TO SIX

INGREDIENTS

- 1 litre/1¾ pints/4 cups coconut milk
- 450g/1lb skinless, boneless chicken breast portions, diced
- 30ml/2 tbsp Thai fish sauce
- 15ml/1 tbsp granulated sugar
- 1–2 drained canned bamboo shoots, total weight about 225g/8oz, rinsed and sliced
- 5 kaffir lime leaves, torn
- salt and ground black pepper
- chopped fresh red chillies and kaffir lime leaves, to garnish

For the red curry paste

- 5ml/1 tsp coriander seeds
- 2.5ml/½ tsp cumin seeds
- 12–15 fresh red chillies, seeded and coarsely chopped
- 4 shallots, thinly sliced
- 2 garlic cloves, chopped
- 15ml/1 tbsp chopped fresh galangal
- 2 lemon grass stalks, chopped
- 3 kaffir lime leaves, chopped
- 4 fresh coriander (cilantro) roots
- 10 black peppercorns
- good pinch ground cinnamon
- 5ml/1 tsp ground turmeric
- 2.5ml/½ tsp shrimp paste
- 5ml/1 tsp salt
- 30ml/2 tbsp vegetable oil

1 Make the curry paste. Dry-fry the coriander seeds and cumin seeds for 1–2 minutes, then put in a mortar or food processor with all the remaining ingredients except the oil. Pound or process to a paste.

2 Add the vegetable oil, a little at a time, mixing or processing well after each addition. Transfer to a screw-top jar, put on the lid and keep in the refrigerator until ready to use.

3 Pour half of the coconut milk into a large, heavy pan. Bring to the boil over a medium heat, stirring constantly until the coconut milk has separated.

4 Stir in 30ml/2 tbsp of the red curry paste and cook the mixture, stirring constantly, for 2–3 minutes, until the curry paste is thoroughly incorporated. The remaining red curry paste can be kept in the closed jar in the refrigerator for up to 3 months.

5 Add the diced chicken, fish sauce and sugar to the pan. Stir well, then lower the heat and cook gently for 5–6 minutes, stirring until the chicken changes colour and is cooked through. Take care that the curry does not stick to the base of the pan.

6 Pour the remaining coconut milk into the pan, then add the sliced bamboo shoots and torn lime leaves. Bring back to the boil over a medium heat, stirring constantly to prevent the mixture from sticking to the pan, then taste and add salt and pepper if necessary.

7 To serve, spoon the curry into a warmed serving dish and garnish with the chopped chillies and lime leaves.

VARIATION

Instead of, or as well as, bamboo shoots, use straw mushrooms. Fresh straw mushrooms are not often seen in the West, but they are available in cans from Asian stores and supermarkets. Drain well and stir into the curry at the end of the recipe. Straw mushrooms are prized for their slippery texture as well as for their delicate, but delicious flavour.

COOK'S TIP

It is essential to use chicken breast portions, rather than any other cut, for this curry, as it is cooked very quickly. To save time, rather than cutting whole portions into bitesize pieces yourself, look for diced chicken or strips of chicken (which are frequently labelled "stir-fry chicken") in the supermarket.

Chicken and Lemon Grass Curry

This fragrant and truly delicious curry is exceptionally easy and takes less than twenty minutes to prepare and cook – a perfect mid-week meal.

SERVES FOUR

INGREDIENTS
- 45ml/3 tbsp vegetable oil
- 2 garlic cloves, crushed
- 500g/1¼lb skinless, boneless chicken thighs, chopped into small pieces
- 45ml/3 tbsp Thai fish sauce
- 120ml/4fl oz/½ cup chicken stock
- 5ml/1 tsp granulated sugar
- 1 lemon grass stalk, chopped into 4 sticks and lightly crushed
- 5 kaffir lime leaves, rolled into cylinders and thinly sliced across, plus extra to garnish
- chopped roasted peanuts and chopped fresh coriander (cilantro), to garnish

For the curry paste
- 1 lemon grass stalk, coarsely chopped
- 2.5cm/1in piece fresh galangal, peeled and coarsely chopped
- 2 kaffir lime leaves, chopped
- 3 shallots, coarsely chopped
- 6 coriander (cilantro) roots, coarsely chopped
- 2 garlic cloves
- 2 fresh green chillies, seeded and coarsely chopped
- 5ml/1 tsp shrimp paste
- 5ml/1 tsp ground turmeric

1 Make the curry paste. Place all the ingredients in a large mortar, or food processor and pound with a pestle or process to a smooth paste.

2 Heat the vegetable oil in a wok or large, heavy frying pan, add the garlic and cook over a low heat, stirring frequently, until golden brown. Be careful not to let the garlic burn or it will taste bitter. Add the curry paste and stir-fry with the garlic for about 30 seconds more.

3 Add the chicken pieces to the pan and stir until thoroughly coated with the curry paste. Stir in the Thai fish sauce and chicken stock, with the sugar, and cook, stirring constantly, for 2 minutes more.

4 Add the lemon grass and lime leaves, reduce the heat and simmer for 10 minutes. If the mixture begins to dry out, add a little more stock or water.

5 Remove the lemon grass, if you like. Spoon the curry into four dishes, garnish with the lime leaves, peanuts and coriander and serve immediately.

YELLOW CHICKEN CURRY

THE PAIRING OF SLIGHTLY SWEET COCONUT MILK AND FRUIT WITH SAVOURY CHICKEN AND SPICES IS AT ONCE A COMFORTING, REFRESHING AND EXOTIC COMBINATION.

SERVES FOUR

INGREDIENTS
- 300ml/½ pint/1¼ cups chicken stock
- 30ml/2 tbsp thick tamarind juice, made by mixing tamarind paste with warm water
- 15ml/1 tbsp granulated sugar
- 200ml/7fl oz/scant 1 cup coconut milk
- 1 green papaya, peeled, seeded and thinly sliced
- 250g/9oz skinless, boneless chicken breast portions, diced
- juice of 1 lime
- lime slices, to garnish

For the curry paste
- 1 fresh red chilli, seeded and coarsely chopped
- 4 garlic cloves, coarsely chopped
- 3 shallots, coarsely chopped
- 2 lemon grass stalks, sliced
- 5cm/2in piece fresh turmeric, coarsely chopped, or 5ml/1 tsp ground turmeric
- 5ml/1 tsp shrimp paste
- 5ml/1 tsp salt

1 Make the yellow curry paste. Put the red chilli, garlic, shallots, lemon grass and turmeric in a mortar or food processor. Add the shrimp paste and salt. Pound or process to a paste, adding a little water if necessary.

COOK'S TIP
Fresh turmeric resembles root ginger in appearance and is a member of the same family. When preparing it, wear gloves to protect your hands from staining.

2 Pour the stock into a wok or medium pan and bring it to the boil. Stir in the curry paste. Bring back to the boil and add the tamarind juice, sugar and coconut milk. Add the papaya and chicken and cook over a medium to high heat for about 15 minutes, stirring frequently, until the chicken is cooked.

3 Stir in the lime juice, transfer to a warm dish and serve immediately, garnished with lime slices.

SOUTHERN CHICKEN CURRY

A MILD COCONUT CURRY FLAVOURED WITH TURMERIC, CORIANDER AND CUMIN SEEDS THAT DEMONSTRATES THE INFLUENCE OF MALAYSIAN COOKING ON THAI CUISINE.

SERVES FOUR

INGREDIENTS

- 60ml/4 tbsp vegetable oil
- 1 large garlic clove, crushed
- 1 chicken, weighing about 1.5kg/3–3½lb, chopped into 12 large pieces
- 400ml/14fl oz/1⅔ cups coconut cream
- 250ml/8fl oz/1 cup chicken stock
- 30ml/2 tbsp Thai fish sauce
- 30ml/2 tbsp sugar
- juice of 2 limes

To garnish

- 2 small fresh red chillies, seeded and finely chopped
- 1 bunch spring onions (scallions), thinly sliced

For the curry paste

- 5ml/1 tsp dried chilli flakes
- 2.5ml/½ tsp salt
- 5cm/2in piece fresh turmeric or 5ml/1 tsp ground turmeric
- 2.5ml/½ tsp coriander seeds
- 2.5ml/½ tsp cumin seeds
- 5ml/1 tsp dried shrimp paste

1 First make the curry paste. Put all the ingredients in a mortar, food processor or spice grinder and pound, process or grind to a smooth paste.

2 Heat the oil in a wok or frying pan and cook the garlic until golden. Add the chicken and cook until golden. Remove the chicken and set aside.

3 Reheat the oil and add the curry paste and then half the coconut cream. Cook for a few minutes until fragrant.

4 Return the chicken to the wok or pan, add the stock, mixing well, then add the remaining coconut cream, the fish sauce, sugar and lime juice. Stir well and bring to the boil, then lower the heat and simmer for 15 minutes.

5 Turn the curry into four warm serving bowls and sprinkle with the chopped fresh chillies and spring onions to garnish. Serve immediately.

COOK'S TIP

Use a large sharp knife or a Chinese cleaver to chop the chicken into pieces. Wash the board, knife and your hands thoroughly afterwards in hot, soapy water as chicken is notorious for harbouring harmful micro-organisms and bacteria.

FRAGRANT GRILLED CHICKEN

IF YOU HAVE TIME, PREPARE THE CHICKEN IN ADVANCE AND LEAVE IT TO MARINATE IN THE REFRIGERATOR FOR SEVERAL HOURS – OR EVEN OVERNIGHT – UNTIL READY TO COOK.

SERVES FOUR

INGREDIENTS
- 450g/1lb boneless chicken breast portions, with the skin on
- 30ml/2 tbsp sesame oil
- 2 garlic cloves, crushed
- 2 coriander (cilantro) roots, finely chopped
- 2 small fresh red chillies, seeded and finely chopped
- 30ml/2 tbsp Thai fish sauce
- 5ml/1 tsp sugar
- cooked rice, to serve
- lime wedges, to garnish

For the sauce
- 90ml/6 tbsp rice vinegar
- 60ml/4 tbsp sugar
- 2.5ml/½ tsp salt
- 2 garlic cloves, crushed
- 1 small fresh red chilli, seeded and finely chopped
- 115g/4oz/4 cups fresh coriander (cilantro), finely chopped

1 Lay the chicken breast portions between two sheets of clear film (plastic wrap), baking parchment or foil and beat with the side of a rolling pin or the flat side of a meat tenderizer until the meat is about half its original thickness. Place in a large, shallow dish or bowl.

2 Mix together the sesame oil, garlic, coriander roots, red chillies, fish sauce and sugar in a jug (pitcher), stirring until the sugar has dissolved. Pour the mixture over the chicken and turn to coat. Cover with clear film and set aside to marinate in a cool place for at least 20 minutes. Meanwhile, make the sauce.

3 Heat the vinegar in a small pan, add the sugar and stir until dissolved. Add the salt and stir until the mixture begins to thicken. Add the remaining sauce ingredients, stir well, then spoon the sauce into a serving bowl.

4 Preheat the grill (broiler) and cook the chicken for 5 minutes. Turn and baste with the marinade, then cook for 5 minutes more, or until cooked through and golden. Serve with rice and the sauce, garnished with lime wedges.

Roast Lime Chicken with Sweet Potatoes

In Thailand, this chicken would be spit-roasted, as ovens are seldom used. However, it works very well as a conventional roast. The sweet potatoes are an inspired addition.

SERVES FOUR

INGREDIENTS

4 garlic cloves, 2 finely chopped and 2 bruised but left whole
small bunch coriander (cilantro), with roots, coarsely chopped
5ml/1 tsp ground turmeric
5cm/2in piece fresh turmeric
1 roasting chicken, about 1.5kg/3¼lb
1 lime, cut in half
4 medium/large sweet potatoes, peeled and cut into thick wedges
300ml/½ pint/1¼ cups chicken or vegetable stock
30ml/2 tbsp soy sauce
salt and ground black pepper

1 Preheat the oven to 190°C/375°F/Gas 5. Calculate the cooking time for the chicken, allowing 20 minutes per 500g/1¼lb, plus 20 minutes. Using a mortar and pestle or food processor, grind the chopped garlic, coriander, 10ml/2 tsp salt and turmeric to a paste.

2 Place the chicken in a roasting pan and smear it with the paste. Squeeze the lime juice over and place the lime halves and garlic cloves in the cavity. Cover with foil and roast in the oven.

3 Meanwhile, bring a pan of water to the boil and par-boil the sweet potatoes for 10–15 minutes, until just tender. Drain well and place them around the chicken in the roasting pan. Baste with the cooking juices and sprinkle with salt and pepper. Replace the foil and return the chicken to the oven.

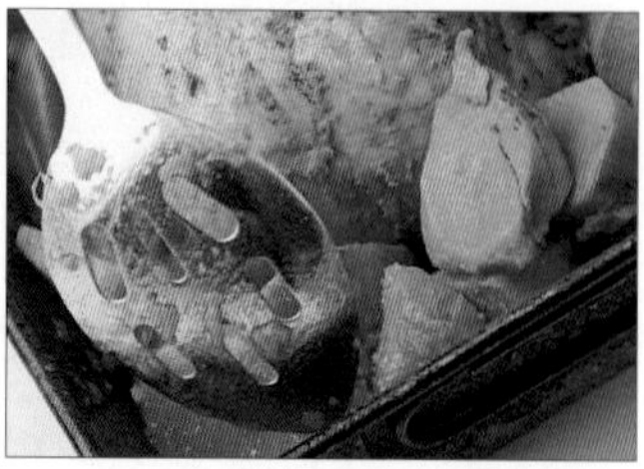

4 About 20 minutes before the end of cooking, remove the foil and baste the chicken. Turn the sweet potatoes over.

5 At the end of the calculated roasting time, check that the chicken is cooked. Lift it out of the roasting pan, tip it so that all the juices collected in the cavity drain into the pan, then place the bird on a carving board. Cover it with tented foil and leave it to rest before carving. Transfer the sweet potatoes to a serving dish and keep them hot in the oven while you make the gravy.

6 Pour away the oil from the roasting pan but keep the juices. Place the roasting pan on top of the stove and heat until the juices are bubbling. Pour in the stock. Bring the mixture to the boil, stirring constantly with a wooden spoon and scraping the base of the pan to incorporate the residue.

7 Stir in the soy sauce and check the seasoning before straining the gravy into a jug (pitcher). Serve it with the carved meat and the sweet potatoes.

COOK'S TIPS

- When the chicken is cooked, the legs should move freely. Insert the tip of a sharp knife or a skewer into the thickest part of one of the thighs. The juices that emerge from the cut should run clear. If there are any traces of pinkness, return the chicken to the oven for a little longer.
- Although originally native to tropical America, sweet potatoes are now a popular food crop throughout South-east Asia. There are many varieties and the flesh ranges in texture from floury to moist and in colour from deep orange through gold to white.

STIR-FRIED CHICKEN WITH BASIL AND CHILLI

This quick and easy chicken dish is an excellent introduction to Thai cuisine. Thai basil, which is sometimes known as holy basil, has a unique, pungent flavour that is both spicy and sharp. Deep-frying the leaves adds another dimension to this dish.

SERVES FOUR TO SIX

INGREDIENTS
- 45ml/3 tbsp vegetable oil
- 4 garlic cloves, thinly sliced
- 2–4 fresh red chillies, seeded and finely chopped
- 450g/1lb skinless boneless chicken breast portions, cut into bitesize pieces
- 45ml/3 tbsp Thai fish sauce
- 10ml/2 tsp dark soy sauce
- 5ml/1 tsp granulated sugar
- 10–12 fresh Thai basil leaves
- 2 fresh red chillies, seeded and finely chopped, and about 20 deep-fried Thai basil leaves, to garnish

1 Heat the oil in a wok or large, heavy frying pan. Add the garlic and chillies and stir-fry over a medium heat for 1–2 minutes until the garlic is golden. Take care not to let the garlic burn, otherwise it will taste bitter.

2 Add the pieces of chicken to the wok or pan, in batches if necessary, and stir-fry until the chicken changes colour.

3 Stir in the fish sauce, soy sauce and sugar. Continue to stir-fry the mixture for 3–4 minutes, or until the chicken is fully cooked and golden brown.

4 Stir in the fresh Thai basil leaves. Spoon the mixture on to a warm platter, or into individual dishes. Garnish with the chopped chillies and deep-fried Thai basil and serve immediately.

COOK'S TIP

To deep-fry Thai basil leaves, first make sure that the leaves are completely dry or they will splutter when added to the oil. Heat vegetable or groundnut (peanut) oil in a wok or deep-fryer to 190°C/375°F or until a cube of bread, added to the oil, browns in about 45 seconds. Add the leaves and deep-fry them briefly until they are crisp and translucent – this will take only about 30–40 seconds. Lift out the leaves using a slotted spoon or wire basket and leave them to drain on kitchen paper before using.

Barbecue Chicken

Chicken cooked on a barbecue is served almost everywhere in Thailand, from roadside stalls to sports stadia. This is the perfect dish for a summer party, but you can also cook this tasty chicken in the oven if the weather proves disappointing.

SERVES FOUR TO SIX

INGREDIENTS

- 1 chicken, about 1.5kg/3–3½lb, cut into 8–10 pieces
- lime wedges and fresh red chillies, to garnish

For the marinade

- 2 lemon grass stalks, roots trimmed
- 2.5cm/1in piece fresh root ginger, peeled and thinly sliced
- 6 garlic cloves, coarsely chopped
- 4 shallots, coarsely chopped
- ½ bunch coriander (cilantro) roots, chopped
- 15ml/1 tbsp palm sugar or light muscovado (brown) sugar
- 120ml/4fl oz/½ cup coconut milk
- 30ml/2 tbsp Thai fish sauce
- 30ml/2 tbsp light soy sauce

1 Make the marinade. Cut off the lower 5cm/2in of the lemon grass stalks and chop them coarsely. Put into a food processor with the ginger, garlic, shallots, coriander, sugar, coconut milk and sauces and process until smooth.

2 Place the chicken pieces in a dish, pour over the marinade and stir to mix well. Cover the dish and leave in a cool place to marinate for at least 4 hours, or leave it in the refrigerator overnight.

3 Prepare the barbecue or preheat the oven to 200°C/400°F/Gas 6. Drain the chicken, reserving the marinade. If you are cooking in the oven, arrange the chicken pieces in a single layer on a rack set over a roasting pan.

4 Cook the chicken on the barbecue over moderately hot coals or on medium heat for a gas barbecue, or bake in the oven for 20–30 minutes. Turn the pieces and brush with the reserved marinade once or twice during cooking.

5 As soon as the chicken pieces are golden brown and cooked through, transfer them to a serving platter, garnish with the lime wedges and red chillies and serve immediately.

COOK'S TIPS

- Coconut milk is available fresh or in cans or cartons from Asian food stores and most supermarkets and you may also find it in powdered form. Alternatively, use 50g/2oz creamed coconut from a packet and stir it into warm water until completely dissolved.
- Coriander roots are more intensely flavoured than the leaves, but the herb is not always available with the roots intact.

Cashew Chicken

Although it is not native to South-east Asia, the cashew tree is highly prized in Thailand and the classic partnership of these slightly sweet nuts with chicken is immensely popular both in Thailand and abroad.

SERVES FOUR TO SIX

INGREDIENTS

- 450g/1lb boneless chicken breast portions
- 1 red (bell) pepper
- 2 garlic cloves
- 4 dried red chillies
- 30ml/2 tbsp vegetable oil
- 30ml/2 tbsp oyster sauce
- 15ml/1 tbsp soy sauce
- pinch of granulated sugar
- 1 bunch spring onions (scallions), cut into 5cm/2in lengths
- 175g/6oz/1½ cups cashews, roasted
- coriander (cilantro) leaves, to garnish

1 Remove and discard the skin from the chicken breasts and trim off any excess fat. With a sharp knife, cut the chicken into bitesize pieces and set aside.

2 Halve the red pepper, scrape out the seeds and membranes and discard, then cut the flesh into 2cm/¾in dice. Peel and thinly slice the garlic and chop the dried red chillies.

3 Preheat a wok and then heat the oil. The best way to do this is to drizzle a "necklace" of oil around the inner rim of the wok, so that it drops down to coat the entire inner surface. Make sure the coating is even by swirling the wok.

4 Add the garlic and dried chillies to the wok and stir-fry over a medium heat until golden. Do not let the garlic burn, otherwise it will taste bitter.

5 Add the chicken to the wok and stir-fry until it is cooked through, then add the red pepper. If the mixture is very dry, add a little water.

6 Stir in the oyster sauce, soy sauce and sugar. Add the spring onions and cashew nuts. Stir-fry for 1–2 minutes more, until heated through. Spoon into a warm dish and serve immediately, garnished with the coriander leaves.

COOK'S TIP

The Thais not only value cashew nuts, but also the "fruit" under which each nut grows. Although they are known as cashew apples, these so-called fruits are actually bulbous portions of the stem. They may be pink, red or yellow in colour and the crisp, sweet flesh can be eaten raw or made into a refreshing drink. They have even been used for making jam. Cashew apples – and undried nuts – are rarely seen outside their growing regions.

JUNGLE CURRY OF GUINEA FOWL

A TRADITIONAL WILD FOOD COUNTRY CURRY FROM THE NORTH-CENTRAL REGION OF THAILAND, THIS DISH CAN BE MADE USING ANY GAME, FISH OR CHICKEN. GUINEA FOWL IS NOT TYPICAL OF THAI CUISINE, BUT IS A POPULAR AND WIDELY AVAILABLE GAME BIRD IN THE WEST.

SERVES FOUR

INGREDIENTS

- 1 guinea fowl or similar game bird
- 15ml/1 tbsp vegetable oil
- 10ml/2 tsp green curry paste
- 15ml/1 tbsp Thai fish sauce
- 2.5cm/1in piece fresh galangal, peeled and finely chopped
- 15ml/1 tbsp fresh green peppercorns
- 3 kaffir lime leaves, torn
- 15ml/1 tbsp whisky, preferably Mekhong
- 300ml/½ pint/1¼ cups chicken stock
- 50g/2oz snake beans or yard-long beans, cut into 2.5cm/1in lengths (about ½ cup)
- 225g/8oz/3¼ cups chestnut mushrooms, sliced
- 1 piece drained canned bamboo shoot, about 50g/2oz, shredded
- 5ml/1 tsp dried chilli flakes, to garnish (optional)

1 Cut up the guinea fowl, remove and discard the skin, then take all the meat off the bones. Chop the meat into bitesize pieces and set aside.

2 Heat the oil in a wok or frying pan and add the curry paste. Stir-fry over a medium heat for 30 seconds, until the paste gives off its aroma.

3 Add the fish sauce and the guinea fowl meat and stir-fry until the meat is browned all over. Add the galangal, peppercorns, lime leaves and whisky, then pour in the stock.

4 Bring to the boil. Add the vegetables, return to a simmer and cook gently for 2–3 minutes, until they are just cooked. Spoon into a dish, sprinkle with chilli flakes, if you like, and serve.

COOK'S TIPS

- Guinea fowl originated in West Africa and was regarded as a game bird. However, it has been domesticated in Europe for over 500 years. They range in size from 675g/1½lb to 2kg/4½lb, but about 1.2kg/2½lb is average. American readers could substitute two or three Cornish hens, depending on size.
- Fresh green peppercorns are simply unripe berries. They are sold on the stem and look rather like miniature Brussels sprout stalks. Look for them at Thai supermarkets. If unavailable, substitute bottled green peppercorns, but rinse well and drain them first.

Chinese Duck Curry

A richly spiced curry that illustrates the powerful Chinese influence on Thai cuisine. The duck is best marinated for as long as possible, although it tastes good even if you only have time to marinate it briefly.

SERVES FOUR

INGREDIENTS

- 4 duck breast portions, skin and bones removed
- 30ml/2 tbsp five-spice powder
- 30ml/2 tbsp sesame oil
- grated rind and juice of 1 orange
- 1 medium butternut squash, peeled and cubed
- 10ml/2 tsp Thai red curry paste
- 30ml/2 tbsp Thai fish sauce
- 15ml/1 tbsp palm sugar or light muscovado (brown) sugar
- 300ml/½ pint/1¼ cups coconut milk
- 2 fresh red chillies, seeded
- 4 kaffir lime leaves, torn
- 450g/1lb thick noodles
- small bunch coriander (cilantro), chopped, to garnish

1 Cut the duck meat into bitesize pieces and place in a bowl with the five-spice powder, sesame oil and orange rind and juice. Stir well to mix all the ingredients and coat the duck in the marinade. Cover the bowl with clear film (plastic wrap) and set aside in a cool place to marinate for at least 15 minutes.

2 Meanwhile, bring a pan of water to the boil. Add the squash and cook for 10–15 minutes, until just tender. Drain well and set aside.

3 Pour the marinade from the duck into a wok and heat until boiling. Stir in the curry paste and cook for 2–3 minutes, until well blended and fragrant. Add the duck and cook for 3–4 minutes, stirring constantly, until browned on all sides.

4 Add the fish sauce and palm sugar and cook for 2 minutes more. Stir in the coconut milk until the mixture is smooth, then add the cooked squash, with the chillies and lime leaves. Simmer gently, stirring frequently, for 5 minutes.

5 Cook the noodles according to the instructions on the packet, then add to the curry and mix well. Sprinkle with the fresh coriander and serve.

DUCK AND SESAME STIR-FRY

This recipe comes from northern Thailand and is intended for game birds, as farmed duck would have too much fat. Use wild duck if you can get it, or even partridge, pheasant or pigeon. If you do use farmed duck, you should remove the skin and fat layer.

SERVES FOUR

INGREDIENTS
- 250g/9oz boneless wild duck meat
- 15ml/1 tbsp sesame oil
- 15ml/1 tbsp vegetable oil
- 4 garlic cloves, finely sliced
- 2.5ml/½ tsp dried chilli flakes
- 15ml/1 tbsp Thai fish sauce
- 15ml/1 tbsp light soy sauce
- 120ml/4fl oz/½ cup water
- 1 head broccoli, cut into small florets
- coriander (cilantro) and 15ml/1 tbsp toasted sesame seeds, to garnish

VARIATIONS

Pak choi (bok choy) or Chinese flowering cabbage can be used instead of broccoli.

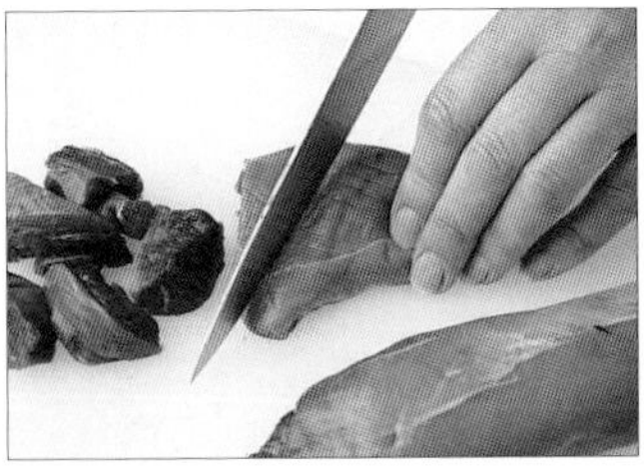

1 Cut the duck meat into bitesize pieces. Heat the oils in a wok or large, heavy frying pan and stir-fry the garlic over a medium heat until it is golden brown – do not let it burn. Add the duck to the pan and stir-fry for a further 2 minutes, until the meat begins to brown.

2 Stir in the chilli flakes, fish sauce, soy sauce and water. Add the broccoli and continue to stir-fry for about 2 minutes, until the duck is just cooked through.

3 Serve on warmed plates, garnished with coriander and sesame seeds.

MEAT DISHES

The majority of meat dishes in Thailand are curries, but curries of such breadth and subtlety that to lump them all together under a single name – and that a name of Indian origin – seems invidious. Thai curries are based on wet pastes, rather than dry spice mixtures, with chillies, garlic, shallots, ginger or galangal the predominant flavourings. Fresh lemon grass and coriander are often included, and coconut milk is what marries the various ingredients together.

GREEN BEEF CURRY WITH THAI AUBERGINES

This is a very quick curry so be sure to use good quality meat. Sirloin is recommended, but tender rump (round) steak could be used instead.

SERVES FOUR TO SIX

INGREDIENTS

- 450g/1lb beef sirloin
- 15ml/1 tbsp vegetable oil
- 45ml/3 tbsp Thai green curry paste
- 600ml/1 pint/2½ cups coconut milk
- 4 kaffir lime leaves, torn
- 15–30ml/1–2 tbsp Thai fish sauce
- 5ml/1 tsp palm sugar or light muscovado (brown) sugar
- 150g/5oz small Thai aubergines (eggplant), halved
- a small handful of fresh Thai basil
- 2 fresh green chillies, to garnish

1 Trim off any excess fat from the beef. Using a sharp knife, cut it into long, thin strips. This is easiest to do if it is well chilled. Set it aside.

2 Heat the oil in a large, heavy pan or wok. Add the curry paste and cook for 1–2 minutes, until it is fragrant.

3 Stir in half the coconut milk, a little at a time. Cook, stirring frequently, for about 5–6 minutes, until an oily sheen appears on the surface of the liquid.

4 Add the beef to the pan with the kaffir lime leaves, Thai fish sauce, sugar and aubergine halves. Cook for 2–3 minutes, then stir in the remaining coconut milk.

5 Bring back to a simmer and cook until the meat and aubergines are tender. Stir in the Thai basil just before serving. Finely shred the green chillies and use to garnish the curry.

COOK'S TIP

To make the green curry paste, put 15 fresh green chillies, 2 chopped lemon grass stalks, 3 sliced shallots, 2 garlic cloves, 15ml/1 tbsp chopped galangal, 4 chopped kaffir lime leaves, 2.5ml/½ tsp grated kaffir lime rind, 5ml/1 tsp chopped coriander root, 6 black peppercorns, 5ml/1 tsp each roasted coriander and cumin seeds, 15ml/1 tbsp granulated sugar, 5ml/1 tsp salt and 5ml/1 tsp shrimp paste into a food processor and process until smooth. Gradually add 30ml/2 tbsp vegetable oil, processing after each addition.

THICK BEEF CURRY IN SWEET PEANUT SAUCE

THIS CURRY IS DELICIOUSLY RICH AND THICKER THAN MOST OTHER THAI CURRIES. SERVE IT WITH BOILED JASMINE RICE AND SALTED DUCK'S EGGS, IF YOU LIKE.

SERVES FOUR TO SIX

INGREDIENTS

- 600ml/1 pint/2½ cups coconut milk
- 45ml/3 tbsp Thai red curry paste
- 45ml/3 tbsp Thai fish sauce
- 30ml/2 tbsp palm sugar or light muscovado (brown) sugar
- 2 lemon grass stalks, bruised
- 450g/1lb rump (round) steak, cut into thin strips
- 75g/3oz/¾ cup roasted peanuts, ground
- 2 fresh red chillies, sliced
- 5 kaffir lime leaves, torn
- salt and ground black pepper
- 2 salted eggs, cut in wedges, and 10–15 Thai basil leaves, to garnish

1 Pour half the coconut milk into a large, heavy pan. Place over a medium heat and bring to the boil, stirring constantly until the milk separates.

2 Stir in the red curry paste and cook for 2–3 minutes until the mixture is fragrant and thoroughly blended. Add the fish sauce, sugar and bruised lemon grass stalks. Mix well.

3 Continue to cook until the colour deepens. Gradually add the remaining coconut milk, stirring constantly. Bring back to the boil.

COOK'S TIP

If you don't have the time to make your own red curry paste, you can buy a ready-made Thai curry paste. There is a wide range available in most Asian stores and large supermarkets.

4 Add the beef and peanuts. Cook, stirring constantly, for 8–10 minutes, or until most of the liquid has evaporated. Add the chillies and lime leaves. Season to taste and serve, garnished with wedges of salted eggs and Thai basil leaves.

MUSSAMAN CURRY

THIS DISH IS TRADITIONALLY BASED ON BEEF, BUT CHICKEN, LAMB OR TOFU CAN BE USED INSTEAD. IT HAS A RICH, SWEET AND SPICY FLAVOUR AND IS BEST SERVED WITH BOILED RICE. MUSSAMAN CURRY PASTE IS AVAILABLE FROM SPECIALIST STORES.

SERVES FOUR TO SIX

INGREDIENTS

- 675g/1½ lb stewing steak
- 600ml/1 pint/2½ cups coconut milk
- 250ml/8fl oz/1 cup coconut cream
- 45ml/3 tbsp Mussaman curry paste
- 30ml/2 tbsp Thai fish sauce
- 15ml/1 tbsp palm sugar or light muscovado (brown) sugar
- 60ml/4 tbsp tamarind juice (tamarind paste mixed with warm water)
- 6 green cardamom pods
- 1 cinnamon stick
- 1 large potato, about 225g/8oz, cut into even chunks
- 1 onion, cut into wedges
- 50g/2oz/½ cup roasted peanuts

1 Trim off any excess fat from the stewing steak, then, using a sharp knife, cut it into 2.5cm/1in chunks.

2 Pour the coconut milk into a large, heavy pan and bring to the boil over a medium heat. Add the chunks of beef, reduce the heat to low, partially cover the pan and simmer gently for about 40 minutes, or until tender.

3 Transfer the coconut cream to a separate pan. Cook over a medium heat, stirring constantly, for about 5 minutes, or until it separates. Stir in the Mussaman curry paste and cook rapidly for 2–3 minutes, until fragrant and thoroughly blended.

4 Return the coconut cream and curry paste mixture to the pan with the beef and stir until thoroughly blended. Simmer for a further 4–5 minutes, stirring occasionally.

5 Stir the fish sauce, sugar, tamarind juice, cardamom pods, cinnamon stick, potato chunks and onion wedges into the beef curry. Continue to simmer for a further 15–20 minutes, or until the potato is cooked and tender.

6 Add the roasted peanuts to the pan and mix well to combine. Cook for about 5 minutes more, then transfer to warmed individual serving bowls and serve immediately.

COOK'S TIP

To make Mussaman curry paste, halve 12 large dried chillies and discard the seeds, then soak the chillies in hot water for about 15 minutes. Remove the chillies from the water and chop finely. Place the chopped chillies in a mortar or food processor and pound or process with 60ml/4 tbsp chopped shallots, 5 garlic cloves, the base of 1 lemon grass stalk and 30ml/2 tbsp chopped fresh galangal. Dry-fry 5ml/1 tsp cumin seeds, 15ml/1 tbsp coriander seeds, 2 cloves and 6 black peppercorns over a low heat for 1–2 minutes. Grind the toasted spices to a powder, then combine with 5ml/1 tsp shrimp paste, 5ml/1 tsp salt, 5ml/1 tsp granulated sugar and 30ml/2 tbsp vegetable oil. Add the shallot mixture to the spice mixture and stir well to make a paste.

DRY BEEF CURRY WITH PEANUT AND LIME

Originating from the mountainous northern regions of Thailand, dry curries are now popular throughout the country. This dry beef curry is usually served with a moist dish such as Northern Fish Curry with Shallots and Lemon Grass.

SERVES FOUR TO SIX

INGREDIENTS

- 400g/14oz can coconut milk
- 900g/2lb stewing steak, finely chopped
- 300ml/½ pint/1¼ cups beef stock
- 30ml/2 tbsp crunchy peanut butter
- juice of 2 limes
- lime slices, shredded coriander (cilantro) and fresh red chilli slices, to garnish

For the red curry paste

- 30ml/2 tbsp coriander seeds
- 5ml/1 tsp cumin seeds
- seeds from 6 green cardamom pods
- 2.5ml/½ tsp grated or ground nutmeg
- 1.5ml/¼ tsp ground cloves
- 2.5ml/½ tsp ground cinnamon
- 20ml/4 tsp paprika
- pared rind of 1 mandarin orange, finely chopped
- 4–5 small fresh red chillies, seeded and finely chopped
- 25ml/5 tsp granulated sugar
- 2.5ml/½ tsp salt
- 1 piece lemon grass, about 10cm/4in long, shredded
- 3 garlic cloves, crushed
- 2cm/¾in piece fresh galangal, peeled and finely chopped
- 4 red shallots, finely chopped
- 1 piece shrimp paste, 2cm/¾in square
- 50g/2oz coriander (cilantro) root or stem, chopped
- juice of ½ lime
- 30ml/2 tbsp vegetable oil

1 Strain the coconut milk into a bowl, retaining the thicker coconut milk in the strainer or sieve.

2 Pour the thin coconut milk from the bowl into a large, heavy pan, then scrape in half the residue from the sieve. Reserve the remaining thick coconut milk. Add the chopped steak. Pour in the beef stock and bring to the boil. Reduce the heat, cover the pan and simmer gently for 50 minutes.

3 Make the curry paste. Dry-fry all the seeds for 1–2 minutes. Tip into a bowl and add the nutmeg, cloves, cinnamon, paprika and orange rind. Pound the chillies with the sugar and salt. Add the spice mixture, lemon grass, garlic, galangal, shallots and shrimp paste and pound to a paste. Work in the coriander, lime juice and oil.

4 Strain the beef, reserving the cooking liquid, and place a cupful of liquid in a wok. Stir in 30–45ml/2–3 tbsp of the curry paste, according to taste. Boil rapidly until all the liquid has evaporated. Stir in the reserved thick coconut milk, the peanut butter and the beef. Simmer, uncovered, for 15–20 minutes, adding a little more cooking liquid if the mixture starts to stick to the pan, but keep the curry dry.

5 Just before serving, stir in the lime juice. Serve in warmed bowls, garnished with the lime slices, shredded coriander and sliced red chillies.

VARIATION

The curry is equally delicious made with lean leg or shoulder of lamb.

BEEF STEW WITH STAR ANISE

Not a Western idea of a stew, but more of a fragrant soup with tender morsels of beef. The beansprouts, spring onion and coriander are added at the end of cooking for a delightful contrast in taste and texture.

SERVES FOUR

INGREDIENTS
- 1 litre/1¾ pints/4 cups vegetable or chicken stock
- 450g/1lb beef steak, cut into slivers
- 3 garlic cloves, finely chopped
- 3 coriander (cilantro) roots, finely chopped
- 2 cinnamon sticks
- 4 star anise
- 30ml/2 tbsp light soy sauce
- 30ml/2 tbsp Thai fish sauce
- 5ml/1 tsp granulated sugar
- 115g/4oz/1⅓ cups beansprouts
- 1 spring onion (scallion), finely chopped
- small bunch fresh coriander (cilantro), coarsely chopped

1 Pour the stock into a large, heavy pan. Add the beef, garlic, chopped coriander roots, cinnamon sticks, star anise, soy sauce, fish sauce and sugar. Bring to the boil, then reduce the heat to low and simmer for 30 minutes. Skim off any foam that rises to the surface of the liquid with a slotted spoon.

2 Meanwhile, divide the beansprouts among four individual serving bowls. Remove and discard the cinnamon sticks and star anise from the stew with a slotted spoon. Ladle the stew over the beansprouts, garnish with the chopped spring onion and chopped fresh coriander and serve immediately.

STIR-FRIED BEEF IN OYSTER SAUCE

ANOTHER SIMPLE BUT DELICIOUS RECIPE. IN THAILAND THIS IS OFTEN MADE WITH JUST STRAW MUSHROOMS, WHICH ARE READILY AVAILABLE FRESH, BUT OYSTER MUSHROOMS MAKE A GOOD SUBSTITUTE AND USING A MIXTURE MAKES THE DISH EXTRA INTERESTING.

SERVES FOUR TO SIX

INGREDIENTS

- 450g/1lb rump (round) steak
- 30ml/2 tbsp soy sauce
- 15ml/1 tbsp cornflour (cornstarch)
- 45ml/3 tbsp vegetable oil
- 15ml/1 tbsp chopped garlic
- 15ml/1 tbsp chopped fresh root ginger
- 225g/8oz/3¼ cups mixed mushrooms such as shiitake, oyster and straw
- 30ml/2 tbsp oyster sauce
- 5ml/1 tsp granulated sugar
- 4 spring onions (scallions), cut into short lengths
- ground black pepper
- 2 fresh red chillies, seeded and cut into strips, to garnish

1 Place the steak in the freezer for 30–40 minutes, until firm, then, using a sharp knife, slice it on the diagonal into long thin strips.

2 Mix together the soy sauce and cornflour in a large bowl. Add the steak, turning to coat well, cover with clear film (plastic wrap) and leave to marinate at room temperature for 1–2 hours.

3 Heat half the oil in a wok or large, heavy frying pan. Add the garlic and ginger and cook for 1–2 minutes, until fragrant. Drain the steak, add it to the wok or pan and stir well to separate the strips. Cook, stirring frequently, for a further 1–2 minutes, until the steak is browned all over and tender. Remove from the wok or pan and set aside.

4 Heat the remaining oil in the wok or pan. Add the shiitake, oyster and straw mushrooms. Stir-fry over a medium heat until golden brown.

5 Return the steak to the wok and mix it with the mushrooms. Spoon in the oyster sauce and sugar, mix well, then add ground black pepper to taste. Toss over the heat until all the ingredients are thoroughly combined.

6 Stir in the spring onions. Tip the mixture on to a serving platter, garnish with the strips of red chilli and serve.

CURRIED PORK WITH PICKLED GARLIC

This very rich curry is best accompanied by lots of plain rice and perhaps a light vegetable dish. It could serve four if served with a vegetable curry. Asian stores sell pickled garlic. It is well worth investing in a jar, as the taste is sweet and delicious.

SERVES TWO

INGREDIENTS

- 130g/4½oz lean pork steaks
- 30ml/2 tbsp vegetable oil
- 1 garlic clove, crushed
- 15ml/1 tbsp Thai red curry paste
- 130ml/4½fl oz/generous ½ cup coconut cream
- 2.5cm/1in piece fresh root ginger, finely chopped
- 30ml/2 tbsp vegetable or chicken stock
- 30ml/2 tbsp Thai fish sauce
- 5ml/1 tsp granulated sugar
- 2.5ml/½ tsp ground turmeric
- 10ml/2 tsp lemon juice
- 4 pickled garlic cloves, finely chopped
- strips of lemon and lime rind, to garnish

1 Place the pork steaks in the freezer for 30–40 minutes, until firm, then, using a sharp knife, cut the meat into fine slivers, trimming off any excess fat.

2 Heat the oil in a wok or large, heavy frying pan and cook the garlic over a low to medium heat until golden brown. Do not let it burn. Add the curry paste and stir it in well.

3 Add the coconut cream and stir until the liquid begins to reduce and thicken. Stir in the pork. Cook for 2 minutes more, until the pork is cooked through.

4 Add the ginger, stock, fish sauce, sugar and turmeric, stirring constantly, then add the lemon juice and pickled garlic. Spoon into bowls, garnish with strips of rind, and serve.

SWEET AND SOUR PORK, THAI-STYLE

IT WAS THE CHINESE WHO ORIGINALLY CREATED SWEET AND SOUR COOKING, BUT THE THAIS ALSO DO IT VERY WELL. THIS VERSION HAS A FRESHER AND CLEANER FLAVOUR THAN THE ORIGINAL. IT MAKES A GOOD ONE-DISH MEAL WHEN SERVED OVER RICE.

SERVES FOUR

INGREDIENTS

- 350g/12oz lean pork
- 30ml/2 tbsp vegetable oil
- 4 garlic cloves, thinly sliced
- 1 small red onion, sliced
- 30ml/2 tbsp Thai fish sauce
- 15ml/1 tbsp granulated sugar
- 1 red (bell) pepper, seeded and diced
- ½ cucumber, seeded and sliced
- 2 plum tomatoes, cut into wedges
- 115g/4oz piece of fresh pineapple, cut into small chunks
- 2 spring onions (scallions), cut into short lengths
- ground black pepper

To garnish

- coriander (cilantro) leaves
- spring onions (scallions), shredded

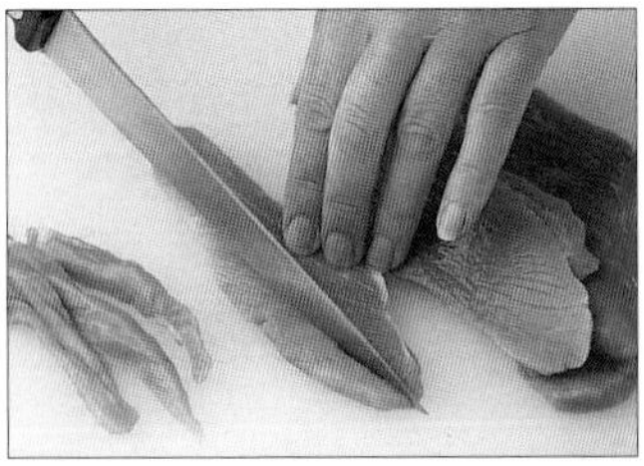

1 Place the pork in the freezer for 30–40 minutes, until firm. Using a sharp knife, cut it into thin strips.

2 Heat the oil in a wok or large frying pan. Add the garlic. Cook over a medium heat until golden, then add the pork and stir-fry for 4–5 minutes. Add the onion slices and toss to mix.

3 Add the fish sauce, sugar and ground black pepper to taste. Toss the mixture over the heat for 3–4 minutes more.

4 Stir in the red pepper, cucumber, tomatoes, pineapple and spring onions. Stir-fry for 3–4 minutes more, then spoon into a bowl. Garnish with the coriander and spring onions and serve.

PORK AND PINEAPPLE COCONUT CURRY

THE HEAT OF THIS CURRY BALANCES OUT ITS SWEETNESS TO MAKE A SMOOTH AND FRAGRANT DISH. IT TAKES VERY LITTLE TIME TO COOK, SO IS IDEAL FOR A QUICK SUPPER BEFORE GOING OUT OR FOR A MID-WEEK FAMILY MEAL ON A BUSY EVENING.

SERVES FOUR

INGREDIENTS

- 400ml/14fl oz can or carton coconut milk
- 10ml/2 tsp Thai red curry paste
- 400g/14oz pork loin steaks, trimmed and thinly sliced
- 15ml/1 tbsp Thai fish sauce
- 5ml/1 tsp palm sugar or light muscovado (brown) sugar
- 15ml/1 tbsp tamarind juice, made by mixing tamarind paste with warm water
- 2 kaffir lime leaves, torn
- ½ medium pineapple, peeled and chopped
- 1 fresh red chilli, seeded and finely chopped

1 Pour the coconut milk into a bowl and let it settle, so that the cream rises to the surface. Scoop the cream into a measuring jug (cup). You should have about 250ml/8fl oz/1 cup. If necessary, add a little of the coconut milk.

2 Pour the coconut cream into a large pan and bring it to the boil.

3 Cook the coconut cream for about 10 minutes, until the cream separates, stirring frequently to prevent it from sticking to the base of the pan and scorching. Add the red curry paste and stir until well mixed. Cook, stirring occasionally, for about 4 minutes, until the paste is fragrant.

4 Add the sliced pork and stir in the fish sauce, sugar and tamarind juice. Cook, stirring constantly, for 1–2 minutes, until the sugar has dissolved and the pork is no longer pink.

5 Add the remaining coconut milk and the lime leaves. Bring to the boil, then stir in the pineapple. Reduce the heat and simmer gently for 3 minutes, or until the pork is fully cooked. Sprinkle over the chilli and serve.

Lemon Grass Pork

Chillies and lemon grass flavour this simple stir-fry, while peanuts add an interesting contrast in texture. Look for jars of chopped lemon grass, which are handy when the fresh vegetable isn't available.

SERVES FOUR

INGREDIENTS
- 675g/1½ lb boneless pork loin
- 2 lemon grass stalks, finely chopped
- 4 spring onions (scallions), thinly sliced
- 5ml/1 tsp salt
- 12 black peppercorns, coarsely crushed
- 30ml/2 tbsp groundnut (peanut) oil
- 2 garlic cloves, chopped
- 2 fresh red chillies, seeded and chopped
- 5ml/1 tsp soft light brown sugar
- 30ml/2 tbsp Thai fish sauce
- 25g/1oz/¼ cup roasted unsalted peanuts, chopped
- ground black pepper
- cooked rice noodles, to serve
- coarsely torn coriander (cilantro) leaves, to garnish

1 Trim any excess fat from the pork. Cut the meat across into 5mm/¼in thick slices, then cut each slice into 5mm/¼in strips. Put the pork into a bowl with the lemon grass, spring onions, salt and crushed peppercorns; mix well. Cover with clear film (plastic wrap) and leave to marinate in a cool place for 30 minutes.

2 Preheat a wok, add the oil and swirl it around. Add the pork mixture and stir-fry over a medium heat for about 3 minutes, until browned all over.

3 Add the garlic and red chillies and stir-fry for a further 5–8 minutes over a medium heat, until the pork is cooked through and tender.

4 Add the sugar, fish sauce and chopped peanuts and toss to mix, then season to taste with black pepper. Serve immediately on a bed of rice noodles, garnished with the coarsely torn coriander leaves.

COOK'S TIP

The heat in chillies is not in the seeds, but in the membranes surrounding them, which are removed along with the seeds.

PORK BELLY WITH FIVE SPICES

THE CHINESE INFLUENCE ON THAI CUISINE STEMS FROM THE EARLY YEARS OF ITS HISTORY, WHEN COLONISTS FROM SOUTHERN CHINA SETTLED IN THE COUNTRY, BRINGING WITH THEM DISHES LIKE THIS, ALTHOUGH THAI COOKS HAVE PROVIDED THEIR OWN UNIQUE IMPRINT.

SERVES FOUR

INGREDIENTS

- 1 large bunch fresh coriander (cilantro) with roots
- 30ml/2 tbsp vegetable oil
- 1 garlic clove, crushed
- 30ml/2 tbsp five-spice powder
- 500g/1¼ lb pork belly, cut into 2.5cm/1in pieces
- 400g/14oz can chopped tomatoes
- 150ml/¼ pint/⅔ cup hot water
- 30ml/2 tbsp dark soy sauce
- 45ml/3 tbsp Thai fish sauce
- 30ml/2 tbsp granulated sugar
- 1 lime, halved

COOK'S TIP

Make sure that you buy Chinese five-spice powder, as the Indian variety is made up from quite different spices.

1 Cut off the coriander roots. Chop five of them finely and freeze the remainder for another occasion. Chop the coriander stalks and leaves and set them aside. Keep the roots separate.

2 Heat the oil in a large pan and cook the garlic until golden brown. Stirring constantly, add the chopped coriander roots and then the five-spice powder.

3 Add the pork and stir-fry until the meat is thoroughly coated in spices and has browned. Stir in the tomatoes and hot water. Bring to the boil, then stir in the soy sauce, fish sauce and sugar.

4 Reduce the heat, cover the pan and simmer for 30 minutes. Stir in the chopped coriander stalks and leaves, squeeze over the lime juice and serve.

PORK CHOPS WITH FIELD MUSHROOMS

IN THAILAND, MEAT IS FREQUENTLY COOKED OVER A BRAZIER OR OPEN FIRE, SO IT ISN'T SURPRISING THAT MANY TASTY BARBECUE-STYLE DISHES COME FROM THERE. THESE FABULOUS PORK CHOPS ARE GREAT FAVOURITES WITH EVERYONE AND ARE DELICIOUS SERVED WITH NOODLES OR RICE.

SERVES FOUR

INGREDIENTS

- 4 pork chops
- 4 large field (portobello) mushrooms
- 45ml/3 tbsp vegetable oil
- 4 fresh red chillies, seeded and thinly sliced
- 45ml/3 tbsp Thai fish sauce
- 90ml/6 tbsp fresh lime juice
- 4 shallots, chopped
- 5ml/1 tsp roasted ground rice
- 30ml/2 tbsp spring onions (scallions), chopped, plus shredded spring onions to garnish
- coriander (cilantro) leaves, to garnish

For the marinade

- 2 garlic cloves, chopped
- 15ml/1 tbsp granulated sugar
- 15ml/1 tbsp Thai fish sauce
- 30ml/2 tbsp soy sauce
- 15ml/1 tbsp sesame oil
- 15ml/1 tbsp whisky or dry sherry
- 2 lemon grass stalks, finely chopped
- 2 spring onions (scallions), chopped

1 Make the marinade. Combine the garlic, sugar, sauces, oil and whisky or sherry in a large, shallow dish. Stir in the lemon grass and spring onions.

2 Add the pork chops, turning to coat them in the marinade. Cover and leave to marinate for 1–2 hours.

3 Lift the chops out of the marinade and place them on a barbecue grid over hot coals or on a grill (broiler) rack. Add the mushrooms and brush them with 15ml/1 tbsp of the oil. Cook the pork chops for 5–7 minutes on each side and the mushrooms for about 2 minutes. Brush both with the marinade while cooking.

4 Heat the remaining oil in a wok or small frying pan, then remove the pan from the heat and stir in the chillies, fish sauce, lime juice, shallots, ground rice and chopped spring onions. Put the pork chops and mushrooms on a large serving plate and spoon over the sauce. Garnish with the coriander leaves and shredded spring onion.

STIR-FRIED PORK WITH DRIED SHRIMP

You might expect the dried shrimp to give this dish a fishy flavour, but instead it simply imparts a delicious savoury taste.

SERVES FOUR

INGREDIENTS

- 250g/9oz pork fillet (tenderloin), sliced
- 30ml/2 tbsp vegetable oil
- 2 garlic cloves, finely chopped
- 45ml/3 tbsp dried shrimp
- 10ml/2 tsp dried shrimp paste or 5mm/¼in piece from block of shrimp paste
- 30ml/2 tbsp soy sauce
- juice of 1 lime
- 15ml/1 tbsp palm sugar or light muscovado (brown) sugar
- 1 small fresh red or green chilli, seeded and finely chopped
- 4 pak choi (bok choy) or 450g/1lb spring greens (collards), shredded

1 Place the pork in the freezer for about 30 minutes, until firm. Using a sharp knife, cut it into thin slices.

2 Heat the oil in a wok or frying pan and cook the garlic until golden brown. Add the pork and stir-fry for about 4 minutes, until just cooked through.

3 Add the dried shrimp, then stir in the shrimp paste, with the soy sauce, lime juice and sugar. Add the chilli and pak choi or spring greens and toss over the heat until the vegetables are just wilted.

4 Transfer the stir-fry to warm individual bowls and serve immediately.

PORK ON LEMON GRASS STICKS

THIS SIMPLE RECIPE MAKES A SUBSTANTIAL SNACK, AND THE LEMON GRASS STICKS NOT ONLY ADD A SUBTLE FLAVOUR BUT ALSO MAKE A GOOD TALKING POINT.

SERVES FOUR

INGREDIENTS

- 300g/11oz minced (ground) pork
- 4 garlic cloves, crushed
- 4 fresh coriander (cilantro) roots, finely chopped
- 2.5ml/½ tsp granulated sugar
- 15ml/1 tbsp soy sauce
- salt and ground black pepper
- 8 x 10cm/4in lengths of lemon grass stalk
- sweet chilli sauce, to serve

VARIATION

Slimmer versions of these pork sticks are perfect for parties. The mixture will be enough for 12 lemon grass sticks if you use it sparingly.

1 Place the minced pork, crushed garlic, chopped coriander root, sugar and soy sauce in a large bowl. Season with salt and pepper to taste and mix well.

2 Divide into eight portions and mould each one into a ball. It may help to dampen your hands before shaping the mixture to prevent it from sticking.

3 Stick a length of lemon grass halfway into each ball, then press the meat mixture around the lemon grass to make a shape like a chicken leg.

4 Cook the pork sticks under a hot grill (broiler) for 3–4 minutes on each side, until golden and cooked through. Serve with the chilli sauce for dipping.

FISH AND SHELLFISH

You need only glance at a map to discover why Thailand has so many wonderful fish and shellfish dishes. The country has a long coastline, most of it on the fish-rich Gulf of Siam, and major rivers provide a wide variety of freshwater fish. Prawns and shrimp are very popular, not just fresh, but also dried. If you've never had a fish curry, do try one of the ones in this chapter. The citrus flavours that are such a feature of Thai curries work very well with fish and shellfish.

Northern Fish Curry with Shallots and Lemon Grass

This is a thin, soupy curry with wonderfully strong flavours. Serve it in bowls with lots of sticky rice to soak up the delicious juices.

SERVES FOUR

INGREDIENTS

- 450g/1lb salmon fillet
- 500ml/17fl oz/2¼ cups vegetable stock
- 4 shallots, finely chopped
- 2 garlic cloves, finely chopped
- 2.5cm/1in piece fresh galangal, finely chopped
- 1 lemon grass stalk, finely chopped
- 2.5ml/½ tsp dried chilli flakes
- 15ml/1 tbsp Thai fish sauce
- 5ml/1 tsp palm sugar or light muscovado (brown) sugar

1 Place the salmon in the freezer for 30–40 minutes to firm up the flesh slightly. Remove and discard the skin, then use a sharp knife to cut the fish into 2.5cm/1in cubes, removing any stray bones with your fingers or with tweezers as you do so.

2 Pour the stock into a large, heavy pan and bring it to the boil over a medium heat. Add the shallots, garlic, galangal, lemon grass, chilli flakes, fish sauce and sugar. Bring back to the boil, stir well, then reduce the heat and simmer gently for 15 minutes.

3 Add the fish, bring back to the boil, then turn off the heat. Leave the curry to stand for 10–15 minutes until the fish is cooked through, then serve.

Mussels and Clams with Lemon Grass and Coconut Cream

Lemon grass has an incomparable aromatic flavour and is widely used with all kinds of seafood in Thailand as the flavours marry so perfectly.

SERVES SIX

INGREDIENTS
- 1.8kg/4lb fresh mussels
- 450g/1lb baby clams
- 120ml/4fl oz/½ cup dry white wine
- 1 bunch spring onions (scallions), chopped
- 2 lemon grass stalks, chopped
- 6 kaffir lime leaves, chopped
- 10ml/2 tsp Thai green curry paste
- 200ml/7fl oz/scant 1 cup coconut cream
- 30ml/2 tbsp chopped fresh coriander (cilantro)
- salt and ground black pepper
- garlic chives, to garnish

1 Clean the mussels by pulling off the beards, scrubbing the shells well and scraping off any barnacles with the blade of a knife. Scrub the clams. Discard any mussels or clams that are damaged or broken or which do not close immediately when tapped sharply.

2 Put the wine in a large pan with the spring onions, lemon grass and lime leaves. Stir in the curry paste. Simmer until the wine has almost evaporated.

COOK'S TIPS
- In these days of marine pollution, it is unwise to gather fresh shellfish yourself. Those available from fish stores have either been farmed or have undergone a purging process to clean them.
- Depending on where you live, you may have difficulty obtaining clams. If so, use a few extra mussels instead.

3 Add the mussels and clams to the pan and increase the heat to high. Cover tightly and steam the shellfish for 5–6 minutes, until they open.

4 Using a slotted spoon, transfer the mussels and clams to a heated serving bowl, cover and keep hot. Discard any shellfish that remain closed. Strain the cooking liquid into a clean pan through a sieve lined with muslin (cheesecloth) and simmer briefly to reduce to about 250ml/8fl oz/1 cup.

5 Stir the coconut cream and chopped coriander into the sauce and season with salt and pepper to taste. Heat through. Pour the sauce over the mussels and clams, garnish with the garlic chives and serve immediately.

PAN-STEAMED MUSSELS WITH THAI HERBS

LIKE SO MANY THAI DISHES, THIS IS VERY EASY TO PREPARE. THE LEMON GRASS AND KAFFIR LIME LEAVES ADD A REFRESHING TANG TO THE MUSSELS.

SERVES FOUR TO SIX

INGREDIENTS

- 1kg/2¼lb fresh mussels
- 2 lemon grass stalks, finely chopped
- 4 shallots, chopped
- 4 kaffir lime leaves, coarsely torn
- 2 fresh red chillies, sliced
- 15ml/1 tbsp Thai fish sauce
- 30ml/2 tbsp fresh lime juice
- thinly sliced spring onions (scallions) and coriander (cilantro) leaves, to garnish

1 Clean the mussels by pulling off the beards, scrubbing the shells well and removing any barnacles. Discard any mussels that are broken or which do not close when tapped sharply.

2 Place the mussels in a large, heavy pan and add the lemon grass, shallots, kaffir lime leaves, chillies, fish sauce and lime juice. Mix well. Cover the pan tightly and steam the mussels over a high heat, shaking the pan occasionally, for 5–7 minutes, until the shells have opened.

3 Using a slotted spoon, transfer the cooked mussels to a warmed serving dish or individual bowls. Discard any mussels that have failed to open.

4 Garnish the mussels with the thinly sliced spring onions and coriander leaves. Serve immediately.

Crab and Tofu Stir-fry

For a year-round light meal, this speedy stir-fry is the ideal choice. As you need only a little crab meat – and you could use the canned variety – this is a very economical dish.

SERVES TWO

INGREDIENTS
- 250g/9oz silken tofu
- 60ml/4 tbsp vegetable oil
- 2 garlic cloves, finely chopped
- 115g/4oz white crab meat
- 130g/4½oz/generous 1 cup baby corn, halved lengthways
- 2 spring onions (scallions), chopped
- 1 fresh red chilli, seeded and finely chopped
- 30ml/2 tbsp soy sauce
- 15ml/1 tbsp Thai fish sauce
- 5ml/1 tsp palm sugar or light muscovado (brown) sugar
- juice of 1 lime
- small bunch fresh coriander (cilantro), chopped, to garnish

1 Using a sharp knife, cut the silken tofu into 1cm/½in cubes.

2 Heat the oil in a wok or large, heavy frying pan. Add the tofu cubes and stir-fry until golden all over, taking care not to break them up. Remove the tofu with a slotted spoon and set aside.

3 Add the garlic to the wok or pan and stir-fry until golden. Add the crab meat, tofu, corn, spring onions, chilli, soy sauce, fish sauce and sugar. Cook, stirring constantly, until the vegetables are just tender. Stir in the lime juice, transfer to warmed bowls, sprinkle with the coriander and serve immediately.

Curried Seafood with Coconut Milk

This curry is based on a Thai classic. The lovely green colour is imparted by the finely chopped chilli and fresh herbs added during the last few moments of cooking.

SERVES FOUR

INGREDIENTS
- 225g/8oz small ready-prepared squid
- 225g/8oz raw tiger prawns (jumbo shrimp)
- 400ml/14fl oz/1⅔ cups coconut milk
- 2 kaffir lime leaves, finely shredded
- 30ml/2 tbsp Thai fish sauce
- 450g/1lb firm white fish fillets, skinned, boned and cut into chunks
- 2 fresh green chillies, seeded and finely chopped
- 30ml/2 tbsp torn fresh basil or coriander (cilantro) leaves
- squeeze of fresh lime juice
- cooked Thai jasmine rice, to serve

For the curry paste
- 6 spring onions (scallions), coarsely chopped
- 4 fresh coriander (cilantro) stems, coarsely chopped, plus 45ml/3 tbsp chopped fresh coriander (cilantro)
- 4 kaffir lime leaves, shredded
- 8 fresh green chillies, seeded and coarsely chopped
- 1 lemon grass stalk, coarsely chopped
- 2.5cm/1in piece fresh root ginger, peeled and coarsely chopped
- 45ml/3 tbsp chopped fresh basil
- 15ml/1 tbsp vegetable oil

1 Make the curry paste. Put all the ingredients, except the oil, in a food processor and process to a paste. Alternatively, pound together in a mortar with a pestle. Stir in the oil.

2 Rinse the squid and pat dry with kitchen paper. Cut the bodies into rings and halve the tentacles, if necessary.

3 Heat a wok until hot, add the prawns and stir-fry, without any oil, for about 4 minutes, until they turn pink.

4 Remove the prawns from the wok and leave to cool slightly, then peel off the shells, saving a few with shells on for the garnish. Make a slit along the back of each one and remove the black vein.

5 Pour the coconut milk into the wok, then bring to the boil over a medium heat, stirring constantly. Add 30ml/2 tbsp of curry paste, the shredded lime leaves and fish sauce and stir well to mix. Reduce the heat to low and simmer gently for about 10 minutes.

6 Add the squid, prawns and chunks of fish and cook for about 2 minutes, until the seafood is tender. Take care not to overcook the squid as it will become tough very quickly.

7 Just before serving, stir in the chillies and basil or coriander. Taste and adjust the flavour with a squeeze of lime juice. Garnish with prawns in their shells, and serve with Thai jasmine rice.

VARIATIONS
- You can use any firm-fleshed white fish for this curry, such as monkfish, cod, haddock or John Dory.
- If you prefer, you could substitute shelled scallops for the squid. Slice them in half horizontally and add them with the prawns (shrimp). As with the squid, be careful not to overcook them.

SATAY PRAWNS

THIS DELICIOUS DISH IS INSPIRED BY THE CLASSIC INDONESIAN SATAY. THE COMBINATION OF MILD PEANUTS, AROMATIC SPICES, SWEET COCONUT MILK AND ZESTY LEMON JUICE IN THE SPICY DIP IS PERFECT AND IS GUARANTEED TO HAVE GUESTS COMING BACK FOR MORE.

SERVES FOUR TO SIX

INGREDIENTS

- 450g/1lb king prawns (jumbo shrimp)
- 25ml/1½ tbsp vegetable oil

For the peanut sauce

- 25ml/1½ tbsp vegetable oil
- 15ml/1 tbsp chopped garlic
- 1 small onion, chopped
- 3–4 fresh red chillies, seeded and chopped
- 3 kaffir lime leaves, torn
- 1 lemon grass stalk, bruised and chopped
- 5ml/1 tsp medium curry paste
- 250ml/8fl oz/1 cup coconut milk
- 1cm/½in piece cinnamon stick
- 75g/3oz/⅓ cup crunchy peanut butter
- 45ml/3 tbsp tamarind juice, made by mixing tamarind paste with warm water
- 30ml/2 tbsp Thai fish sauce
- 30ml/2 tbsp palm sugar or light muscovado (brown) sugar
- juice of ½ lemon

For the garnish

- ½ bunch fresh coriander (cilantro) leaves (optional)
- 4 fresh red chillies, finely sliced (optional)
- spring onions (scallions), cut diagonally

1 Remove the heads from the prawns and peel, leaving the tail ends intact. Slit each prawn along the back with a small, sharp knife and remove the black vein. Rinse under cold running water, pat completely dry on kitchen paper and set the prawns aside.

2 Make the peanut sauce. Heat half the oil in a wok or large, heavy frying pan. Add the garlic and onion and cook over a medium heat, stirring occasionally, for 3–4 minutes, until the mixture has softened but not browned.

3 Add the chillies, kaffir lime leaves, lemon grass and curry paste. Stir well and cook for a further 2–3 minutes, then stir in the coconut milk, cinnamon stick, peanut butter, tamarind juice, fish sauce, sugar and lemon juice. Cook, stirring constantly, until well blended.

4 Bring to the boil, then reduce the heat to low and simmer gently for 15–20 minutes, until the sauce thickens. Stir occasionally with a wooden spoon to prevent the sauce from sticking to the base of the wok or frying pan.

5 Thread the prawns on to skewers and brush with a little oil. Cook under a preheated grill (broiler) for 2 minutes on each side until they turn pink and are firm to the touch. Alternatively, pan-fry the prawns, then thread on to skewers.

6 Remove the cinnamon stick from the sauce and discard. Arrange the skewered prawns on a warmed platter, garnish with spring onions and coriander leaves and sliced red chillies, if liked, and serve with the sauce.

VARIATIONS

- For a curry-style dish, heat the oil in a wok or large frying pan. Add the prawns (shrimp) and stir-fry for 3–4 minutes, or until pink. Mix the prawns with the sauce and serve with jasmine rice.
- You can use this basic sauce for satay pork or chicken, too. With a sharp knife, cut pork fillet (tenderloin) or skinless, boneless chicken breast portions into long thin strips and stir-fry in hot oil until golden brown all over and cooked through. Then stir into the sauce instead of the king prawns (jumbo shrimp).
- You could use Thai red or green curry paste for this recipe. Make your own or buy a good-quality product from an Asian food store. Once opened, jars of curry paste should be kept in the refrigerator and used within 2 months.
- You can make the satay sauce in advance and leave it to cool. Transfer to a bowl, cover with clear film (plastic wrap) and store in the refrigerator. Reheat gently, stirring occasionally, before stir-frying the prawns (shrimp).

STIR-FRIED PRAWNS WITH TAMARIND

The sour, tangy flavour that is characteristic of many Thai dishes comes from tamarind. Fresh tamarind pods from the tamarind tree can sometimes be bought, but preparing them for cooking is a laborious process. It is much easier to use a block of tamarind paste.

SERVES FOUR TO SIX

INGREDIENTS
- 6 dried red chillies
- 30ml/2 tbsp vegetable oil
- 30ml/2 tbsp chopped onion
- 30ml/2 tbsp palm sugar or light muscovado (brown) sugar
- 30ml/2 tbsp chicken stock or water
- 15ml/1 tbsp Thai fish sauce
- 90ml/6 tbsp tamarind juice, made by mixing tamarind paste with warm water
- 450g/1lb raw prawns (shrimp), peeled
- 15ml/1 tbsp fried chopped garlic
- 30ml/2 tbsp fried sliced shallots
- 2 spring onions (scallions), chopped, to garnish

1 Heat a wok or large frying pan, but do not add any oil at this stage. Add the dried chillies and dry-fry them by pressing them against the surface of the wok or pan with a spatula, turning them occasionally. Do not let them burn. Set them aside to cool slightly.

2 Add the oil to the wok or pan and reheat. Add the chopped onion and cook over a medium heat, stirring occasionally, for 2–3 minutes, until softened and golden brown.

3 Add the sugar, stock or water, fish sauce, dry-fried red chillies and the tamarind juice, stirring constantly until the sugar has dissolved. Bring to the boil, then lower the heat slightly.

4 Add the prawns, garlic and shallots. Toss over the heat for 3–4 minutes, until the prawns are cooked. Garnish with the spring onions and serve.

COOK'S TIP
Leave a few prawns (shrimp) in their shells for a garnish, if you like.

SALMON MARINATED WITH THAI SPICES

THIS RECIPE IS AN ASIAN INTERPRETATION OF GRAVADLAX, A SCANDINAVIAN SPECIALITY. USE VERY FRESH SALMON. THE RAW FISH IS MARINATED FOR SEVERAL DAYS IN A BRINE FLAVOURED WITH THAI SPICES, WHICH EFFECTIVELY "COOKS" IT.

SERVES FOUR TO SIX

INGREDIENTS
- tail piece of 1 salmon, weighing about 675g/1½lb, cleaned, scaled and filleted (see Cook's Tip)
- 20ml/4 tsp coarse sea salt
- 20ml/4 tsp granulated sugar
- 2.5cm/1in piece fresh root ginger, peeled and grated
- 2 lemon grass stalks, coarse outer leaves removed, thinly sliced
- 4 kaffir lime leaves, finely chopped or shredded
- grated rind of 1 lime
- 1 fresh red chilli, seeded and finely chopped
- 5ml/1 tsp black peppercorns, coarsely crushed
- 30ml/2 tbsp chopped fresh coriander (cilantro)
- fresh coriander (cilantro) sprigs and quartered kaffir limes, to garnish

For the dressing
- 150ml/¼ pint/⅔ cup mayonnaise
- juice of ½ lime
- 10ml/2 tsp chopped fresh coriander (cilantro)

1 Remove any remaining bones from the salmon – a pair of tweezers is the best tool for doing this, as they are likely to be both tiny and slippery.

2 Put the coarse sea salt, sugar, ginger, lemon grass, lime leaves, lime rind, chopped chilli, crushed black peppercorns and chopped coriander in a bowl and mix together.

3 Place one-quarter of the spice mixture in a shallow dish. Place one salmon fillet, skin down, on top. Spread two-thirds of the remaining mixture over the flesh, then place the remaining fillet on top, flesh side down. Sprinkle the rest of the spice mixture over the fish.

4 Cover with foil, then place a board on top. Add some weights, such as clean cans of fruit. Chill for 2–5 days, turning the fish daily in the spicy brine.

5 Make the dressing by mixing the mayonnaise, lime juice and chopped coriander in a bowl.

6 Scrape the spices off the fish. Slice it as thinly as possible. Garnish with the coriander and kaffir limes, and serve with the lime dressing.

COOK'S TIP

Ask your fishmonger to scale the fish, split it lengthways and remove it from the backbone in two matching fillets.

STIR-FRIED SQUID WITH GINGER

THE ABUNDANCE OF FISH AROUND THE GULF OF THAILAND SUSTAINS THRIVING MARKETS FOR THE RESTAURANT AND HOTEL TRADE, AND EVERY MARKET NATURALLY FEATURES STALLS WHERE DELICIOUS, FRESHLY-CAUGHT SEAFOOD IS COOKED AND SERVED. THIS RECIPE IS POPULAR AMONG STREET TRADERS.

SERVES TWO

INGREDIENTS

- 4 ready-prepared baby squid, total weight about 250g/9oz
- 15ml/1 tbsp vegetable oil
- 2 garlic cloves, finely chopped
- 30ml/2 tbsp soy sauce
- 2.5cm/1in piece fresh root ginger, peeled and finely chopped
- juice of ½ lemon
- 5ml/1 tsp granulated sugar
- 2 spring onions (scallions), chopped

VARIATIONS

This dish is often prepared with fresh galangal rather than ginger and works well with most kinds of seafood, including prawns (shrimp) and scallops.

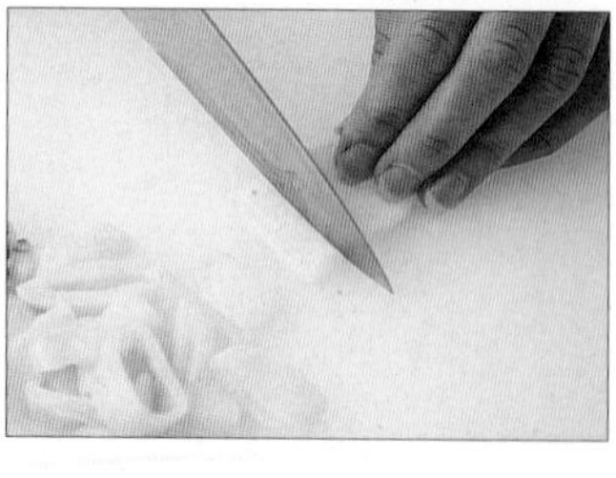

1 Rinse the squid well and pat dry with kitchen paper. Cut the bodies into rings and halve the tentacles, if necessary.

2 Heat the oil in a wok or frying pan and cook the garlic until golden brown, but do not let it burn. Add the squid and stir-fry for 30 seconds over a high heat.

3 Add the soy sauce, ginger, lemon juice, sugar and spring onions. Stir-fry a further 30 seconds, then serve.

COOK'S TIP

Squid has an undeserved reputation for being rubbery in texture. This is always a result of overcooking it.

STIR-FRIED PRAWNS WITH NOODLES

ONE OF THE MOST APPEALING ASPECTS OF THAI FOOD IS ITS APPEARANCE. INGREDIENTS ARE CAREFULLY CHOSEN SO THAT EACH DISH, EVEN A SIMPLE STIR-FRY LIKE THIS ONE, IS BALANCED IN TERMS OF COLOUR, TEXTURE AND FLAVOUR.

SERVES FOUR

INGREDIENTS

- 130g/4½oz rice noodles
- 30ml/2 tbsp groundnut (peanut) oil
- 1 large garlic clove, crushed
- 150g/5oz large prawns (shrimp), peeled and deveined
- 15g/½oz dried shrimp
- 1 piece mooli (daikon), about 75g/3oz, grated
- 15ml/1 tbsp Thai fish sauce
- 30ml/2 tbsp soy sauce
- 30ml/2 tbsp palm sugar or light muscovado (brown) sugar
- 30ml/2 tbsp fresh lime juice
- 90g/3½oz/1¾ cups beansprouts
- 40g/1½oz/⅓ cup peanuts, chopped
- 15ml/1 tbsp sesame oil
- chopped coriander (cilantro), 5ml/1 tsp dried chilli flakes and 2 shallots, finely chopped, to garnish

1 Soak the noodles in a bowl of boiling water for 5 minutes, or according to the packet instructions. Heat the oil in a wok or large frying pan. Add the garlic, and stir-fry over a medium heat for 2–3 minutes, until golden brown.

2 Add the prawns, dried shrimp and grated mooli and stir-fry for a further 2 minutes. Stir in the fish sauce, soy sauce, sugar and lime juice.

3 Drain the noodles thoroughly, then snip them into smaller lengths with scissors. Add to the wok or pan with the beansprouts, peanuts and sesame oil. Toss to mix, then stir-fry for 2 minutes. Serve immediately, garnished with the coriander, chilli flakes and shallots.

COOK'S TIP

Some cooks salt the mooli and leave it to drain, then rinse and dry before use.

SWEET AND SOUR FISH

WHEN FISH SUCH AS RED MULLET OR SNAPPER IS COOKED IN THIS WAY THE SKIN BECOMES CRISP, WHILE THE FLESH INSIDE REMAINS MOIST AND JUICY. THE SWEET AND SOUR SAUCE, WITH ITS COLOURFUL CHERRY TOMATOES, COMPLEMENTS THE FISH BEAUTIFULLY.

SERVES FOUR TO SIX

INGREDIENTS

- 1 large or 2 medium fish, such as snapper or mullet, heads removed
- 20ml/4 tsp cornflour (cornstarch)
- 120ml/4fl oz/½ cup vegetable oil
- 15ml/1 tbsp chopped garlic
- 15ml/1 tbsp chopped fresh root ginger
- 30ml/2 tbsp chopped shallots
- 225g/8oz cherry tomatoes
- 30ml/2 tbsp red wine vinegar
- 30ml/2 tbsp granulated sugar
- 30ml/2 tbsp tomato ketchup
- 15ml/1 tbsp Thai fish sauce
- 45ml/3 tbsp water
- salt and ground black pepper
- coriander (cilantro) leaves and shredded spring onions (scallions), to garnish

1 Rinse and dry the fish. Score the skin diagonally on both sides, then coat the fish lightly all over with 15ml/1 tbsp of the cornflour. Shake off any excess.

2 Heat the oil in a wok or large frying pan. Add the fish and cook over a medium heat for 6–7 minutes. Turn the fish over and cook for 6–7 minutes more, until it is crisp and brown.

3 Remove the fish with a metal spatula or fish slice and place on a large platter. Pour off all but 30ml/2 tbsp of the oil from the wok or pan and reheat. Add the garlic, ginger and shallots and cook over a medium heat, stirring occasionally, for 3–4 minutes, until golden.

4 Add the cherry tomatoes and cook until they burst open. Stir in the vinegar, sugar, tomato ketchup and fish sauce. Lower the heat and simmer gently for 1–2 minutes, then taste and adjust the seasoning, adding more vinegar, sugar and/or fish sauce, if necessary.

5 In a cup, mix the remaining 5ml/1 tsp cornflour to a paste with the water. Stir into the sauce. Heat, stirring, until it thickens. Pour the sauce over the fish, garnish with coriander leaves and shredded spring onions and serve.

STEAMED FISH WITH CHILLI SAUCE

STEAMING IS ONE OF THE BEST METHODS OF COOKING FISH. BY LEAVING THE FISH WHOLE AND ON THE BONE, MAXIMUM FLAVOUR IS RETAINED AND THE FLESH REMAINS BEAUTIFULLY MOIST. THE BANANA LEAF IS BOTH AUTHENTIC AND ATTRACTIVE, BUT YOU CAN USE BAKING PARCHMENT.

SERVES FOUR

INGREDIENTS

- 1 large or 2 medium firm fish such as sea bass or grouper, scaled and cleaned
- 30ml/2 tbsp rice wine
- 3 fresh red chillies, seeded and thinly sliced
- 2 garlic cloves, finely chopped
- 2cm/¾in piece fresh root ginger, peeled and finely shredded
- 2 lemon grass stalks, crushed and finely chopped
- 2 spring onions (scallions), chopped
- 30ml/2 tbsp Thai fish sauce
- juice of 1 lime
- 1 fresh banana leaf

For the chilli sauce

- 10 fresh red chillies, seeded and chopped
- 4 garlic cloves, chopped
- 60ml/4 tbsp Thai fish sauce
- 15ml/1 tbsp granulated sugar
- 75ml/5 tbsp fresh lime juice

1 Thoroughly rinse the fish under cold running water. Pat it dry with kitchen paper. With a sharp knife, slash the skin of the fish a few times on both sides.

2 Mix together the rice wine, chillies, garlic, shredded ginger, lemon grass and spring onions in a non-metallic bowl. Add the fish sauce and lime juice and mix to a paste. Place the fish on the banana leaf and spread the spice paste evenly over it, rubbing it in well where the skin has been slashed.

3 Put a rack or a small upturned plate in the base of a wok. Pour in boiling water to a depth of 5cm/2in. Lift the banana leaf, together with the fish, and place it on the rack or plate. Cover with a lid and steam for 10–15 minutes, or until the fish is cooked.

4 Meanwhile, make the sauce. Place all the ingredients in a food processor and process until smooth. If the mixture seems to be too thick, add a little cold water. Scrape into a serving bowl.

5 Serve the fish hot, on the banana leaf if you like, with the sweet chilli sauce to spoon over the top.

Hot and Fragrant Trout

This wickedly hot spice paste could be used as a marinade for any fish or meat. It also makes a wonderful spicy dip for grilled meat.

SERVES FOUR

INGREDIENTS
- 2 large fresh green chillies, seeded and coarsely chopped
- 5 shallots, peeled
- 5 garlic cloves, peeled
- 30ml/2 tbsp fresh lime juice
- 30ml/2 tbsp Thai fish sauce
- 15ml/1 tbsp palm sugar or light muscovado (brown) sugar
- 4 kaffir lime leaves, rolled into cylinders and thinly sliced
- 2 trout or similar firm-fleshed fish, about 350g/12oz each, cleaned
- fresh garlic chives, to garnish
- boiled rice, to serve

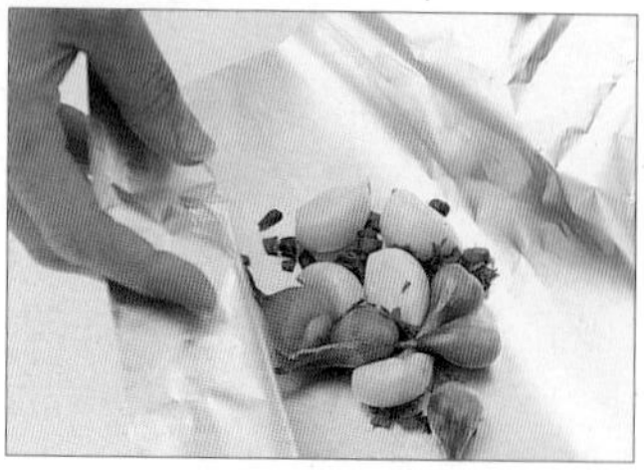

1 Wrap the chillies, shallots and garlic in a foil package. Place under a hot grill (broiler) for 10 minutes, until softened.

2 When the package is cool enough to handle, tip the contents into a mortar or food processor and pound with a pestle or process to a paste.

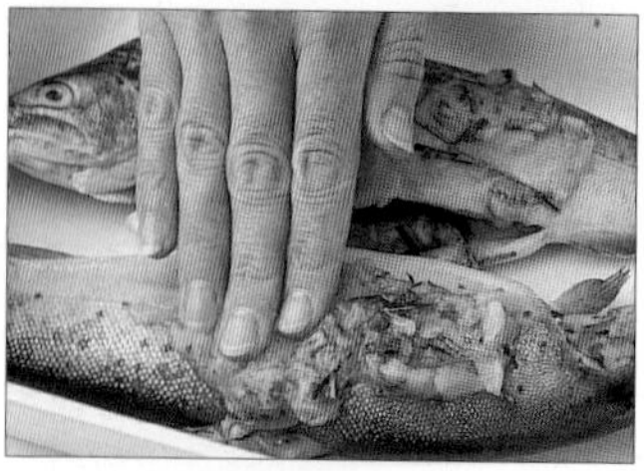

3 Add the lime juice, fish sauce, sugar and lime leaves and mix well. With a teaspoon, stuff this paste inside the fish. Smear a little on the skin too. Grill (broil) the fish for about 5 minutes on each side, until just cooked through. Lift the fish on to a platter, garnish with garlic chives and serve with rice.

TROUT WITH TAMARIND AND CHILLI SAUCE

SOMETIMES TROUT CAN TASTE RATHER BLAND, BUT THIS SPICY SAUCE REALLY GIVES IT A ZING. IF YOU LIKE YOUR FOOD VERY SPICY, ADD AN EXTRA CHILLI.

SERVES FOUR

INGREDIENTS
- 4 trout, cleaned
- 6 spring onions (scallions), sliced
- 60ml/4 tbsp soy sauce
- 15ml/1 tbsp vegetable oil
- 30ml/2 tbsp chopped fresh coriander (cilantro) and strips of fresh red chilli, to garnish

For the sauce
- 50g/2oz tamarind pulp
- 105ml/7 tbsp boiling water
- 2 shallots, coarsely chopped
- 1 fresh red chilli, seeded and chopped
- 1cm/½in piece fresh root ginger, peeled and chopped
- 5ml/1 tsp soft light brown sugar
- 45ml/3 tbsp Thai fish sauce

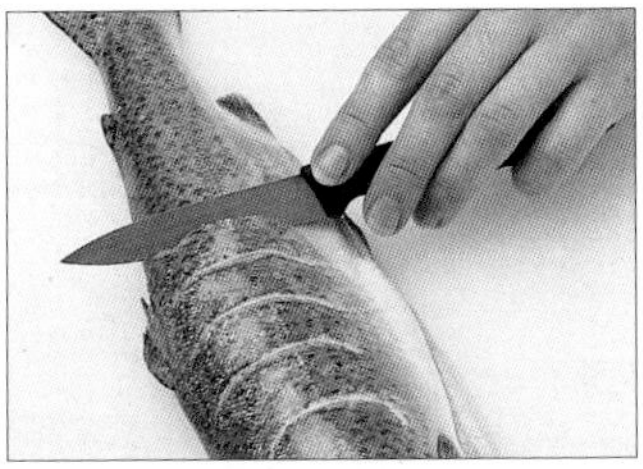

1 Slash the trout diagonally four or five times on each side. Place them in a shallow dish that is large enough to hold them all in a single layer.

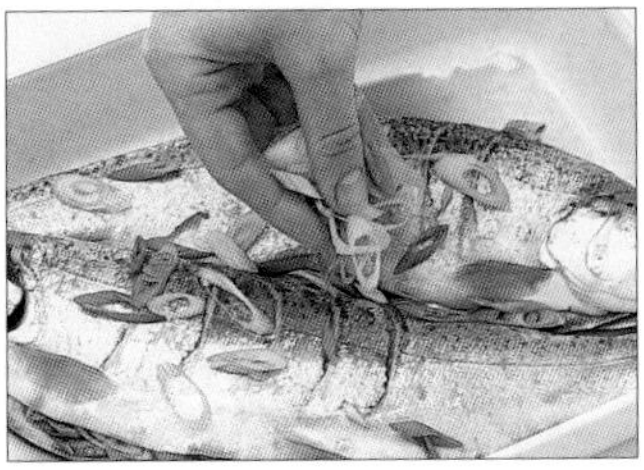

2 Fill the cavities with spring onions and douse each fish with soy sauce. Carefully turn the fish over to coat both sides with the sauce. Sprinkle any remaining spring onions over the top.

3 Make the sauce. Put the tamarind pulp in a small bowl and pour on the boiling water. Mash well with a fork until softened. Tip the tamarind mixture into a food processor or blender, and add the shallots, fresh chilli, ginger, sugar and fish sauce. Process to a coarse pulp. Scrape into a bowl.

4 Heat the oil in a large frying pan or wok and cook the trout, one at a time if necessary, for about 5 minutes on each side, until the skin is crisp and browned and the flesh cooked. Put on warmed plates and spoon over some of the sauce. Sprinkle with the coriander and chilli and serve with the remaining sauce.

Vegetable Main Dishes

To talk of Thai main dishes is somewhat inappropriate, since all dishes are traditionally served together. However, the term provides a useful way of distinguishing more substantial dishes, composed of a relatively large number of ingredients, from what Westerners might term side dishes. Delicious vegetable curries, unusual stir-fries, stuffed vegetables and a tasty tempura are included here. Most are very quick and easy to make, with the majority of time required for preparation,

THAI VEGETABLE CURRY WITH LEMON GRASS RICE

FRAGRANT JASMINE RICE, SUBTLY FLAVOURED WITH LEMON GRASS AND CARDAMOM, IS THE PERFECT ACCOMPANIMENT FOR THIS RICHLY SPICED VEGETABLE CURRY.

SERVES FOUR

INGREDIENTS

- 10ml/2 tsp vegetable oil
- 400ml/14fl oz/1⅔ cups coconut milk
- 300ml/½ pint/1¼ cups vegetable stock
- 225g/8oz new potatoes, halved or quartered, if large
- 8 baby corn cobs
- 5ml/1 tsp golden caster (superfine) sugar
- 185g/6½oz/1¼ cups broccoli florets
- 1 red (bell) pepper, seeded and sliced lengthways
- 115g/4oz spinach, tough stalks removed, leaves shredded
- 30ml/2 tbsp chopped fresh coriander (cilantro)
- salt and ground black pepper

For the spice paste

- 1 fresh red chilli, seeded and chopped
- 3 fresh green chillies, seeded and chopped
- 1 lemon grass stalk, outer leaves removed and lower 5cm/2in finely chopped
- 2 shallots, chopped
- finely grated rind of 1 lime
- 2 garlic cloves, chopped
- 5ml/1 tsp ground coriander
- 2.5ml/½ tsp ground cumin
- 1cm/½in piece fresh galangal, finely chopped, or 2.5ml/½ tsp dried galangal (optional)
- 30ml/2 tbsp chopped fresh coriander (cilantro)
- 15ml/1 tbsp chopped fresh coriander (cilantro) roots and stems (optional)

For the rice

- 225g/8oz/1¼ cups jasmine rice, rinsed
- 6 cardamom pods, bruised
- 1 lemon grass stalk, outer leaves removed, cut into 3 pieces
- 475ml/16fl oz/2 cups water

1 Make the spice paste. Place all the ingredients in a food processor and process to a coarse paste. Heat the oil in a large, heavy pan. Add the paste and stir-fry over a medium heat for 1–2 minutes, until fragrant.

2 Pour in the coconut milk and stock and bring to the boil. Reduce the heat, add the potatoes and simmer gently for about 15 minutes, until almost tender.

3 Meanwhile, put the rice into a large pan with the cardamoms and lemon grass. Pour in the water. Bring to the boil, reduce the heat, cover, and cook for 10–15 minutes, until the water has been absorbed and the rice is tender.

4 When the rice is cooked and slightly sticky, season to taste with salt, then replace the lid and leave to stand for about 10 minutes.

5 Add the baby corn to the potatoes, season with salt and pepper to taste, then cook for 2 minutes. Stir in the sugar, broccoli and red pepper, and cook for 2 minutes more, or until the vegetables are tender.

6 Stir the shredded spinach and half the fresh coriander into the vegetable mixture. Cook for 2 minutes, then spoon the curry into a warmed serving dish.

7 Remove and discard the cardamom pods and lemon grass from the rice and fluff up the grains with a fork. Garnish the curry with the remaining fresh coriander and serve with the rice.

COOK'S TIP

Cardamom pods may be dark brown, cream, or pale green. The brown pods are usually larger, coarser and do not have such a good flavour as the others. Always remove them before serving.

Vegetable Forest Curry

This is a thin, soupy curry with lots of fresh green vegetables and robust flavours. In the forested regions of Thailand, where it originated, it would be made using edible wild leaves and roots. Serve it with rice or noodles for a simple lunch or supper.

SERVES TWO

INGREDIENTS
- 600ml/1 pint/2½ cups water
- 5ml/1 tsp Thai red curry paste
- 5cm/2in piece fresh galangal or fresh root ginger
- 90g/3½oz/scant 1 cup green beans
- 2 kaffir lime leaves, torn
- 8 baby corn cobs, halved widthways
- 2 heads Chinese broccoli, chopped
- 90g/3½oz/generous 3 cups beansprouts
- 15ml/1 tbsp drained bottled green peppercorns, crushed
- 10ml/2 tsp granulated sugar
- 5ml/1 tsp salt

1 Heat the water in a large pan. Add the red curry paste and stir until it has dissolved completely. Bring to the boil.

2 Meanwhile, using a sharp knife, peel and finely chop the fresh galangal or root ginger.

3 Add the galangal or ginger, green beans, lime leaves, baby corn cobs, broccoli and beansprouts to the pan. Stir in the crushed peppercorns, sugar and salt. Bring back to the boil, then reduce the heat to low and simmer for 2 minutes. Serve immediately.

TOFU AND GREEN BEAN RED CURRY

THIS IS ONE OF THOSE VERSATILE RECIPES THAT SHOULD BE IN EVERY COOK'S REPERTOIRE. THIS VERSION USES GREEN BEANS, BUT OTHER TYPES OF VEGETABLE WORK EQUALLY WELL. THE TOFU TAKES ON THE FLAVOUR OF THE SPICE PASTE AND ALSO BOOSTS THE NUTRITIONAL VALUE.

SERVES FOUR TO SIX

INGREDIENTS

- 600ml/1 pint/2½ cups canned coconut milk
- 15ml/1 tbsp Thai red curry paste
- 45ml/3 tbsp Thai fish sauce
- 10ml/2 tsp palm sugar or light muscovado (brown) sugar
- 225g/8oz/3¼ cups button (white) mushrooms
- 115g/4oz/scant 1 cup green beans, trimmed
- 175g/6oz firm tofu, rinsed, drained and cut in 2cm/¾in cubes
- 4 kaffir lime leaves, torn
- 2 fresh red chillies, seeded and sliced
- fresh coriander (cilantro) leaves, to garnish

1 Pour about one-third of the coconut milk into a wok or pan. Cook until it starts to separate and an oily sheen appears on the surface.

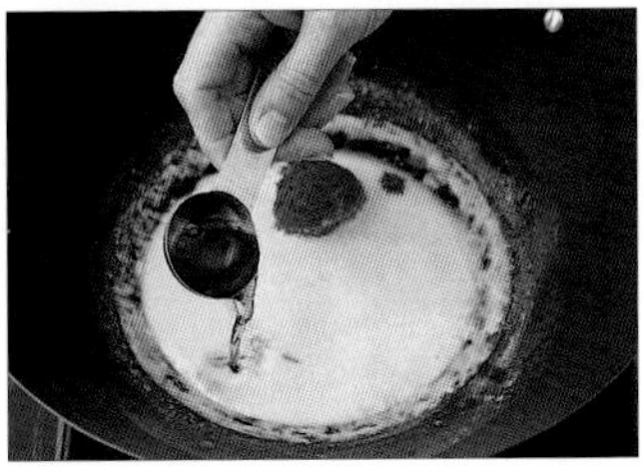

2 Add the red curry paste, fish sauce and sugar to the coconut milk. Mix thoroughly, then add the mushrooms. Stir and cook for 1 minute.

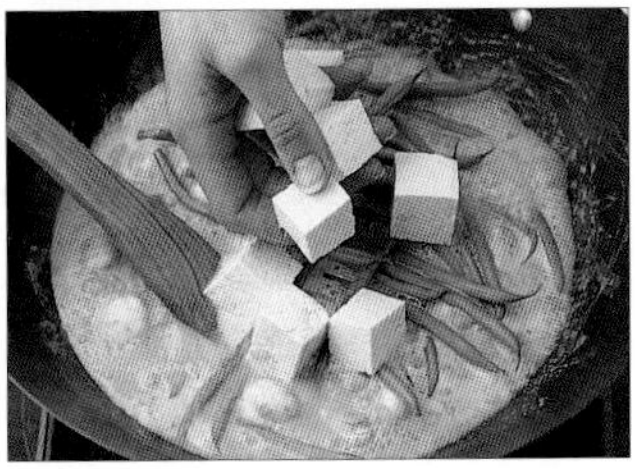

3 Stir in the remaining coconut milk. Bring back to the boil, then add the green beans and tofu cubes. Simmer gently for 4–5 minutes more.

4 Stir in the kaffir lime leaves and sliced red chillies. Spoon the curry into a serving dish, garnish with the coriander leaves and serve immediately.

Aubergine and Sweet Potato Stew with Coconut Milk

Scented with fragrant lemon grass, ginger and lots of garlic, this is a particularly good combination of flavours. Aubergines and sweet potatoes go well together and the coconut milk adds a mellow note.

SERVES SIX

INGREDIENTS

- 400g/14oz baby aubergines (eggplant) or 2 standard aubergines
- 60ml/4 tbsp groundnut (peanut) oil
- 225g/8oz Thai red shallots or other small shallots or pickling onions
- 5ml/1 tsp fennel seeds, lightly crushed
- 4–5 garlic cloves, thinly sliced
- 25ml/1½ tbsp finely chopped fresh root ginger
- 475ml/16fl oz/2 cups vegetable stock
- 2 lemon grass stalks, outer layers discarded, finely chopped or minced
- 15g/½oz/⅔ cup fresh coriander (cilantro), stalks and leaves chopped separately
- 3 kaffir lime leaves, lightly bruised
- 2–3 small fresh red chillies
- 45–60ml/3–4 tbsp Thai green curry paste
- 675g/1½lb sweet potatoes, peeled and cut into thick chunks
- 400ml/14fl oz/1⅔ cups coconut milk
- 2.5–5ml/½–1 tsp palm sugar or light muscovado (brown) sugar
- 250g/9oz/3½ cups mushrooms, thickly sliced
- juice of 1 lime, to taste
- salt and ground black pepper
- boiled rice and 18 fresh Thai basil or ordinary basil leaves, to serve

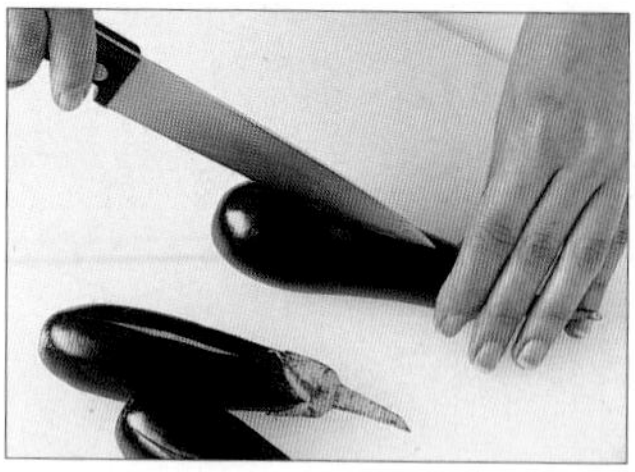

1 Trim the aubergines. Slice baby aubergines in half lengthways. Cut standard aubergines into chunks.

2 Heat half the oil in a wide pan or deep, lidded frying pan. Add the aubergines and cook (uncovered) over a medium heat, stirring occasionally, until lightly browned on all sides. Remove from the pan and set aside.

3 Slice 4–5 of the shallots. Cook the whole shallots in the oil remaining in the pan, adding a little more oil if necessary, until lightly browned. Set aside with the aubergines. Add the remaining oil to the pan and cook the sliced shallots, fennel seeds, garlic and ginger over a low heat for 5 minutes.

4 Pour in the vegetable stock, then add the lemon grass, chopped coriander stalks and any roots, lime leaves and whole chillies. Cover and simmer over a low heat for 5 minutes.

5 Stir in 30ml/2 tbsp of the curry paste and the sweet potatoes. Simmer gently for about 10 minutes, then return the aubergines and browned shallots to the pan and cook for a further 5 minutes.

6 Stir in the coconut milk and the sugar. Season to taste with salt and pepper, then stir in the mushrooms and simmer gently for 5 minutes, or until all the vegetables are cooked and tender.

7 Stir in more curry paste and lime juice to taste, followed by the chopped coriander leaves. Adjust the seasoning, if necessary, and ladle the vegetables into warmed bowls. Sprinkle basil leaves over the stew and serve with rice.

COOK'S TIP

Although this is called a stew, green curry paste is an important ingredient, as it is in most of these recipes. The quantity given is only a guide, however, so use less if you prefer.

SWEET PUMPKIN AND PEANUT CURRY

A HEARTY, SOOTHING CURRY PERFECT FOR AUTUMN OR WINTER EVENINGS. ITS CHEERFUL COLOUR ALONE WILL BRIGHTEN YOU UP – AND IT TASTES TERRIFIC.

SERVES FOUR

INGREDIENTS

- 30ml/2 tbsp vegetable oil
- 4 garlic cloves, crushed
- 4 shallots, finely chopped
- 30ml/2 tbsp yellow curry paste
- 600ml/1 pint/2½ cups vegetable stock
- 2 kaffir lime leaves, torn
- 15ml/1 tbsp chopped fresh galangal
- 450g/1lb pumpkin, peeled, seeded and diced
- 225g/8oz sweet potatoes, diced
- 90g/3½oz/scant 1 cup peanuts, roasted and chopped
- 300ml/½ pint/1¼ cups coconut milk
- 90g/3½oz/1½ cups chestnut mushrooms, sliced
- 15ml/1 tbsp soy sauce
- 30ml/2 tbsp Thai fish sauce
- 50g/2oz/⅓ cup pumpkin seeds, toasted, and fresh green chilli flowers, to garnish

1 Heat the oil in a large pan. Add the garlic and shallots and cook over a medium heat, stirring occasionally, for 10 minutes, until softened and golden. Do not let them burn.

2 Add the yellow curry paste and stir-fry over a medium heat for 30 seconds, until fragrant, then add the stock, lime leaves, galangal, pumpkin and sweet potatoes. Bring to the boil, stirring frequently, then reduce the heat to low and simmer gently for 15 minutes.

3 Add the peanuts, coconut milk and mushrooms. Stir in the soy sauce and fish sauce and simmer for 5 minutes more. Spoon into warmed individual serving bowls, garnish with the pumpkin seeds and chillies and serve.

COOK'S TIP

The well-drained vegetables from any of these curries would make a very tasty filling for a pastry or pie. This may not be a Thai tradition, but it is a good example of fusion food.

CORN AND CASHEW NUT CURRY

A SUBSTANTIAL CURRY, THIS COMBINES ALL THE ESSENTIAL FLAVOURS OF SOUTHERN THAILAND. IT IS DELICIOUSLY AROMATIC, BUT THE FLAVOUR IS FAIRLY MILD.

SERVES FOUR

INGREDIENTS

- 30ml/2 tbsp vegetable oil
- 4 shallots, chopped
- 90g/3½oz/scant 1 cup cashew nuts
- 5ml/1 tsp Thai red curry paste
- 400g/14oz potatoes, peeled and cut into chunks
- 1 lemon grass stalk, finely chopped
- 200g/7oz can chopped tomatoes
- 600ml/1 pint/2½ cups boiling water
- 200g/7oz/generous 1 cup drained canned whole kernel corn
- 4 celery sticks, sliced
- 2 kaffir lime leaves, rolled into cylinders and thinly sliced
- 15ml/1 tbsp tomato ketchup
- 15ml/1 tbsp light soy sauce
- 5ml/1 tsp palm sugar or light muscovado (brown) sugar
- 5ml/1 tsp Thai fish sauce
- 4 spring onions (scallions), thinly sliced
- small bunch fresh basil, chopped

COOK'S TIP

Rolling the lime leaves into cylinders before slicing produces very fine strips – a technique known as cutting *en chiffonnade*. Remove the central rib from the leaves before cutting them.

1 Heat the oil in a large, heavy pan or wok. Add the shallots and stir-fry over a medium heat for 2–3 minutes, until softened. Add the cashew nuts and stir-fry for a few minutes until golden.

2 Stir in the red curry paste. Stir-fry for 1 minute, then add the potatoes, lemon grass, tomatoes and boiling water.

3 Bring back to the boil, then reduce the heat to low, cover and simmer gently for 15–20 minutes, or until the potatoes are tender.

4 Stir the corn, celery, lime leaves, tomato ketchup, soy sauce, sugar and fish sauce into the pan or wok. Simmer for a further 5 minutes, until heated through, then spoon into warmed serving bowls. Sprinkle with the sliced spring onions and basil and serve.

Tofu and Vegetable Thai Curry

Traditional Thai ingredients – chillies, galangal, lemon grass and kaffir lime leaves – give this curry a wonderfully fragrant aroma. The tofu needs to marinate for at least 2 hours, so bear this in mind when timing your meal.

SERVES FOUR

INGREDIENTS
- 175g/6oz firm tofu
- 45ml/3 tbsp dark soy sauce
- 15ml/1 tbsp sesame oil
- 5ml/1 tsp chilli sauce
- 2.5cm/1in piece fresh root ginger, peeled and finely grated
- 1 head broccoli, about 225g/8oz
- ½ head cauliflower, about 225g/8oz
- 30ml/2 tbsp vegetable oil
- 1 onion, sliced
- 400ml/14fl oz/1⅔ cups coconut milk
- 150ml/¼ pint/⅔ cup water
- 1 red (bell) pepper, seeded and chopped
- 175g/6oz/generous 1 cup green beans, halved
- 115g/4oz/1½ cups shiitake or button (white) mushrooms, halved
- shredded spring onions (scallions), to garnish
- boiled jasmine rice or noodles, to serve

For the curry paste
- 2 fresh red or green chillies, seeded and chopped
- 1 lemon grass stalk, chopped
- 2.5cm/1in piece fresh galangal, chopped
- 2 kaffir lime leaves
- 10ml/2 tsp ground coriander
- a few fresh coriander (cilantro) sprigs, including the stalks
- 45ml/3 tbsp water

1 Rinse and drain the tofu. Using a sharp knife, cut it into 2.5cm/1in cubes. Place the cubes in an ovenproof dish that is large enough to hold them all in a single layer.

2 Mix together the soy sauce, sesame oil, chilli sauce and grated ginger in a jug (pitcher) and pour over the tofu. Toss gently to coat all the cubes evenly, cover with clear film (plastic wrap) and leave to marinate for at least 2 hours or overnight if possible, turning and basting the tofu occasionally.

3 Make the curry paste. Place the chillies, lemon grass, galangal, lime leaves, ground coriander and fresh coriander in a food processor and process until well blended. Add the water and process to a thick paste.

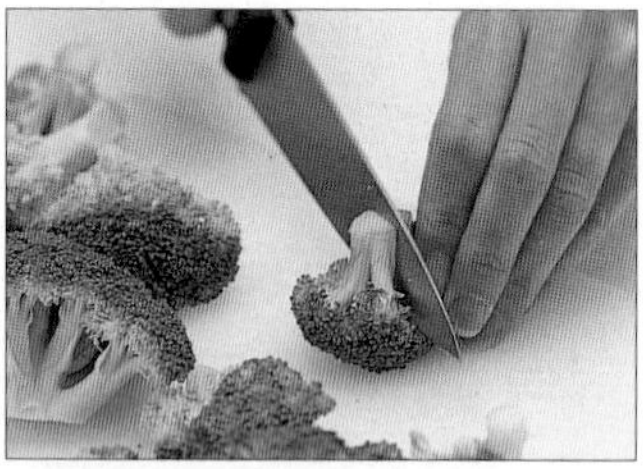

4 Preheat the oven to 190°C/375°F/Gas 5. Cut the broccoli and cauliflower into small florets. Cut any stalks into thin slices.

5 Heat the vegetable oil in a frying pan and add the sliced onion. Cook over a low heat for about 8 minutes, until soft and lightly browned. Stir in the curry paste and the coconut milk. Add the water and bring to the boil.

6 Stir in the red pepper, green beans, broccoli and cauliflower. Transfer to a Chinese sand pot or earthenware casserole. Cover and place towards the bottom of the oven.

7 Stir the tofu and marinade, then place the dish on a shelf near the top of the oven. Cook for 30 minutes. Remove both the dish and the sand pot or casserole from the oven. Add the tofu, with any remaining marinade, to the curry, with the mushrooms, and stir well.

8 Return the sand pot or casserole to the oven, reduce the temperature to 180°C/350°F/Gas 4 and cook for about 15 minutes, or until the vegetables are tender. Garnish with the spring onions and serve with the rice or noodles.

COOK'S TIP

Tofu or beancurd is made from soya beans and is sold in blocks. It is a creamy white colour and has a solid gel-like texture. Tofu has a bland flavour and its absorbent nature means that it takes on the flavours of marinades or other foods with which it is cooked.

SNAKE BEANS WITH TOFU

ANOTHER NAME FOR SNAKE BEANS IS YARD-LONG BEANS. THIS IS SOMETHING OF AN EXAGGERATION BUT THEY DO GROW TO LENGTHS OF 35CM/14IN AND MORE. LOOK FOR THEM IN ASIAN STORES AND MARKETS, BUT IF YOU CAN'T FIND ANY, SUBSTITUTE OTHER GREEN BEANS.

SERVES FOUR

INGREDIENTS

- 500g/1¼lb long beans, thinly sliced
- 200g/7oz silken tofu, cut into cubes
- 2 shallots, thinly sliced
- 200ml/7fl oz/scant 1 cup coconut milk
- 115g/4oz/1 cup roasted peanuts, chopped
- juice of 1 lime
- 10ml/2 tsp palm sugar or light muscovado (brown) sugar
- 60ml/4 tbsp soy sauce
- 5ml/1 tsp dried chilli flakes

VARIATIONS

The sauce also works very well with mangetouts (snow peas). Alternatively, stir in sliced yellow or red (bell) pepper.

1 Bring a pan of lightly salted water to the boil. Add the beans and blanch them for 30 seconds.

2 Drain the beans immediately, then refresh under cold water and drain again, shaking well to remove as much water as possible. Place in a serving bowl and set aside.

3 Put the tofu and shallots in a pan with the coconut milk. Heat gently, stirring, until the tofu begins to crumble.

4 Add the peanuts, lime juice, sugar, soy sauce and chilli flakes. Heat, stirring, until the sugar has dissolved. Pour the sauce over the beans, toss to combine and serve immediately.

MUSHROOMS WITH GARLIC AND CHILLI SAUCE

WHEN YOU ARE PLANNING A BARBECUE FOR FRIENDS AND FAMILY, IT CAN BE TRICKY FINDING SOMETHING REALLY SPECIAL FOR THE VEGETARIANS IN THE PARTY. THESE TASTY MUSHROOM KEBABS ARE IDEAL BECAUSE THEY LOOK, SMELL AND TASTE WONDERFUL.

SERVES FOUR

INGREDIENTS

- 12 large field (portobello), chestnut or oyster mushrooms or a mixture, cut in half
- 4 garlic cloves, coarsely chopped
- 6 coriander (cilantro) roots, coarsely chopped
- 15ml/1 tbsp granulated sugar
- 30ml/2 tbsp light soy sauce
- ground black pepper

For the dipping sauce

- 15ml/1 tbsp granulated sugar
- 90ml/6 tbsp rice vinegar
- 5ml/1 tsp salt
- 1 garlic clove, crushed
- 1 small fresh red chilli, seeded and finely chopped

1 If using wooden skewers, soak eight of them in cold water for at least 30 minutes to prevent them burning over the barbecue or under the grill.

2 Make the dipping sauce by heating the sugar, rice vinegar and salt in a small pan, stirring occasionally until the sugar and salt have dissolved. Add the garlic and chilli, pour into a serving dish and keep warm.

3 Thread three mushroom halves on to each skewer. Lay the filled skewers side by side in a shallow dish.

4 In a mortar or spice grinder pound or blend the garlic and coriander roots. Scrape into a bowl and mix with the sugar, soy sauce and a little pepper.

5 Brush the soy sauce mixture over the mushrooms and leave to marinate for 15 minutes. Prepare the barbecue or preheat the grill (broiler) and cook the mushrooms for 2–3 minutes on each side. Serve with the dipping sauce.

Aubergine and Pepper Tempura with Sweet Chilli Dip

These crunchy vegetables in a beautifully light batter are quick and easy to make and taste very good with the piquant dip. Although tempura is a signature dish of Japanese cuisine, it has now become popular throughout Asia, with each country adding its own characteristic touch – in the case of Thailand, this chilli-flavoured sauce.

SERVES FOUR

INGREDIENTS

- 2 aubergines (eggplant)
- 2 red (bell) peppers
- vegetable oil, for deep-frying

For the tempura batter

- 250g/9oz/2¼ cups plain (all-purpose) flour
- 2 egg yolks
- 500ml/17fl oz/2¼ cups iced water
- 5ml/1 tsp salt

For the dip

- 150ml/¼ pint/⅔ cup water
- 10ml/2 tsp granulated sugar
- 1 fresh red chilli, seeded and finely chopped
- 1 garlic clove, crushed
- juice of ½ lime
- 5ml/1 tsp rice vinegar
- 35ml/2½ tbsp Thai fish sauce
- ½ small carrot, finely grated

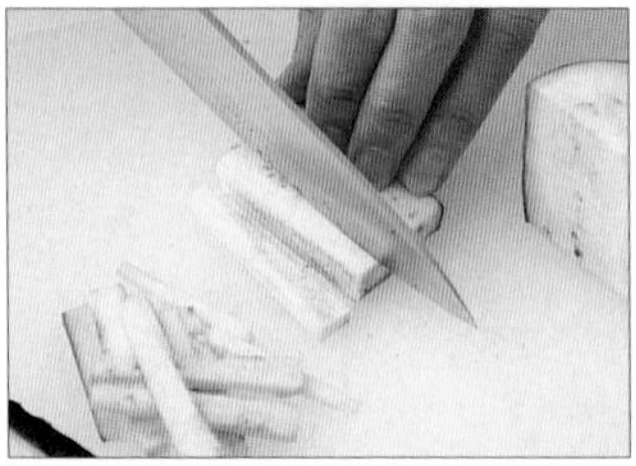

1 Using a sharp knife or a mandolin, slice the aubergines into thin batons. Halve, seed and slice the red peppers thinly.

2 Make the dip. Mix together all the ingredients in a bowl and stir until the sugar has dissolved. Cover with clear film (plastic wrap) and set aside.

VARIATIONS

Tempura batter is also good with pieces of fish or whole shellfish, such as large prawns (jumbo shrimp) or baby squid, as well as with a variety of vegetables.

3 Make the tempura batter. Set aside 30ml/2 tbsp of the flour. Put the egg yolks in a large bowl and beat in the iced water. Tip in the remaining flour with the salt and stir briefly together – the mixture should resemble thick pancake batter but be lumpy and not properly mixed. If it is too thick, add a little more iced water. Do not leave the batter to stand; use it immediately.

4 Pour the oil for deep-frying into a wok or deep-fryer and heat to 190°C/375°F or until a cube of bread, added to the oil, browns in about 30 seconds.

5 Pick up a small, haphazard handful of aubergine batons and pepper slices, dust it with the reserved flour, then dip it into the batter. Immediately drop the batter-coated vegetables into the hot oil, taking care as the oil will froth up furiously. Repeat to make two or three more fritters, but do not cook any more than this at one time, or the oil may overflow.

6 Cook the fritters for 3–4 minutes, until they are golden and crisp all over, then lift them out with a metal basket or slotted spoon. Drain thoroughly on kitchen paper and keep hot.

7 Repeat until all the vegetables have been coated in batter and cooked. Serve immediately, with the dip.

STUFFED SWEET PEPPERS

THIS IS AN UNUSUAL RECIPE IN THAT THE STUFFED PEPPERS ARE STEAMED RATHER THAN BAKED, BUT THE RESULT IS BEAUTIFULLY LIGHT AND TENDER. THE FILLING INCORPORATES TYPICAL THAI INGREDIENTS SUCH AS RED CURRY PASTE AND FISH SAUCE.

SERVES FOUR

INGREDIENTS

- 3 garlic cloves, finely chopped
- 2 coriander (cilantro) roots, finely chopped
- 400g/14oz/3 cups mushrooms, quartered
- 5ml/1 tsp Thai red curry paste
- 1 egg, lightly beaten
- 15ml/1 tbsp Thai fish sauce
- 15ml/1 tbsp light soy sauce
- 2.5ml/½ tsp granulated sugar
- 3 kaffir lime leaves, finely chopped
- 4 yellow (bell) peppers, halved lengthways and seeded

VARIATIONS

Use red or orange (bell) peppers if you prefer, or a combination of the two.

1 In a mortar or spice grinder pound or blend the garlic with the coriander roots. Scrape into a bowl.

2 Put the mushrooms in a food processor and pulse briefly until they are finely chopped. Add to the garlic mixture, then stir in the curry paste, egg, sauces, sugar and lime leaves.

3 Place the pepper halves in a single layer in a steamer basket. Spoon the mixture loosely into the pepper halves. Do not pack the mixture down tightly or the filling will dry out too much. Bring the water in the steamer to the boil, then lower the heat to a simmer. Steam the peppers for 15 minutes, or until the flesh is tender. Serve hot.

SWEET AND SOUR VEGETABLES WITH TOFU

BIG, BOLD AND BEAUTIFUL, THIS IS A HEARTY STIR-FRY THAT WILL SATISFY THE HUNGRIEST GUESTS. STIR-FRIES ARE ALWAYS A GOOD CHOICE WHEN ENTERTAINING AS YOU CAN PREPARE THE INGREDIENTS AHEAD OF TIME AND THEN THEY TAKE SUCH A SHORT TIME TO COOK.

SERVES FOUR

INGREDIENTS

- 4 shallots
- 3 garlic cloves
- 30ml/2 tbsp groundnut (peanut) oil
- 250g/9oz Chinese leaves (Chinese cabbage), shredded
- 8 baby corn cobs, sliced on the diagonal
- 2 red (bell) peppers, seeded and thinly sliced
- 200g/7oz/1¾ cups mangetouts (snow peas), trimmed and sliced
- 250g/9oz tofu, rinsed, drained and cut in 1cm/½in cubes
- 60ml/4 tbsp vegetable stock
- 30ml/2 tbsp light soy sauce
- 15ml/1 tbsp granulated sugar
- 30ml/2 tbsp rice vinegar
- 2.5ml/½ tsp dried chilli flakes
- small bunch coriander (cilantro), chopped

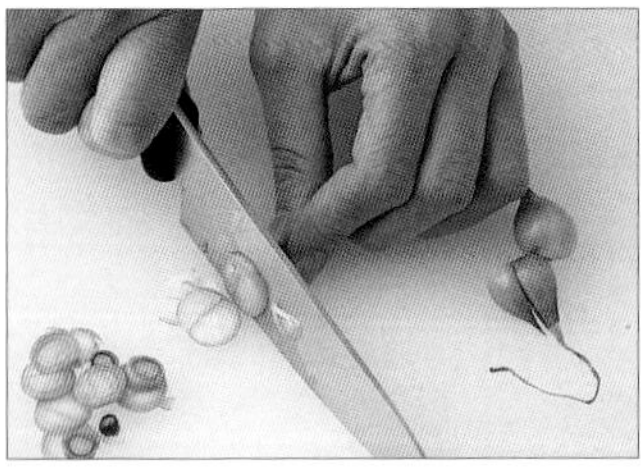

1 Slice the shallots thinly using a sharp knife. Finely chop the garlic.

2 Heat the oil in a wok or large frying pan and cook the shallots and garlic for 2–3 minutes over a medium heat, until golden. Do not let the garlic burn or it will taste bitter.

3 Add the shredded cabbage, toss over the heat for 30 seconds, then add the corn cobs and repeat the process.

4 Add the red peppers, mangetouts and tofu in the same way, each time adding a single ingredient and tossing it over the heat for about 30 seconds before adding the next ingredient.

5 Pour in the stock and soy sauce. Mix together the sugar and vinegar in a small bowl, stirring until the sugar has dissolved, then add to the wok or pan. Sprinkle over the chilli flakes and coriander, toss to mix well and serve.

STIR-FRIED CRISPY TOFU

THE ASPARAGUS GROWN IN ASIA TENDS TO HAVE SLENDER STALKS. LOOK FOR IT IN THAI MARKETS OR SUBSTITUTE THE THIN ASPARAGUS POPULARLY KNOWN AS SPRUE.

SERVES TWO

INGREDIENTS

- 250g/9oz fried tofu cubes
- 30ml/2 tbsp groundnut (peanut) oil
- 15ml/1 tbsp Thai green curry paste
- 30ml/2 tbsp light soy sauce
- 2 kaffir lime leaves, rolled into cylinders and thinly sliced
- 30ml/2 tbsp granulated sugar
- 150ml/¼ pint/⅔ cup vegetable stock
- 250g/9oz Asian asparagus, trimmed and sliced into 5cm/2in lengths
- 30ml/2 tbsp roasted peanuts, finely chopped

VARIATION

Substitute slim carrot sticks or broccoli florets for the asparagus.

1 Preheat the grill (broiler) to medium. Place the tofu cubes in a grill pan and grill (broil) for 2–3 minutes, then turn them over and continue to cook until they are crisp and golden brown all over. Watch them carefully; they must not be allowed to burn.

2 Heat the oil in a wok or heavy frying pan. Add the green curry paste and cook over a medium heat, stirring constantly, for 1–2 minutes, until it gives off its aroma.

3 Stir the soy sauce, lime leaves, sugar and vegetable stock into the wok or pan and mix well. Bring to the boil, then reduce the heat to low so that the mixture is just simmering.

4 Add the asparagus and simmer gently for 5 minutes. Meanwhile, chop each piece of tofu into four, then add to the pan with the peanuts.

5 Toss to coat all the ingredients in the sauce, then spoon into a warmed dish and serve immediately.

STIR-FRIED SEEDS AND VEGETABLES

THE CONTRAST BETWEEN THE CRUNCHY SEEDS AND VEGETABLES AND THE RICH, SAVOURY SAUCE IS WHAT MAKES THIS DISH SO DELICIOUS. SERVE IT SOLO, OR WITH RICE OR NOODLES.

SERVES FOUR

INGREDIENTS
- 30ml/2 tbsp vegetable oil
- 30ml/2 tbsp sesame seeds
- 30ml/2 tbsp sunflower seeds
- 30ml/2 tbsp pumpkin seeds
- 2 garlic cloves, finely chopped
- 2.5cm/1in piece fresh root ginger, peeled and finely chopped
- 2 large carrots, cut into batons
- 2 large courgettes (zucchini), cut into batons
- 90g/3½oz/1½ cups oyster mushrooms, torn in pieces
- 150g/5oz watercress or spinach leaves, coarsely chopped
- small bunch fresh mint or coriander (cilantro), leaves and stems chopped
- 60ml/4 tbsp black bean sauce
- 30ml/2 tbsp light soy sauce
- 15ml/1 tbsp palm sugar or light muscovado (brown) sugar
- 30ml/2 tbsp rice vinegar

1 Heat the oil in a wok or large frying pan. Add the seeds. Toss over a medium heat for 1 minute, then add the garlic and ginger and continue to stir-fry until the ginger is aromatic and the garlic is golden. Do not let the garlic burn or it will taste bitter.

2 Add the carrot and courgette batons and the sliced mushrooms to the wok or pan and stir-fry over a medium heat for a further 5 minutes, or until all the vegetables are crisp-tender and are golden at the edges.

3 Add the watercress or spinach with the fresh herbs. Toss over the heat for 1 minute, then stir in the black bean sauce, soy sauce, sugar and vinegar. Stir-fry for 1–2 minutes, until combined and hot. Serve immediately.

COOK'S TIP

Oyster mushrooms have acquired their name because of their texture, rather than flavour, which is quite superb. They are delicate, so it is usually better to tear them into pieces along the lines of the gills, rather than slice them with a knife.

Rice Dishes

Thailand is one of the world's major producers of both long grain and glutinous rice. Thai fragrant rice, also known as jasmine rice, is valued the world over for its subtle fragrance. It goes well with both savoury and sweet dishes and is particularly delicious when cooked in coconut milk or served with toasted coconut strips, as in the recipe for Thai Fried Rice. The grains are slightly sticky when cooked, although not so sticky as those of glutinous rice.

Coconut Rice

This rich dish is usually served with a tangy papaya salad to balance the sweetness of the coconut milk and sugar. It is one of those comforting treats that everyone enjoys.

SERVES FOUR TO SIX

INGREDIENTS
- 250ml/8fl oz/1 cup water
- 475ml/16fl oz/2 cups coconut milk
- 2.5ml/½ tsp salt
- 30ml/2 tbsp granulated sugar
- 450g/1lb/2⅔ cups jasmine rice

COOK'S TIP

For a special occasion serve in a halved papaya and garnish with thin shreds of fresh coconut. Use a vegetable peeler to pare the coconut finely, as you would when making curls of Parmesan cheese.

1 Place the measured water, coconut milk, salt and sugar in a heavy pan. Wash the rice in several changes of cold water until it runs clear.

2 Add the jasmine rice, cover tightly with a lid and bring to the boil over a medium heat. Reduce the heat to low and simmer gently, without lifting the lid unnecessarily, for 15–20 minutes, until the rice is tender and cooked through. Test it by biting a grain.

3 Turn off the heat and leave the rice to rest in the pan, still covered with the lid, for a further 5–10 minutes.

4 Gently fluff up the rice grains with chopsticks or a fork before transferring it to a warmed dish and serving.

Brown Rice with Lime and Lemon Grass

It is unusual to find brown rice given the Thai treatment, but the nutty flavour of the grains is enhanced by the fragrance of limes and lemon grass in this delicious dish.

SERVES FOUR

INGREDIENTS
- 2 limes
- 1 lemon grass stalk
- 225g/8oz/generous 1 cup brown long grain rice
- 15ml/1 tbsp olive oil
- 1 onion, chopped
- 2.5cm/1in piece fresh root ginger, peeled and finely chopped
- 7.5ml/1½ tsp coriander seeds
- 7.5ml/1½ tsp cumin seeds
- 750ml/1¼ pints/3 cups vegetable stock
- 60ml/4 tbsp chopped fresh coriander (cilantro)
- spring onion (scallion) green and toasted coconut strips, to garnish
- lime wedges, to serve

1 Pare the limes, using a cannelle knife (zester) or fine grater, taking care to avoid cutting the bitter pith. Set the rind aside. Finely chop the lower portion of the lemon grass stalk and set it aside.

2 Rinse the rice in plenty of cold water until the water runs clear. Tip it into a sieve and drain thoroughly.

3 Heat the oil in a large pan. Add the onion, ginger, coriander and cumin seeds, lemon grass and lime rind and cook over a low heat for 2–3 minutes.

4 Add the rice to the pan and cook, stirring constantly, for 1 minute, then pour in the stock and bring to the boil. Reduce the heat to very low and cover the pan. Cook gently for 30 minutes, then check the rice. If it is still crunchy, cover the pan and cook for 3–5 minutes more. Remove from the heat.

5 Stir in the fresh coriander, fluff up the rice grains with a fork, cover the pan and leave to stand for 10 minutes. Transfer to a warmed dish, garnish with spring onion green and toasted coconut strips, and serve with lime wedges.

FESTIVE RICE

THIS PRETTY THAI DISH IS TRADITIONALLY SHAPED INTO A CONE AND SURROUNDED BY A VARIETY OF ACCOMPANIMENTS BEFORE BEING SERVED.

SERVES EIGHT

INGREDIENTS
- 450g/1lb/2⅔ cups jasmine rice
- 60ml/4 tbsp oil
- 2 garlic cloves, crushed
- 2 onions, thinly sliced
- 2.5ml/½ tsp ground turmeric
- 750ml/1¼ pints/3 cups water
- 400ml/14fl oz can coconut milk
- 1–2 lemon grass stalks, bruised

For the accompaniments
- omelette strips
- 2 fresh red chillies, seeded and shredded
- cucumber chunks
- tomato wedges
- deep-fried onions
- prawn (shrimp) crackers

1 Put the jasmine rice in a large strainer and rinse it thoroughly under cold water. Drain well.

COOK'S TIP
Jasmine rice is widely available in most supermarkets and Asian stores. It is also known as Thai fragrant rice.

2 Heat the oil in a frying pan with a lid. Cook the garlic, onions and turmeric over a low heat for 2–3 minutes, until the onions have softened. Add the rice and stir well to coat in oil.

3 Pour in the water and coconut milk and add the lemon grass. Bring to the boil, stirring. Cover the pan and cook gently for 12 minutes, or until all the liquid has been absorbed by the rice.

4 Remove the pan from the heat and lift the lid. Cover with a clean dishtowel, replace the lid and leave to stand in a warm place for 15 minutes. Remove the lemon grass, mound the rice mixture in a cone on a serving platter and garnish with the accompaniments, then serve.

THAI FRIED RICE

THIS SUBSTANTIAL AND TASTY DISH IS BASED ON JASMINE RICE. DICED CHICKEN, RED PEPPER AND CORN KERNELS ADD COLOUR AND EXTRA FLAVOUR.

SERVES FOUR

INGREDIENTS

- 475ml/16fl oz/2 cups water
- 50g/2oz/½ cup coconut milk powder
- 350g/12oz/1¾ cups jasmine rice, rinsed
- 30ml/2 tbsp groundnut (peanut) oil
- 2 garlic cloves, chopped
- 1 small onion, finely chopped
- 2.5cm/1in piece of fresh root ginger, peeled and grated
- 225g/8oz skinless, boneless chicken breast portions, cut into 1cm/½in dice
- 1 red (bell) pepper, seeded and sliced
- 115g/4oz/1 cup drained canned whole kernel corn
- 5ml/1 tsp chilli oil
- 5ml/1 tsp hot curry powder
- 2 eggs, beaten
- salt
- spring onion (scallion) shreds, to garnish

1 Pour the water into a pan and whisk in the coconut milk powder. Add the rice and bring to the boil. Reduce the heat, cover and cook for 12 minutes, or until the rice is tender and the liquid has been absorbed. Spread the rice on a baking sheet and leave until cold.

2 Heat the oil in a wok, add the garlic, onion and ginger and stir-fry over a medium heat for 2 minutes.

COOK'S TIP

It is important that the rice is completely cold before being fried.

3 Push the onion mixture to the sides of the wok, add the chicken to the centre and stir-fry for 2 minutes. Add the rice and toss well. Stir-fry over a high heat for about 3 minutes more, until the chicken is cooked through.

4 Stir in the sliced red pepper, corn, chilli oil and curry powder, with salt to taste. Toss over the heat for 1 minute. Stir in the beaten eggs and cook for 1 minute more. Garnish with the spring onion shreds and serve.

SAVOURY FRIED RICE

THIS IS TYPICAL THAI STREET FOOD, EATEN AT ALL TIMES OF THE DAY. THE RECIPE CAN BE ADAPTED TO USE WHATEVER VEGETABLES YOU HAVE AVAILABLE AND YOU COULD ALSO ADD MEAT OR SHELLFISH.

SERVES TWO

INGREDIENTS

- 30ml/2 tbsp vegetable oil
- 2 garlic cloves, finely chopped
- 1 small fresh red chilli, seeded and finely chopped
- 50g/2oz/½ cup cashew nuts, toasted
- 50g/2oz/⅔ cup desiccated (dry unsweetened shredded) coconut, toasted
- 2.5ml/½ tsp palm sugar or light muscovado (brown) sugar
- 30ml/2 tbsp light soy sauce
- 15ml/1 tbsp rice vinegar
- 1 egg
- 115g/4oz/1 cup green beans, sliced
- ½ spring cabbage or 115g/4oz spring greens (collards) or pak choi (bok choy), shredded
- 90g/3½oz jasmine rice, cooked
- lime wedges, to serve

1 Heat the oil in a wok or large, heavy frying pan. Add the garlic and cook over a medium to high heat until golden. Do not let it burn or it will taste bitter.

2 Add the red chilli, cashew nuts and toasted coconut to the wok or pan and stir-fry briefly, taking care to prevent the coconut from scorching. Stir in the sugar, soy sauce and rice vinegar. Toss over the heat for 1–2 minutes.

3 Push the stir-fry to one side of the wok or pan and break the egg into the empty side. When the egg is almost set stir it into the garlic and chilli mixture with a wooden spatula or spoon.

4 Add the green beans, greens and cooked rice. Stir over the heat until the greens have just wilted, then spoon into a dish to serve. Offer the lime wedges separately, for squeezing over the rice.

FRIED JASMINE RICE WITH PRAWNS AND THAI BASIL

THAI BASIL (BAI GRAPAO), ALSO KNOWN AS HOLY BASIL, HAS A UNIQUE, PUNGENT FLAVOUR THAT IS BOTH SPICY AND SHARP. IT CAN BE FOUND IN MOST ASIAN FOOD MARKETS.

SERVES FOUR TO SIX

INGREDIENTS

- 45ml/3 tbsp vegetable oil
- 1 egg, beaten
- 1 onion, chopped
- 15ml/1 tbsp chopped garlic
- 15ml/1 tbsp shrimp paste
- 1kg/2¼lb/4 cups cooked jasmine rice
- 350g/12oz cooked shelled prawns (shrimp)
- 50g/2oz thawed frozen peas
- oyster sauce, to taste
- 2 spring onions (scallions), chopped
- 15–20 Thai basil leaves, roughly snipped, plus an extra sprig, to garnish

1 Heat 15ml/1 tbsp of the oil in a wok or frying pan. Add the beaten egg and swirl it around to set like a thin pancake.

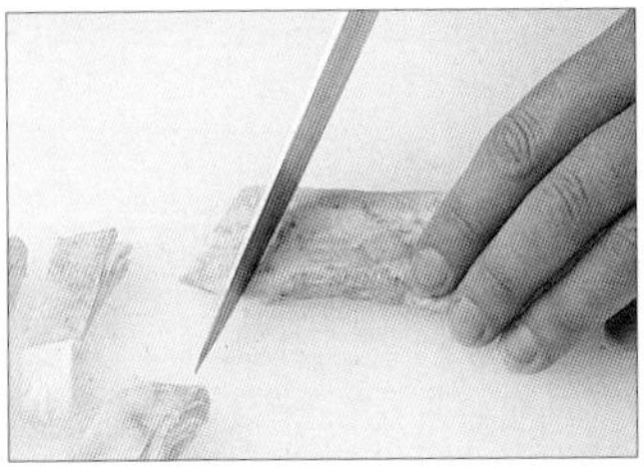

2 Cook the pancake (on one side only) over a gentle heat until golden. Slide the pancake on to a board, roll up and cut into thin strips. Set aside.

3 Heat the remaining oil in the wok or pan, add the onion and garlic and stir-fry for 2–3 minutes. Stir in the shrimp paste and mix well until thoroughly combined.

4 Add the rice, prawns and peas and toss and stir together, until everything is heated through.

5 Season with oyster sauce to taste, taking great care as the shrimp paste is salty. Mix in the spring onions and basil leaves. Transfer to a serving dish and top with the strips of egg pancake. Serve, garnished with a sprig of basil.

FRIED RICE WITH PORK

THIS CLASSIC RICE DISH LOOKS PARTICULARLY PRETTY GARNISHED WITH STRIPS OF OMELETTE, AS IN THE RECIPE FOR FRIED JASMINE RICE WITH PRAWNS AND THAI BASIL.

SERVES FOUR TO SIX

INGREDIENTS

- 45ml/3 tbsp vegetable oil
- 1 onion, chopped
- 15ml/1 tbsp chopped garlic
- 115g/4oz pork, cut into small cubes
- 2 eggs, beaten
- 1kg/2¼ lb/4 cups cooked rice
- 30ml/2 tbsp Thai fish sauce
- 15ml/1 tbsp dark soy sauce
- 2.5ml/½ tsp caster (superfine) sugar
- 4 spring onions (scallions), finely sliced, to garnish
- 2 red chillies, sliced, to garnish
- 1 lime, cut into wedges, to garnish

COOK'S TIP

To make 1kg/2¼ lb/4 cups cooked rice, you will need approximately 400g/14oz/2 cups uncooked rice.

1 Heat the oil in a wok or large frying pan. Add the onion and garlic and cook for about 2 minutes until softened.

2 Add the pork to the softened onion and garlic. Stir-fry until the pork changes colour and is cooked.

3 Add the eggs and cook until scrambled into small lumps.

4 Add the rice and continue to stir and toss, to coat it with the oil and prevent it from sticking.

5 Add the fish sauce, soy sauce and sugar and mix well. Continue to fry until the rice is thoroughly heated. Spoon into warmed individual bowls and serve, garnished with sliced spring onions, chillies and lime wedges.

FRIED RICE WITH BEEF

ONE OF THE JOYS OF THAI COOKING IS THE EASE AND SPEED WITH WHICH A REALLY GOOD MEAL CAN BE PREPARED. THIS ONE CAN BE ON THE TABLE IN 15 MINUTES.

SERVES FOUR

INGREDIENTS
- 200g/7oz beef steak
- 15ml/1 tbsp vegetable oil
- 2 garlic cloves, finely chopped
- 1 egg
- 250g/9oz/2¼ cups cooked jasmine rice
- ½ medium head broccoli, coarsely chopped
- 30ml/2 tbsp dark soy sauce
- 15ml/1 tbsp light soy sauce
- 5ml/1 tsp palm sugar or light muscovado (brown) sugar
- 15ml/1 tbsp Thai fish sauce
- ground black pepper
- chilli sauce, to serve

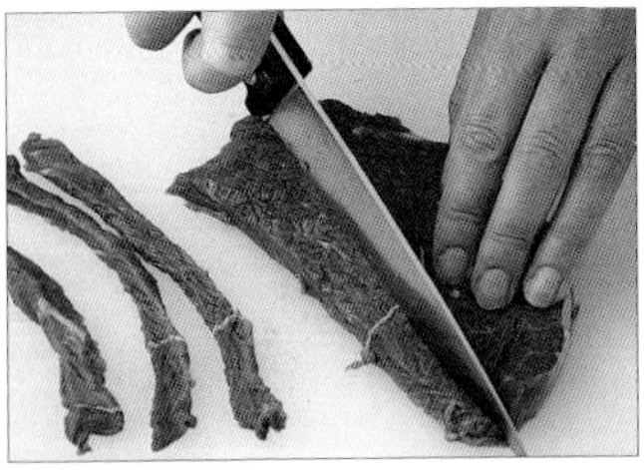

1 Trim the steak and cut into very thin strips with a sharp knife.

2 Heat the oil in a wok or frying pan and cook the garlic over a low to medium heat until golden. Do not let it burn. Increase the heat to high, add the steak and stir-fry for 2 minutes.

3 Move the pieces of beef to the edges of the wok or pan and break the egg into the centre. When the egg starts to set, stir-fry it with the meat.

4 Add the rice and toss all the contents of the wok together, scraping up any residue on the base, then add the broccoli, soy sauces, sugar and fish sauce and stir-fry for 2 minutes more. Season to taste with pepper and serve immediately with chilli sauce.

COOK'S TIP

Soy sauce is made from fermented soya beans. The first extraction is sold as light soy sauce and has a delicate, "beany" fragrance. Dark soy sauce has been allowed to mature for longer.

CURRIED CHICKEN AND RICE

THIS SIMPLE ONE-POT MEAL IS PERFECT FOR CASUAL ENTERTAINING. IT CAN BE MADE USING VIRTUALLY ANY MEAT OR VEGETABLES THAT YOU HAVE TO HAND.

SERVES FOUR

INGREDIENTS

- 60ml/4 tbsp vegetable oil
- 4 garlic cloves, finely chopped
- 1 chicken (about 1.5kg/3–3½ lb) or chicken pieces, skin and bones removed and meat cut into bitesize pieces
- 5ml/1 tsp garam masala
- 450g/1lb/2⅔ cups jasmine rice, rinsed and drained
- 10ml/2 tsp salt
- 1 litre/1¾ pints/4 cups chicken stock
- small bunch fresh coriander (cilantro), chopped, to garnish

COOK'S TIP

You will probably need to brown the chicken in batches, so don't be tempted to add too much chicken at once.

1 Heat the oil in a wok or flameproof casserole, which has a lid. Add the garlic and cook over a low to medium heat until golden brown. Add the chicken, increase the heat and brown the pieces on all sides (see Cook's Tip).

2 Add the garam masala, stir well to coat the chicken all over in the spice, then tip in the drained rice. Add the salt and stir to mix.

3 Pour in the stock, stir well, then cover the wok or casserole and bring to the boil. Reduce the heat to low and simmer gently for 10 minutes, until the rice is cooked and tender.

4 Lift the wok or casserole off the heat, leaving the lid on, and leave for 10 minutes. Fluff up the rice grains with a fork and spoon on to a platter. Sprinkle with the coriander and serve immediately.

RICE CAKES WITH A PRAWN AND COCONUT DIP

THESE WONDERFULLY CRUNCHY RICE CAKES TAKE SOME TIME TO PREPARE BUT ARE VERY EASY TO MAKE. THE DIP IS DELICIOUS AND GOES WELL WITH OTHER DISHES; TRY IT WITH BALLS OF STICKY RICE.

SERVES FOUR TO SIX

INGREDIENTS

- 150g/5oz/scant 1 cup jasmine rice
- 400ml/14fl oz/1⅔ cups boiling water

For the dip

- 1 garlic clove, coarsely chopped
- small bunch fresh coriander (cilantro), coarsely chopped
- 90g/3½oz cooked prawns (shrimp), peeled and deveined
- 250ml/8fl oz/1 cup coconut milk
- 15ml/1 tbsp Thai fish sauce
- 15ml/1 tbsp light soy sauce
- 15ml/1 tbsp tamarind juice, made by mixing tamarind pulp with warm water
- 5ml/1 tsp palm sugar or light muscovado (brown) sugar
- 30ml/2 tbsp roasted peanuts, coarsely chopped
- 1 fresh red chilli, seeded and chopped

1 Rinse the rice in a sieve under running cold water until the water runs clear, then place the rice in a large, heavy pan and pour over the measured boiling water. Stir, bring back to the boil, then reduce the heat and simmer, uncovered, for 15 minutes, by which time almost all the water should have been absorbed or evaporated.

2 Reduce the heat to the lowest possible setting – use a heat diffuser if you have one. Cook the rice for a further 2 hours, by which time it should be crisp and stuck to the base of the pan. Continue to cook for a further 5–10 minutes, until the sides of the rice cake begin to come away from the edges of the pan.

VARIATION

If you don't have time to make your own rice cakes, you could use the ones sold in packets in supermarkets. The texture of the bought product is very different and the flavour bland, but it will be improved by the dip.

3 Preheat the oven to 180°C/350°F/Gas 4. Remove the rice cake by gently easing the tip of a knife under the edges to loosen it all around. Place it on a baking sheet. Bake the rice cake for 20 minutes, until it is golden and crisp, then leave it to cool.

4 Meanwhile, make the dip. Place all the ingredients in a food processor and process to a smooth paste. Tip into a wide serving bowl. Serve the rice cake with the dip. It can either be left whole for guests to break, or sliced or broken into pieces by the cook.

Noodle Dishes

In Thailand, you are never very far from a noodle seller. This popular food is bought from breakfast to bedtime, from special restaurants and kiosks, floating barges or streetside stalls. Most of the noodles on sale are made from rice, although you will also find mung bean noodles, whose almost glassy appearance makes them a popular choice for stir-fries. Their bland taste means that they are a good vehicle for other flavours, and they are often served simply, with a selection of condiments or dips.

PLAIN NOODLES WITH FOUR FLAVOURS

A WONDERFULLY SIMPLE WAY OF SERVING NOODLES, THIS DISH ALLOWS EACH INDIVIDUAL DINER TO SEASON THEIR OWN, SPRINKLING OVER THE FOUR FLAVOURS AS THEY LIKE. FLAVOURINGS ARE ALWAYS PUT OUT IN LITTLE BOWLS WHENEVER NOODLES ARE SERVED.

SERVES FOUR

INGREDIENTS

- 4 small fresh red or green chillies
- 60ml/4 tbsp Thai fish sauce
- 60ml/4 tbsp rice vinegar
- granulated sugar
- mild or hot chilli powder
- 350g/12oz fresh or dried noodles

1 Prepare the four flavours. For the first, finely chop 2 small red or green chillies, discarding the seeds or leaving them in, depending on how hot you like your flavouring. Place them in a small bowl and add the Thai fish sauce.

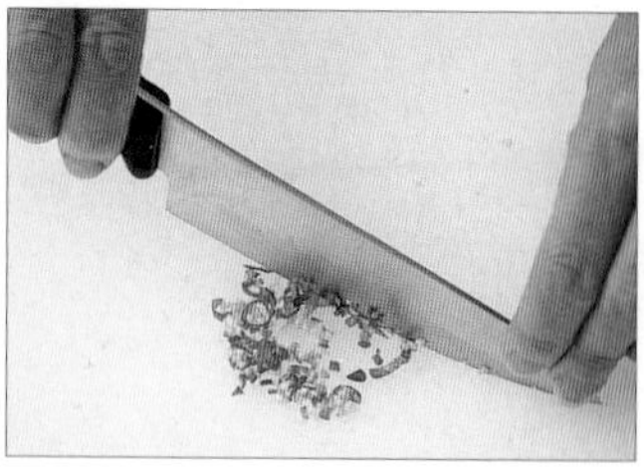

2 For the second flavour, chop the remaining chillies finely and mix them with the rice vinegar in a small bowl. Put the sugar and chilli powder in separate small bowls.

3 Cook the noodles until tender, following the instructions on the packet. Drain well, tip into a large bowl and serve immediately with the four flavours handed separately.

THAI NOODLES WITH CHINESE CHIVES

THIS RECIPE REQUIRES A LITTLE TIME FOR PREPARATION, BUT THE COOKING TIME IS VERY FAST. EVERYTHING IS COOKED IN A HOT WOK AND SHOULD BE EATEN IMMEDIATELY. THIS IS A FILLING AND TASTY VEGETARIAN DISH, IDEAL FOR A WEEKEND LUNCH.

SERVES FOUR

INGREDIENTS

- 350g/12oz dried rice noodles
- 1cm/½in piece fresh root ginger, peeled and grated
- 30ml/2 tbsp light soy sauce
- 45ml/3 tbsp vegetable oil
- 225g/8oz Quorn (mycoprotein), cut into small cubes
- 2 garlic cloves, crushed
- 1 large onion, cut into thin wedges
- 115g/4oz fried tofu, thinly sliced
- 1 fresh green chilli, seeded and thinly sliced
- 175g/6oz/2 cups beansprouts
- 2 large bunches garlic chives, total weight about 115g/4oz, cut into 5cm/2in lengths
- 50g/2oz/½ cup roasted peanuts, ground
- 30ml/2 tbsp dark soy sauce
- 30ml/2 tbsp chopped fresh coriander (cilantro), and 1 lemon, cut into wedges, to garnish

1 Place the noodles in a bowl, cover with warm water and leave to soak for 30 minutes. Drain and set aside.

2 Mix the ginger, light soy sauce and 15ml/1 tbsp of the oil in a bowl. Add the Quorn, then set aside for 10 minutes. Drain, reserving the marinade.

3 Heat 15ml/1 tbsp of the remaining oil in a frying pan and cook the garlic for a few seconds. Add the Quorn and stir-fry for 3–4 minutes. Using a slotted spoon, transfer to a plate and set aside.

4 Heat the remaining oil in the pan and stir-fry the onion for 3–4 minutes, until softened and tinged with brown. Add the tofu and chilli, stir-fry briefly and then add the noodles. Stir-fry over a medium heat for 4–5 minutes.

5 Stir in the beansprouts, garlic chives and most of the ground peanuts, reserving a little for the garnish. Stir well, then add the Quorn, the dark soy sauce and the reserved marinade.

6 When hot, spoon on to serving plates and garnish with the remaining ground peanuts, the coriander and lemon.

THAI FRIED NOODLES

PHAT THAI *HAS A FASCINATING FLAVOUR AND TEXTURE. IT IS MADE WITH RICE NOODLES AND IS CONSIDERED ONE OF THE NATIONAL DISHES OF THAILAND.*

SERVES FOUR TO SIX

INGREDIENTS
- 16 raw tiger prawns (jumbo shrimp)
- 350g/12oz rice noodles
- 45ml/3 tbsp vegetable oil
- 15ml/1 tbsp chopped garlic
- 2 eggs, lightly beaten
- 15ml/1 tbsp dried shrimp, rinsed
- 30ml/2 tbsp pickled mooli (daikon)
- 50g/2oz fried tofu, cut into small slivers
- 2.5ml/½ tsp dried chilli flakes
- 1 large bunch garlic chives, about 115g/4oz, cut into 5cm/2in lengths
- 225g/8oz/2½ cups beansprouts
- 50g/2oz/½ cup roasted peanuts, coarsely ground
- 5ml/1 tsp granulated sugar
- 15ml/1 tbsp dark soy sauce
- 30ml/2 tbsp Thai fish sauce
- 30ml/2 tbsp tamarind juice, made by mixing tamarind paste with warm water

To garnish
- fresh coriander (cilantro) leaves
- lime wedges

1 Peel the prawns, leaving the tails intact. Carefully cut along the back of each prawn and remove the dark vein.

2 Place the rice noodles in a large bowl, add warm water to cover and leave to soak for 20–30 minutes, then drain thoroughly and set aside.

3 Heat 15ml/1 tbsp of the oil in a wok. Stir-fry the garlic until golden. Stir in the prawns and cook for 1–2 minutes, until pink. Remove and set aside.

4 Heat 15ml/1 tbsp of the remaining oil in the wok. Add the eggs and tilt the wok to make a thin layer. Stir to scramble and break up. Remove from the wok and set aside with the prawns.

5 Heat the remaining oil in the same wok. Add the dried shrimp, pickled mooli, tofu slivers and dried chilli flakes. Stir briefly. Add the noodles and stir-fry for about 5 minutes.

6 Add the garlic chives, half the beansprouts and half the peanuts. Add the granulated sugar, then season with soy sauce, fish sauce and tamarind juice. Mix well and cook until the noodles are heated through.

7 Return the prawn and egg mixture to the wok and mix with the noodles. Serve topped with the remaining beansprouts and peanuts, and garnished with the coriander leaves and lime wedges.

COOK'S TIP

There are numerous species of prawns (shrimp) and they range in colour from black to white, although most turn pink when cooked. Genuine Indo-Pacific tiger prawns, of which there are several types, have a fine flavour and a good texture. They grow up to 28cm/11in in length. However, not all large, warm water varieties are so succulent, and even farmed prawns tend to be quite expensive.

Spicy Fried Noodles

This is a wonderfully versatile dish as you can adapt it to include your favourite ingredients – just as long as you keep a balance of flavours, textures and colours.

SERVES FOUR

INGREDIENTS
- 225g/8oz egg thread noodles
- 60ml/4 tbsp vegetable oil
- 2 garlic cloves, finely chopped
- 175g/6oz pork fillet (tenderloin), sliced into thin strips
- 1 skinless, boneless chicken breast portion (about 175g/6oz), sliced into thin strips
- 115g/4oz/1 cup cooked peeled prawns (shrimp), rinsed if canned
- 45ml/3 tbsp fresh lemon juice
- 45ml/3 tbsp Thai fish sauce
- 30ml/2 tbsp soft light brown sugar
- 2 eggs, beaten
- ½ fresh red chilli, seeded and finely chopped
- 50g/2oz/⅔ cup beansprouts
- 60ml/4 tbsp roasted peanuts, chopped
- 3 spring onions (scallions), cut into 5cm/2in lengths and shredded
- 45ml/3 tbsp chopped fresh coriander (cilantro)

1 Bring a large pan of water to the boil. Add the noodles, remove the pan from the heat and leave for 5 minutes.

2 Meanwhile, heat 45ml/3 tbsp of the oil in a wok or large frying pan, add the garlic and cook for 30 seconds. Add the pork and chicken and stir-fry until lightly browned, then add the prawns and stir-fry for 2 minutes.

3 Stir in the lemon juice, then add the fish sauce and sugar. Stir-fry until the sugar has dissolved.

4 Drain the noodles and add to the wok or pan with the remaining 15ml/1 tbsp oil. Toss all the ingredients together.

5 Pour the beaten eggs over the noodles and stir-fry until almost set, then add the chilli and beansprouts.

6 Divide the roasted peanuts, spring onions and coriander leaves into two equal portions, add one portion to the pan and stir-fry for about 2 minutes.

7 Tip the noodles on to a serving platter. Sprinkle on the remaining roasted peanuts, spring onions and chopped coriander and serve immediately.

COOK'S TIP

Store beansprouts in the refrigerator and use within a day of purchase, as they tend to lose their crispness and become slimy and unpleasant quite quickly. The most commonly used beansprouts are sprouted mung beans, but you could use other types of beansprouts instead.

SPECIAL CHOW MEIN

ANOTHER EXAMPLE OF THE CHINESE INFLUENCE IN THAI COOKING. LAP CHEONG IS A SPECIAL AIR-DRIED CHINESE SAUSAGE AND IS AVAILABLE FROM MOST CHINESE SUPERMARKETS.

SERVES FOUR TO SIX

INGREDIENTS

- 450g/1lb egg noodles
- 45ml/3 tbsp vegetable oil
- 2 garlic cloves, sliced
- 5ml/1 tsp chopped fresh root ginger
- 2 fresh red chillies, seeded and chopped
- 2 lap cheong, total weight about 75g/3oz, rinsed and sliced (optional)
- 1 skinless, boneless chicken breast portion, thinly sliced
- 16 uncooked tiger prawns (jumbo shrimp), peeled, tails left intact, and deveined
- 115g/4oz/2 cups green beans
- 225g/8oz/2½ cups beansprouts
- small bunch garlic chives, about 50g/2oz
- 30ml/2 tbsp soy sauce
- 15ml/1 tbsp oyster sauce
- 15ml/1 tbsp sesame oil
- salt and ground black pepper
- 2 shredded spring onions (scallions) and fresh coriander (cilantro) leaves, to garnish

1 Cook the noodles in a large pan of boiling water, according to the instructions on the packet. Drain well.

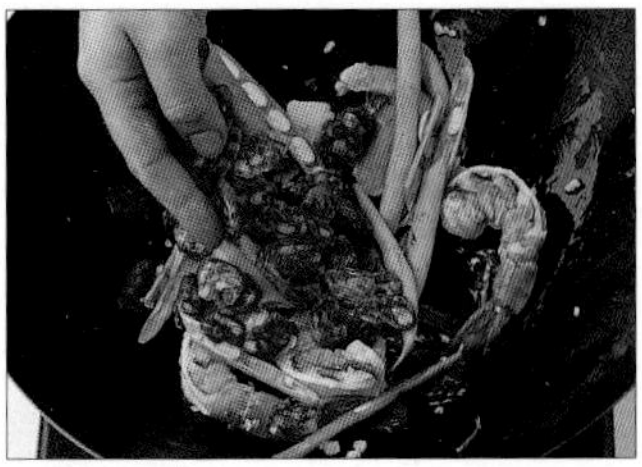

2 Heat 15ml/1 tbsp of the oil in a wok or large frying pan and stir-fry the garlic, ginger and chillies for 2 minutes. Add the lap cheong, if using, chicken, prawns and beans. Stir-fry over a high heat for 2 minutes more, or until the chicken and prawns are cooked. Transfer the mixture to a bowl and set aside.

3 Heat the rest of the oil in the wok. Add the beansprouts and garlic chives and stir-fry for 1–2 minutes.

4 Add the drained noodles and toss over the heat to mix. Season with the soy sauce, oyster sauce and salt and pepper to taste. Return the prawn mixture to the wok. Mix well with the noodles and toss until heated through.

5 Stir the sesame oil into the noodles. Spoon into a warmed bowl and serve immediately, garnished with the spring onions and coriander leaves.

MEE KROB

THE NAME OF THIS DISH MEANS "DEEP-FRIED NOODLES" AND IT IS VERY POPULAR IN THAILAND. THE TASTE IS A STUNNING COMBINATION OF SWEET AND HOT, SALTY AND SOUR, WHILE THE TEXTURE CONTRIVES TO BE BOTH CRISP AND CHEWY. TO SOME WESTERN PALATES, IT MAY SEEM RATHER UNUSUAL, BUT THIS DELICIOUS DISH IS WELL WORTH MAKING.

SERVES ONE

INGREDIENTS

- vegetable oil, for deep-frying
- 130g/4½oz rice vermicelli noodles

For the sauce

- 30ml/2 tbsp vegetable oil
- 130g/4½oz fried tofu, cut into thin strips
- 2 garlic cloves, finely chopped
- 2 small shallots, finely chopped
- 15ml/1 tbsp light soy sauce
- 30ml/2 tbsp palm sugar or light muscovado (brown) sugar
- 60ml/4 tbsp vegetable stock
- juice of 1 lime
- 2.5ml/½ tsp dried chilli flakes

For the garnish

- 15ml/1 tbsp vegetable oil
- 1 egg, lightly beaten with 15ml/1 tbsp cold water
- 25g/1oz/⅓ cup beansprouts
- 1 spring onion (scallion), thinly shredded
- 1 fresh red chilli, seeded and finely chopped
- 1 whole head pickled garlic, sliced across the bulb so each slice looks like a flower

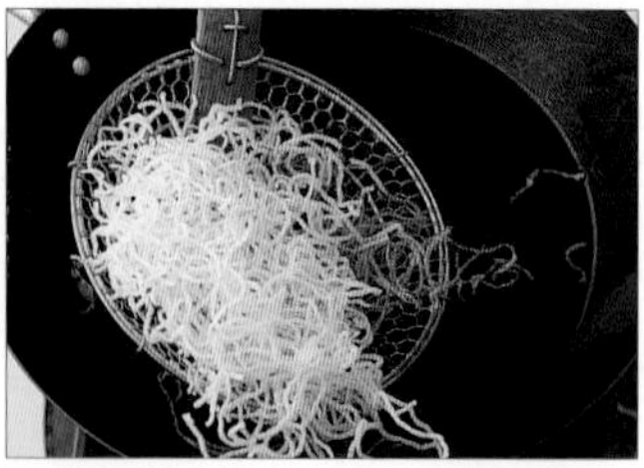

1 Heat the oil for deep-frying in a wok or large pan to 190°C/375°F or until a cube of bread, added to the oil, browns in about 45 seconds. Add the noodles and deep-fry until golden and crisp. Drain on kitchen paper and set aside.

2 Make the sauce. Heat the oil in a wok, add the fried tofu and cook over a medium heat until crisp. Using a slotted spoon, transfer it to a plate.

3 Add the garlic and shallots to the wok and cook until golden brown. Stir in the soy sauce, sugar, stock, lime juice and chilli flakes. Cook, stirring, until the mixture begins to caramelize.

4 Add the reserved tofu and stir until it has soaked up some of the liquid. Remove the wok from the heat and set aside.

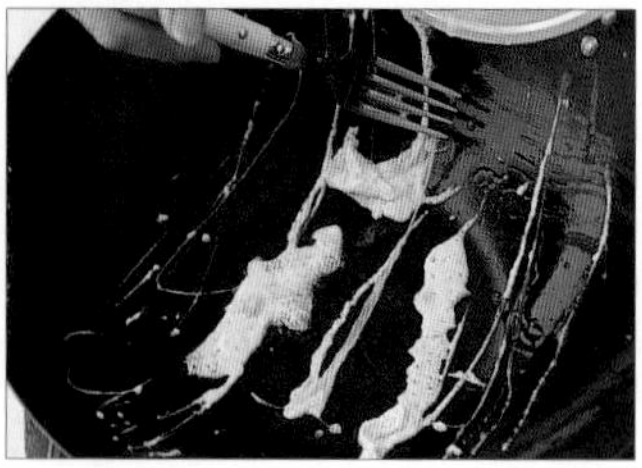

5 Prepare the egg garnish. Heat the oil in a wok or frying pan. Pour in the egg in a thin stream to form trails. As soon as it sets, lift it out with a fish slice or metal spatula and place on a plate.

6 Crumble the noodles into the tofu sauce, mix well, then spoon into warmed serving bowls. Sprinkle with the beansprouts, spring onion, fried egg strips, chilli and pickled garlic "flowers" and serve immediately.

COOK'S TIP

Successful deep-frying depends, to a large extent, on the type of oil used and the temperature to which it is heated. A bland-tasting oil, such as sunflower, will not alter the flavour of the food. All fats have a "smoke point" – the temperature at which they begin to decompose. Most vegetable oils have a high smoke point, with groundnut (peanut) oil the highest of all and so also the safest.

SWEET AND HOT VEGETABLE NOODLES

This noodle dish has the colour of fire, but only the mildest suggestion of heat. Ginger and plum sauce give it its fruity flavour, while lime adds a delicious tang.

SERVES FOUR

INGREDIENTS

- 130g/4½oz dried rice noodles
- 30ml/2 tbsp groundnut (peanut) oil
- 2.5cm/1in piece fresh root ginger, sliced into thin batons
- 1 garlic clove, crushed
- 130g/4½oz drained canned bamboo shoots, sliced into thin batons
- 2 medium carrots, sliced into batons
- 130g/4½oz/1½ cups beansprouts
- 1 small white cabbage, shredded
- 30ml/2 tbsp Thai fish sauce
- 30ml/2 tbsp soy sauce
- 30ml/2 tbsp plum sauce
- 10ml/2 tsp sesame oil
- 15ml/1 tbsp palm sugar or light muscovado (brown) sugar
- juice of ½ lime
- 90g/3½oz mooli (daikon), sliced into thin batons
- small bunch fresh coriander (cilantro), chopped
- 60ml/4 tbsp sesame seeds, toasted

1 Cook the noodles in a large pan of boiling water, following the instructions on the packet. Meanwhile, heat the oil in a wok or large frying pan and stir-fry the ginger and garlic for 2–3 minutes over a medium heat, until golden.

2 Drain the noodles and set them aside. Add the bamboo shoots to the wok, increase the heat to high and stir-fry for 5 minutes. Add the carrots, beansprouts and cabbage and stir-fry for a further 5 minutes, until they are beginning to char on the edges.

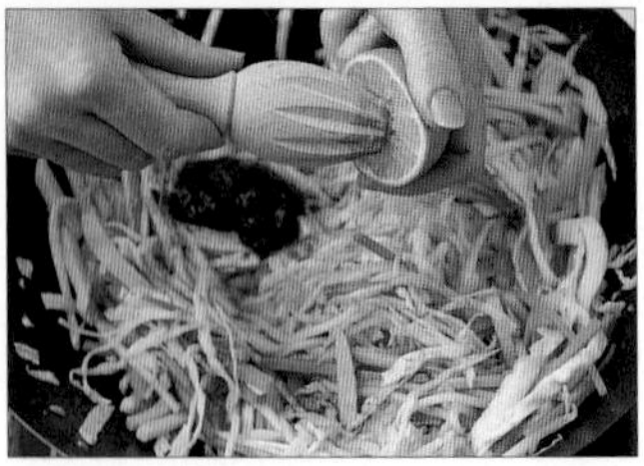

3 Stir in the sauces, sesame oil, sugar and lime juice. Add the mooli and coriander, toss to mix, then spoon into a warmed bowl, sprinkle with toasted sesame seeds and serve immediately.

COOK'S TIP

Use a large, sharp knife for shredding cabbage. Remove any tough outer leaves, if necessary, then cut the cabbage into quarters. Cut off and discard the hard core from each quarter, place flat side down, then slice the cabbage very thinly to make fine shreds.

SOUTHERN CURRIED NOODLES

CHICKEN OR PORK CAN BE USED TO PROVIDE THE PROTEIN IN THIS TASTY DISH. IT IS SO QUICK AND EASY TO PREPARE AND COOK, IT MAKES THE PERFECT SNACK FOR BUSY PEOPLE.

SERVES TWO

INGREDIENTS

- 30ml/2 tbsp vegetable oil
- 10ml/2 tsp magic paste
- 1 lemon grass stalk, finely chopped
- 5ml/1 tsp Thai red curry paste
- 90g/3½ oz skinless, boneless chicken breast portion or pork fillet (tenderloin), sliced into slivers
- 30ml/2 tbsp light soy sauce
- 400ml/14fl oz/1⅔ cups coconut milk
- 2 kaffir lime leaves, rolled into cylinders and thinly sliced
- 250g/9oz dried medium egg noodles
- 90g/3½ oz Chinese leaves (Chinese cabbage), shredded
- 90g/3½ oz spinach or watercress (leaves), shredded
- juice of 1 lime
- small bunch fresh coriander (cilantro), chopped

1 Heat the oil in a wok or large, heavy frying pan. Add the magic paste and lemon grass and stir-fry over a low to medium heat for 4–5 seconds, until they give off their aroma.

2 Stir in the curry paste, then add the chicken or pork. Stir-fry over a medium to high heat for 2 minutes, until the chicken or pork is coated in the paste and seared on all sides.

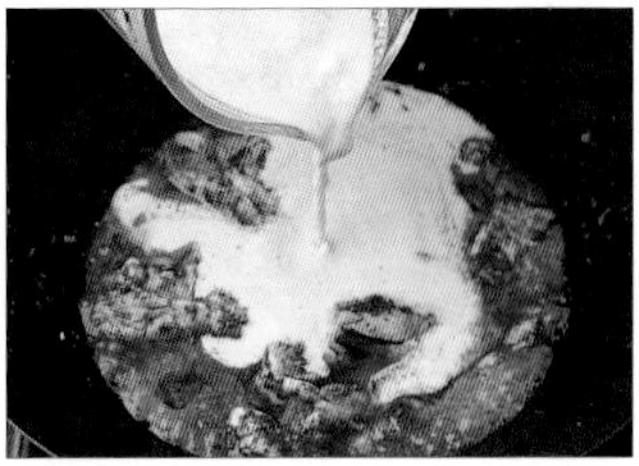

3 Add the soy sauce, coconut milk and sliced lime leaves. Bring to a simmer, then add the noodles. Simmer gently for 4 minutes, tossing the mixture occasionally to make sure that the noodles cook evenly.

4 Add the Chinese leaves and the watercress. Stir well, then add the lime juice. Spoon into a warmed bowl, sprinkle with the coriander and serve.

CHIANG MAI NOODLES

AN INTERESTING NOODLE DISH THAT COMBINES SOFT, BOILED NOODLES WITH CRISP DEEP-FRIED ONES AND ADDS THE USUAL PANOPLY OF THAI SWEET, HOT AND SOUR FLAVOURS.

SERVES FOUR

INGREDIENTS
- 250ml/8fl oz/1 cup coconut cream
- 15ml/1 tbsp magic paste
- 5ml/1 tsp Thai red curry paste
- 450g/1lb chicken thigh meat, chopped into small pieces
- 30ml/2 tbsp dark soy sauce
- 2 red (bell) peppers, seeded and finely diced
- 600ml/1 pint/2½ cups chicken or vegetable stock
- 90g/3½oz fresh or dried rice noodles

For the garnishes
- vegetable oil, for deep-frying
- 90g/3½oz fine dried rice noodles
- 2 pickled garlic cloves, chopped
- small bunch fresh coriander (cilantro), chopped
- 2 limes, cut into wedges

1 Pour the coconut cream into a large wok or frying pan and bring to the boil over a medium heat. Continue to boil, stirring frequently, for 8–10 minutes, until the milk separates and an oily sheen appears on the surface.

2 Add the magic paste and red curry paste and cook, stirring constantly, for 3–5 seconds, until fragrant.

3 Add the chicken and toss over the heat until sealed on all sides. Stir in the soy sauce and the diced peppers and stir-fry for 3–4 minutes. Pour in the stock. Bring to the boil, then lower the heat and simmer for 10–15 minutes, until the chicken is fully cooked.

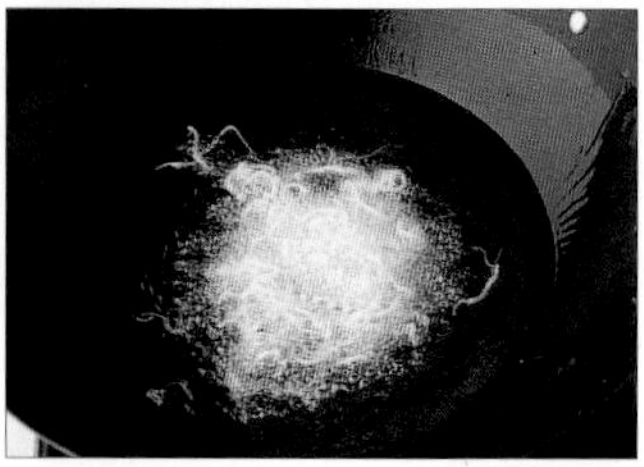

4 Meanwhile, make the noodle garnish. Heat the oil in a pan or deep-fryer to 190°C/375°F or until a cube of bread, added to the oil, browns in 45 seconds. Break all the noodles in half, then divide them into four portions. Add one portion at a time to the hot oil. They will puff up on contact. As soon as they are crisp, lift the noodles out with a slotted spoon and drain on kitchen paper.

5 Bring a large pan of water to the boil and cook the fresh or dried noodles until tender, following the instructions on the packet. Drain well, divide among four warmed individual dishes, then spoon the curry sauce over them. Top each portion with a cluster of fried noodles. Sprinkle the chopped pickled garlic and coriander over the top and serve immediately, offering lime wedges for squeezing.

COOK'S TIP

If you are planning to serve this dish to guests, you can save on preparation time by making the noodle garnish in advance. Deep-fry the noodles a few hours before you need them and drain well on kitchen paper. Transfer the crispy noodles to a wire rack lined with fresh sheets of kitchen paper and set aside until ready to use.

CELLOPHANE NOODLES WITH PORK

SIMPLE, SPEEDY AND SATISFYING, THIS IS AN EXCELLENT WAY OF USING MUNG BEAN NOODLES. THE DISH IS POPULAR ALL OVER THAILAND.

SERVES TWO

INGREDIENTS
- 200g/7oz cellophane noodles
- 30ml/2 tbsp vegetable oil
- 15ml/1 tbsp magic paste
- 200g/7oz minced (ground) pork
- 1 fresh green or red chilli, seeded and finely chopped
- 300g/11oz/3½ cups beansprouts
- bunch spring onions (scallions), finely chopped
- 30ml/2 tbsp soy sauce
- 30ml/2 tbsp Thai fish sauce
- 30ml/2 tbsp sweet chilli sauce
- 15ml/1 tbsp palm sugar or light muscovado (brown) sugar
- 30ml/2 tbsp rice vinegar
- 30ml/2 tbsp roasted peanuts, chopped, to garnish
- small bunch fresh coriander (cilantro), chopped, to garnish

1 Place the noodles in a large bowl, cover with boiling water and soak for 10 minutes. Drain the noodles and set aside until ready to use.

2 Heat the oil in a wok or large, heavy frying pan. Add the magic paste and stir-fry for 2–3 seconds, then add the pork. Stir-fry the meat, breaking it up with a wooden spatula, for 2–3 minutes, until browned all over.

3 Add the chopped chilli to the meat and stir-fry for 3–4 seconds, then add the beansprouts and chopped spring onions, stir-frying for a few seconds after each addition.

4 Snip the noodles into 5cm/2in lengths and add to the wok, with the soy sauce, Thai fish sauce, sweet chilli sauce, sugar and rice vinegar.

5 Toss the ingredients together over the heat until well combined and the noodles have warmed through. Pile on to a platter or into a large bowl. Sprinkle over the peanuts and coriander and serve immediately.

VARIATION

This dish is also very good made with chicken. Replace the pork with the same quantity of minced (ground) chicken.

Noodles and Vegetables in Coconut Sauce

When everyday vegetables are given the Thai treatment, the result is a delectable dish which everyone will enjoy. Noodles add bulk and a welcome contrast in texture.

SERVES FOUR TO SIX

INGREDIENTS

- 30ml/2 tbsp sunflower oil
- 1 lemon grass stalk, finely chopped
- 15ml/1 tbsp Thai red curry paste
- 1 onion, thickly sliced
- 3 courgettes (zucchini), thickly sliced
- 115g/4oz Savoy cabbage, thickly sliced
- 2 carrots, thickly sliced
- 150g/5oz broccoli, stem thickly sliced and head separated into florets
- 2 × 400ml/14fl oz cans coconut milk
- 475ml/16fl oz/2 cups vegetable stock
- 150g/5oz dried egg noodles
- 15ml/1 tbsp Thai fish sauce
- 30ml/2 tbsp soy sauce
- 60ml/4 tbsp chopped fresh coriander (cilantro)

For the garnish

- 2 lemon grass stalks
- 1 bunch fresh coriander (cilantro)
- 8–10 small fresh red chillies

1 Heat the oil in a large pan or wok. Add the lemon grass and red curry paste and stir-fry for 2–3 seconds. Add the onion and cook over a medium heat, stirring occasionally, for about 5–10 minutes, until the onion has softened but not browned.

2 Add the courgettes, cabbage, carrots and slices of broccoli stem. Using two spoons, toss the vegetables with the onion mixture. Reduce the heat to low and cook gently, stirring occasionally, for a further 5 minutes.

3 Increase the heat to medium, stir in the coconut milk and vegetable stock and bring to the boil. Add the broccoli florets and the noodles, lower the heat and simmer gently for 20 minutes.

4 Meanwhile, make the garnish. Split the lemon grass stalks lengthways through the root. Gather the coriander into a small bouquet and lay it on a platter, following the curve of the rim.

5 Tuck the lemon grass halves into the coriander bouquet and add the chillies to resemble flowers.

6 Stir the fish sauce, soy sauce and chopped coriander into the noodle mixture. Spoon on to the platter, taking care not to disturb the herb bouquet, and serve immediately.

THAI CRISPY NOODLES WITH BEEF

RICE VERMICELLI IS DEEP-FRIED BEFORE BEING ADDED TO THIS DISH, AND IN THE PROCESS THE VERMICELLI EXPANDS TO AT LEAST FOUR TIMES ITS ORIGINAL SIZE.

SERVES FOUR

INGREDIENTS
- 450g/1lb rump (round) steak
- teriyaki sauce, for brushing
- 175g/6oz rice vermicelli
- groundnut (peanut) oil, for deep-frying and stir-frying
- 8 spring onions (scallions), diagonally sliced
- 2 garlic cloves, crushed
- 4–5 carrots, cut into julienne strips
- 1–2 fresh red chillies, seeded and finely sliced
- 2 small courgettes (zucchini), diagonally sliced
- 5ml/1 tsp grated fresh root ginger
- 60ml/4 tbsp rice vinegar
- 90ml/6 tbsp light soy sauce
- about 475ml/16fl oz/2 cups spicy stock

1 Beat the steak to about 2.5cm/1in thick. Place in a shallow dish, brush generously with the teriyaki sauce and set aside for 2–4 hours to marinate.

2 Separate the rice vermicelli into manageable loops. Pour oil into a large wok to a depth of about 5cm/2in, and heat until a strand of vermicelli cooks as soon as it is lowered into the oil.

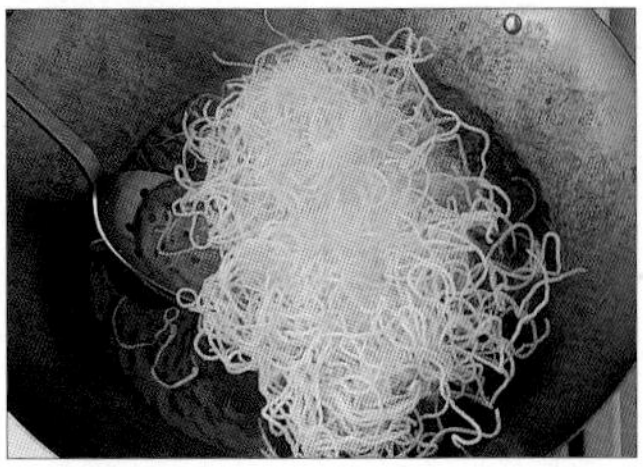

3 Carefully add a loop of vermicelli to the oil. Almost immediately, turn to cook on the other side, then remove and drain on kitchen paper. Repeat with the remaining loops. Transfer the cooked noodles to a separate wok or deep serving bowl and keep them warm while you cook the steak and vegetables.

4 Strain the oil from the wok into a heatproof bowl and set it aside. Heat 15ml/1 tbsp groundnut oil in the clean wok. When it sizzles, fry the steak for about 30 seconds on each side, until browned. Transfer to a board and cut into thick slices. The meat should be well browned on the outside but still pink inside. Set aside.

5 Add a little extra oil to the wok, add the spring onions, garlic and carrots and stir-fry over a medium heat for 5–6 minutes, until the carrots are slightly soft and have a glazed appearance. Add the chillies, courgettes and ginger and stir-fry for 1–2 minutes.

6 Stir in the rice vinegar, soy sauce and stock. Cook for 4 minutes, or until the sauce has thickened slightly. Return the slices of steak to the wok and cook for a further 1–2 minutes.

7 Spoon the steak, vegetables and sauce over the noodles and toss lightly and carefully to mix. Serve immediately.

COOK'S TIP

As soon as you add the meat mixture to the noodles, they will begin to soften in the sauce. If you wish to keep a few crispy noodles, leave some on the surface so that they do not come into contact with the hot liquid.

Side Dishes

Strictly speaking, a traditional Thai meal consists of several dishes, rather than a main dish served with side dishes. However, to make menu-planning easier, this chapter contains a selection of vegetable dishes and salads that go particularly well with the meat, poultry, fish and vegetable dishes. Their classic combination of crisp textures and sweet, sharp, spicy and aromatic flavours provides a refreshing complement and perfect balance to the curries and main dishes included in this book.

Green Papaya Salad

This salad appears in many guises in South-east Asia. As green papaya is not easy to get hold of, finely grated carrots, cucumber or even crisp green apple can be used instead. Alternatively, use very thinly sliced white cabbage.

SERVES FOUR

INGREDIENTS

- 1 green papaya
- 4 garlic cloves, coarsely chopped
- 15ml/1 tbsp chopped shallots
- 3–4 fresh red chillies, seeded and sliced
- 2.5ml/½ tsp salt
- 2–3 snake beans or 6 green beans, cut into 2cm/¾in lengths
- 2 tomatoes, cut into thin wedges
- 45ml/3 tbsp Thai fish sauce
- 15ml/1 tbsp caster (superfine) sugar
- juice of 1 lime
- 30ml/2 tbsp crushed roasted peanuts
- sliced fresh red chillies, to garnish

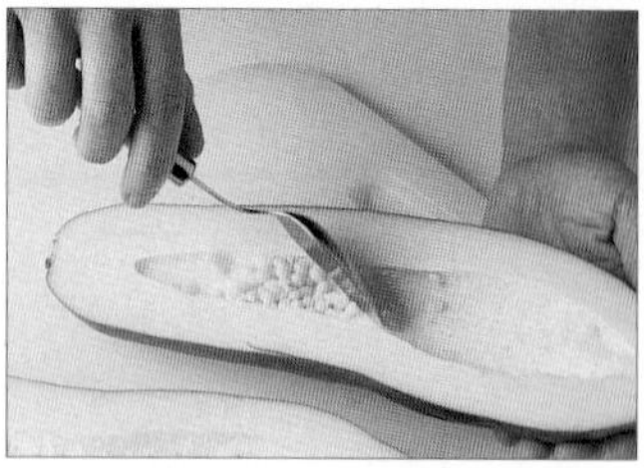

1 Cut the papaya in half lengthways. Scrape out the seeds with a spoon and discard, then peel, using a swivel vegetable peeler or a small sharp knife. Shred the flesh finely in a food processor or using a grater.

2 Put the garlic, shallots, red chillies and salt in a large mortar and grind to a paste with a pestle. Add the shredded papaya, a small amount at a time, pounding with the pestle until it becomes slightly limp and soft.

3 Add the sliced snake or green beans and wedges of tomato to the mortar and crush them lightly with the pestle until they are incorporated.

4 Season the mixture with the fish sauce, sugar and lime juice. Transfer the salad to a serving dish and sprinkle with the crushed roasted peanuts. Garnish with the sliced red chillies and serve the salad immediately.

RAW VEGETABLE YAM

IN THIS CONTEXT, THE WORD "YAM" DOES NOT REFER TO THE STARCHY VEGETABLE THAT RESEMBLES SWEET POTATO, BUT RATHER TO A UNIQUE STYLE OF THAI COOKING. YAM DISHES ARE SALADS MADE WITH RAW OR LIGHTLY COOKED VEGETABLES, DRESSED WITH A SPECIAL SPICY SAUCE.

SERVES FOUR

INGREDIENTS

- 50g/2oz watercress or baby spinach, chopped
- ½ cucumber, finely diced
- 2 celery sticks, finely diced
- 2 carrots, finely diced
- 1 red (bell) pepper, seeded and finely diced
- 2 tomatoes, seeded and finely diced
- small bunch fresh mint, chopped
- 90g/3½oz cellophane noodles

For the yam

- 2 small fresh red chillies, seeded and finely chopped
- 60ml/4 tbsp light soy sauce
- 45ml/3 tbsp lemon juice
- 5ml/1 tsp palm sugar or light muscovado (brown) sugar
- 60ml/4 tbsp water
- 1 head pickled garlic, finely chopped, plus 15ml/1 tbsp vinegar from the jar
- 50g/2oz/scant ½ cup peanuts, roasted and chopped
- 90g/3½oz fried tofu, finely chopped
- 15ml/1 tbsp sesame seeds, toasted

1 Place the watercress or spinach, cucumber, celery, carrots, red pepper and tomatoes in a bowl. Add the chopped mint and toss together.

2 Soak the noodles in boiling water for 3 minutes, or according to the packet instructions, then drain well and snip with scissors into shorter lengths. Add them to the vegetables.

3 Make the yam. Put the chopped chillies in a pan and add the soy sauce, lemon juice, sugar and water. Place over a medium heat and stir until the sugar has dissolved. Add the garlic, with the pickling vinegar from the jar, then mix in the chopped nuts, tofu and toasted sesame seeds.

4 Pour the yam over the vegetables and noodles, toss together until well mixed, and serve immediately.

VARIATIONS

Any salad vegetables could be used for this recipe. Instead of dicing them, you could cut them into thin batons, preferably using a mandolin. The Thais like all the vegetable components in a dish like this to be of a small and uniform size so that all the different flavours and textures are experienced in a single mouthful.

SOUTHERN-STYLE YAM

THE FOOD OF THE SOUTHERN REGION IS NOTORIOUSLY HOT AND BECAUSE OF THE PROXIMITY TO THE BORDERS WITH MALAYSIA, THAILAND'S MUSLIM MINORITY ARE MOSTLY TO BE FOUND IN THIS AREA. THEY HAVE INTRODUCED RICHER CURRY FLAVOURS REMINISCENT OF INDIAN FOOD.

SERVES FOUR

INGREDIENTS

- 90g/3½oz Chinese leaves (Chinese cabbage), shredded
- 90g/3½oz/generous 1 cup beansprouts
- 90g/3½oz/scant 1 cup green beans, trimmed
- 90g/3½oz broccoli, preferably the purple sprouting variety, divided into florets
- 15ml/1 tbsp sesame seeds, toasted

For the yam

- 60ml/4 tbsp coconut cream
- 5ml/1 tsp Thai red curry paste
- 90g/3½oz/1¼ cups oyster mushrooms or field (portabello) mushrooms, sliced
- 60ml/4 tbsp coconut milk
- 5ml/1 tsp ground turmeric
- 5ml/1 tsp thick tamarind juice, made by mixing tamarind paste with warm water
- juice of ½ lemon
- 60ml/4 tbsp light soy sauce
- 5ml/1 tsp palm sugar or light muscovado (brown) sugar

1 Steam the shredded Chinese leaves, beansprouts, green beans and broccoli separately or blanch them in boiling water for 1 minute per batch. Drain, place in a serving bowl and leave to cool.

2 Make the yam. Pour the coconut cream into a wok or frying pan and heat gently for 2–3 minutes, until it separates. Stir in the red curry paste. Cook over a low heat for 30 seconds, until the mixture is fragrant.

3 Increase the heat to high and add the mushrooms to the wok or pan. Cook for a further 2–3 minutes.

4 Pour in the coconut milk and add the ground turmeric, tamarind juice, lemon juice, soy sauce and sugar to the wok or pan. Mix thoroughly.

5 Pour the mixture over the prepared vegetables and toss well to combine. Sprinkle with the toasted sesame seeds and serve immediately.

COOK'S TIPS

- There's no need to buy coconut cream especially for this dish. Use a carton or can of coconut milk. Skim the cream off the top and cook 60ml/4 tbsp of it before adding the curry paste. Add the measured coconut milk later, as described in the recipe.
- Oyster mushrooms may have fawn, peacock-blue or yellow caps, depending on the variety.

THAI FRUIT AND VEGETABLE SALAD

This fruit salad is traditionally presented with the main course and serves as a cooler to counteract the heat of the chillies that will inevitably be present in the other dishes. It is a typically harmonious balance of flavours.

SERVES FOUR TO SIX

INGREDIENTS

1 small pineapple
1 small mango, peeled and sliced
1 green apple, cored and sliced
6 rambutans or lychees, peeled and stoned (pitted)
115g/4oz/1 cup green beans, trimmed and halved
1 red onion, sliced
1 small cucumber, cut into short sticks
115g/4oz/1⅓ cups beansprouts
2 spring onions (scallions), sliced
1 ripe tomato, quartered
225g/8oz cos, romaine or iceberg lettuce leaves

For the coconut dipping sauce

30ml/2 tbsp coconut cream
30ml/2 tbsp granulated sugar
75ml/5 tbsp boiling water
1.5ml/¼ tsp chilli sauce
15ml/1 tbsp Thai fish sauce
juice of 1 lime

1 Make the coconut dipping sauce. Spoon the coconut cream, sugar and boiling water into a screw-top jar. Add the chilli and fish sauces and lime juice, close tightly and shake to mix.

2 Trim both ends of the pineapple with a serrated knife, then cut away the outer skin. Remove the central core with an apple corer. Alternatively, quarter the pineapple lengthways and remove the portion of core from each wedge with a knife. Chop the pineapple and set aside with the other fruits.

3 Bring a small pan of lightly salted water to the boil over a medium heat. Add the green beans and cook for 3–4 minutes, until just tender but still retaining some "bite". Drain, refresh under cold running water, drain well again and set aside.

4 To serve, arrange all the fruits and vegetables in small heaps on a platter or in a shallow bowl. Pour the coconut sauce into a small serving bowl and serve separately as a dip.

BAMBOO SHOOT SALAD

THIS HOT, SHARP-FLAVOURED SALAD ORIGINATED IN NORTH-EASTERN THAILAND. USE CANNED WHOLE BAMBOO SHOOTS, IF YOU CAN FIND THEM – THEY HAVE MORE FLAVOUR THAN SLICED ONES.

SERVES FOUR

INGREDIENTS

- 400g/14oz canned bamboo shoots, in large pieces
- 25g/1oz/about 3 tbsp glutinous rice
- 30ml/2 tbsp chopped shallots
- 15ml/1 tbsp chopped garlic
- 45ml/3 tbsp chopped spring onions (scallions)
- 30ml/2 tbsp Thai fish sauce
- 30ml/2 tbsp fresh lime juice
- 5ml/1 tsp granulated sugar
- 2.5ml/½ tsp dried chilli flakes
- 20–25 small fresh mint leaves
- 15ml/1 tbsp toasted sesame seeds

COOK'S TIP

Glutinous rice does not, in fact, contain any gluten – it's just sticky.

1 Rinse the bamboo shoots under cold running water, then drain them and pat them thoroughly dry with kitchen paper and set them aside.

2 Dry-roast the rice in a frying pan until it is golden brown. Leave to cool slightly, then tip into a mortar and grind to fine crumbs with a pestle.

3 Transfer the rice to a bowl and add the shallots, garlic, spring onions, fish sauce, lime juice, sugar, chillies and half the mint leaves. Mix well.

4 Add the bamboo shoots to the bowl and toss to mix. Serve sprinkled with the toasted sesame seeds and the remaining mint leaves.

CABBAGE SALAD

THIS IS A SIMPLE AND DELICIOUS WAY OF SERVING A SOMEWHAT MUNDANE VEGETABLE. CLASSIC THAI FLAVOURS PERMEATE THIS COLOURFUL WARM SALAD.

SERVES FOUR TO SIX

INGREDIENTS
- 30ml/2 tbsp vegetable oil
- 2 large fresh red chillies, seeded and cut into thin strips
- 6 garlic cloves, thinly sliced
- 6 shallots, thinly sliced
- 1 small cabbage, shredded
- 30ml/2 tbsp coarsely chopped roasted peanuts, to garnish

For the dressing
- 30ml/2 tbsp Thai fish sauce
- grated rind of 1 lime
- 30ml/2 tbsp fresh lime juice
- 120ml/4fl oz/½ cup coconut milk

VARIATION
Other vegetables, such as cauliflower, broccoli and Chinese leaves (Chinese cabbage), can be cooked in this way.

1 Make the dressing by mixing the fish sauce, lime rind and juice and coconut milk in a bowl. Whisk until thoroughly combined, then set aside.

2 Heat the oil in a wok. Stir-fry the chillies, garlic and shallots over a medium heat for 3–4 minutes, until the shallots are brown and crisp. Remove with a slotted spoon and set aside.

3 Bring a large pan of lightly salted water to the boil. Add the cabbage and blanch for 2–3 minutes. Tip it into a colander, drain well and put into a bowl.

4 Whisk the dressing again, add it to the warm cabbage and toss to mix. Transfer the salad to a serving dish. Sprinkle with the fried shallot mixture and the peanuts. Serve immediately.

Fragrant Mushrooms in Lettuce Leaves

This quick and easy vegetable dish is served on lettuce leaf "saucers" so can be eaten with the fingers – a great treat for children.

SERVES TWO

INGREDIENTS

- 30ml/2 tbsp vegetable oil
- 2 garlic cloves, finely chopped
- 2 baby cos or romaine lettuces, or 2 Little Gem (Bibb) lettuces
- 1 lemon grass stalk, finely chopped
- 2 kaffir lime leaves, rolled in cylinders and thinly sliced
- 200g/7oz/3 cups oyster or chestnut mushrooms, sliced
- 1 small fresh red chilli, seeded and finely chopped
- juice of ½ lemon
- 30ml/2 tbsp light soy sauce
- 5ml/1 tsp palm sugar or light muscovado (brown) sugar
- small bunch fresh mint, leaves removed from the stalks

1 Heat the oil in a wok or frying pan. Add the garlic and cook over a medium heat, stirring occasionally, until golden. Do not let it burn or it will taste bitter.

2 Meanwhile, separate the individual lettuce leaves and set aside.

3 Increase the heat under the wok or pan and add the lemon grass, lime leaves and sliced mushrooms. Stir-fry for about 2 minutes.

4 Add the chilli, lemon juice, soy sauce and sugar to the wok or pan. Toss the mixture over the heat to combine the ingredients together, then stir-fry for a further 2 minutes.

5 Arrange the lettuce leaves on a large plate. Spoon a small amount of the mushroom mixture on to each leaf, top with a mint leaf and serve.

THAI ASPARAGUS

THIS IS AN EXCITINGLY DIFFERENT WAY OF COOKING ASPARAGUS. THE CRUNCHY TEXTURE IS RETAINED AND THE FLAVOUR IS COMPLEMENTED BY THE ADDITION OF GALANGAL AND CHILLI.

SERVES FOUR

INGREDIENTS

- 350g/12oz asparagus stalks
- 30ml/2 tbsp vegetable oil
- 1 garlic clove, crushed
- 15ml/1 tbsp sesame seeds, toasted
- 2.5cm/1in piece fresh galangal, finely shredded
- 1 fresh red chilli, seeded and finely chopped
- 15ml/1 tbsp Thai fish sauce
- 15ml/1 tbsp light soy sauce
- 45ml/3 tbsp water
- 5ml/1 tsp palm sugar or light muscovado (brown) sugar

VARIATIONS

Try this with broccoli or pak choi (bok choy). The sauce also works very well with green beans.

1 Snap the asparagus stalks. They will break naturally at the junction between the woody base and the more tender portion of the stalk. Discard the woody parts of the stems.

2 Heat the oil in a wok and stir-fry the garlic, sesame seeds and galangal for 3–4 seconds, until the garlic is just beginning to turn golden.

3 Add the asparagus stalks and chilli, toss to mix, then add the fish sauce, soy sauce, water and sugar. Using two spoons, toss over the heat for a further 2 minutes, or until the asparagus just begins to soften and the liquid is reduced by half.

4 Carefully transfer to a warmed platter and serve immediately.

PAK CHOI WITH LIME DRESSING

THE COCONUT DRESSING FOR THIS THAI SPECIALITY IS TRADITIONALLY MADE USING FISH SAUCE, BUT VEGETARIANS COULD USE MUSHROOM SAUCE INSTEAD. BEWARE, THIS IS A FIERY DISH!

SERVES FOUR

INGREDIENTS
- 30ml/2 tbsp oil
- 3 fresh red chillies, cut into thin strips
- 4 garlic cloves, thinly sliced
- 6 spring onions (scallions), sliced diagonally
- 2 pak choi (bok choy), shredded
- 15ml/1 tbsp crushed peanuts

For the dressing
- 30ml/2 tbsp fresh lime juice
- 15–30ml/1–2 tbsp Thai fish sauce
- 250ml/8fl oz/1 cup coconut milk

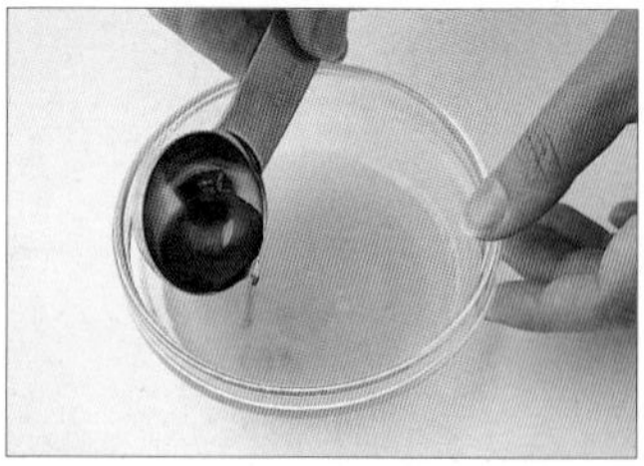

1 Make the dressing. Put the lime juice and fish sauce in a bowl and mix well together, then gradually whisk in the coconut milk until combined.

2 Heat the oil in a wok and stir-fry the chillies for 2–3 minutes, until crisp. Transfer to a plate using a slotted spoon. Add the garlic to the wok and stir-fry for 30–60 seconds, until golden brown. Transfer to the plate.

3 Stir-fry the white parts of the spring onions for about 2–3 minutes, then add the green parts and stir-fry for 1 minute more. Transfer to the plate.

4 Bring a large pan of lightly salted water to the boil and add the pak choi. Stir twice, then drain immediately.

5 Place the pak choi in a large bowl, add the dressing and toss to mix. Spoon into a large serving bowl and sprinkle with the crushed peanuts and the stir-fried chilli mixture. Serve warm or cold.

VARIATION

If you don't like particularly spicy food, substitute red (bell) pepper strips for some or all of the chillies.

FRIED VEGETABLES WITH NAM PRIK

Nam prik is the universal Thai sauce. It can be served as a condiment, but it is more often used as a dip for fresh or cooked vegetables.

SERVES FOUR

INGREDIENTS

- 3 large (US extra large) eggs
- 1 aubergine (eggplant), halved lengthways and cut into long, thin slices
- ½ small butternut squash, peeled, seeded and cut into long, thin slices
- 2 courgettes (zucchini), trimmed and cut into long, thin slices
- 105ml/7 tbsp vegetable or sunflower oil
- salt and ground black pepper
- nam prik or sweet chilli sauce, to serve (see Cook's Tip)

1 Beat the eggs in a large bowl. Add the aubergine, butternut squash and courgette slices. Toss the vegetables until coated all over in the egg, then season with salt and pepper.

2 Heat the oil in a wok. When it is hot, add the vegetables, one strip at a time, making sure that each strip has plenty of egg clinging to it. Do not cook more than eight strips at a time or the oil will cool down too much.

COOK'S TIP

Nam prik is quite a complex sauce, numbering dried shrimp, tiny aubergines (eggplant), shrimp paste and lime or lemon juice among its ingredients.

3 As each strip turns golden and is cooked, lift it out, using a wire basket or slotted spoon, and drain on kitchen paper. Keep hot while cooking the remaining vegetables. Transfer to a warmed dish and serve with the nam prik or sweet chilli sauce as a dip.

STEAMED MORNING GLORY WITH FRIED GARLIC AND SHALLOTS

MORNING GLORY GOES BY VARIOUS NAMES, INCLUDING WATER SPINACH, WATER CONVOLVULUS AND SWAMP CABBAGE. IT IS A GREEN LEAFY VEGETABLE WITH LONG JOINTED STEMS AND ARROW-SHAPED LEAVES. THE STEMS REMAIN CRUNCHY WHILE THE LEAVES WILT LIKE SPINACH WHEN COOKED.

SERVES FOUR

INGREDIENTS

- 2 bunches morning glory, total weight about 250g/9oz, trimmed and coarsely chopped into 2.5cm/1in lengths
- 30ml/2 tbsp vegetable oil
- 4 shallots, thinly sliced
- 6 large garlic cloves, thinly sliced
- sea salt
- 1.5ml/¼ tsp dried chilli flakes

VARIATIONS

Use spinach instead of morning glory, or substitute young spring greens (collards), sprouting broccoli or Swiss chard.

1 Place the morning glory in a steamer and steam over a pan of boiling water for 30 seconds, until just wilted. If necessary, cook it in batches. Place the leaves in a bowl or spread them out on a large serving plate.

2 Heat the oil in a wok and stir-fry the shallots and garlic over a medium to high heat until golden. Spoon the mixture over the morning glory, sprinkle with a little sea salt and the chilli flakes and serve immediately.

STEAMED VEGETABLES WITH CHIANG MAI SPICY DIP

In Thailand, steamed vegetables are often partnered with raw ones to create the contrasting textures that are such a feature of the national cuisine. By happy coincidence, it is an extremely healthy way to serve them.

SERVES FOUR

INGREDIENTS
- 1 head broccoli, divided into florets
- 130g/4½oz 1 cup green beans, trimmed
- 130g/4½oz asparagus, trimmed
- ½ head cauliflower, divided into florets
- 8 baby corn cobs
- 130g/4½oz mangetouts (snow peas) or sugar snap peas
- salt

For the dip
- 1 fresh green chilli, seeded
- 4 garlic cloves, peeled
- 4 shallots, peeled
- 2 tomatoes, halved
- 5 pea aubergines (eggplant)
- 30ml/2 tbsp lemon juice
- 30ml/2 tbsp soy sauce
- 2.5ml/½ tsp salt
- 5ml/1 tsp granulated sugar

COOK'S TIP
Cauliflower varieties with pale green curds have a more delicate flavour than those with white curds.

1 Place the broccoli, green beans, asparagus and cauliflower in a steamer and steam over boiling water for about 4 minutes, until just tender but still with a "bite". Transfer them to a bowl and add the corn cobs and mangetouts or sugar snap peas. Season to taste with a little salt. Toss to mix, then set aside.

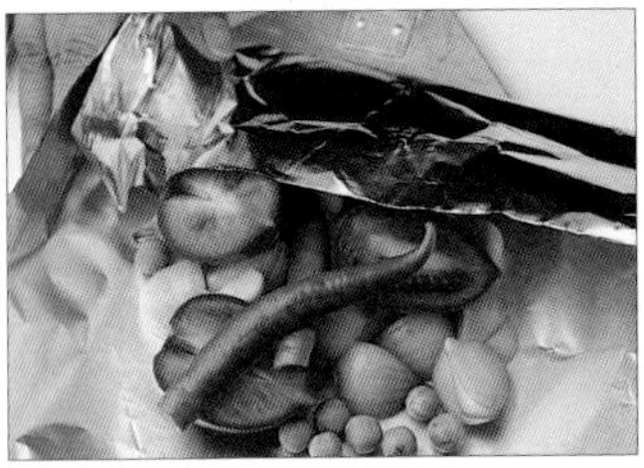

2 Make the dip. Preheat the grill (broiler). Wrap the chilli, garlic cloves, shallots, tomatoes and aubergines in a foil package. Grill (broil) for 10 minutes, until the vegetables have softened, turning the package over once or twice.

3 Unwrap the foil and tip its contents into a mortar or food processor. Add the lemon juice, soy sauce, salt and sugar. Pound with a pestle or process to a fairly liquid paste.

4 Scrape the dip into a serving bowl or four individual bowls. Serve, surrounded by the steamed and raw vegetables.

VARIATIONS
You can use a combination of other vegetables if you like. Use pak choi (bok choy) instead of the cauliflower or substitute raw baby carrots for the corn cobs and mushrooms in place of the mangetouts (snow peas).

STIR-FRIED PINEAPPLE WITH GINGER

THIS DISH MAKES AN INTERESTING ACCOMPANIMENT TO GRILLED MEAT OR STRONGLY-FLAVOURED FISH SUCH AS TUNA OR SWORDFISH. IF THE IDEA SEEMS STRANGE, THINK OF IT AS RESEMBLING A FRESH MANGO CHUTNEY, BUT WITH PINEAPPLE AS THE PRINCIPAL INGREDIENT.

SERVES FOUR

INGREDIENTS

- 1 pineapple
- 15ml/1 tbsp vegetable oil
- 2 garlic cloves, finely chopped
- 2 shallots, finely chopped
- 5cm/2in piece fresh root ginger, peeled and finely shredded
- 30ml/2 tbsp light soy sauce
- juice of ½ lime
- 1 large fresh red chilli, seeded and finely shredded

VARIATION

This also tastes excellent if peaches or nectarines are substituted for the diced pineapple. Use three or four, depending on their size.

1 Trim and peel the pineapple. Cut out the core and dice the flesh.

2 Heat the oil in a wok or frying pan. Stir-fry the garlic and shallots over a medium heat for 2–3 minutes, until golden. Do not let the garlic burn or the dish will taste bitter.

3 Add the pineapple. Stir-fry for about 2 minutes, or until the pineapple cubes start to turn golden on the edges.

4 Add the ginger, soy sauce, lime juice and chopped chilli. Toss together until well mixed. Cook over a low heat for a further 2 minutes, then serve.

HOT THAI PICKLED SHALLOTS

PICKLING THAI SHALLOTS IN THIS WAY DEMANDS SOME PATIENCE, WHILE THE VINEGAR AND SPICES WORK THEIR MAGIC, BUT THE RESULTS ARE DEFINITELY WORTH THE WAIT. THINLY SLICED, THE SHALLOTS ARE OFTEN USED AS A CONDIMENT WITH SOUTH-EAST ASIAN MEALS.

MAKES TWO TO THREE JARS

INGREDIENTS
- 5–6 small red or green bird's eye chillies
- 500g/1¼lb Thai pink shallots, peeled
- 2 large garlic cloves, peeled, halved and green shoots removed

For the vinegar
- 40g/1½oz/3 tbsp granulated sugar
- 10ml/2 tsp salt
- 5cm/2in piece fresh root ginger, peeled and sliced
- 15ml/1 tbsp coriander seeds
- 2 lemon grass stalks, cut in half lengthways
- 4 kaffir lime leaves or pared strips of lime rind
- 600ml/1 pint/2½ cups cider vinegar
- 15ml/1 tbsp chopped fresh coriander (cilantro)

1 The chillies can be left whole or halved and seeded. The pickle will be hotter if you leave the seeds in. If leaving the chillies whole, prick them several times with a cocktail stick (toothpick). Bring a large pan of water to the boil. Add the chillies, shallots and garlic. Blanch for 1–2 minutes, then drain. Rinse all the vegetables under cold water, then drain again.

2 Prepare the vinegar. Put the sugar, salt, ginger, coriander seeds, lemon grass and lime leaves or lime rind in a pan, pour in the vinegar and bring to the boil. Reduce the heat to low and simmer for 3–4 minutes. Leave to cool.

3 Remove and discard the ginger, then bring the vinegar back to the boil. Add the fresh coriander, garlic and chillies and cook for 1 minute.

4 Pack the shallots into sterilized jars, distributing the lemon grass, lime leaves, chillies and garlic among them. Pour over the hot vinegar. Cool, then seal and store in a cool, dark place for 2 months before eating.

COOK'S TIPS
- Always be careful when making pickles to be sure that bowls and pans used for vinegar are non-reactive, that is, they are not chemically affected by the acid of the vinegar. China and glass bowls and stainless steel pans are suitable. Kilner and Mason jars are ideal containers.
- When packing pickles, make sure that metal lids will not come in contact with the pickle. The acid in the vinegar will corrode the metal. Use plastic-coated or glass lids with rubber rings. Alternatively, cover the top of the jar with a circle of cellophane or waxed paper to prevent direct contact when using metal lids.
- Take care when handling hot jars. Let them cool slightly after sterilizing and before filling to avoid burning yourself. However, do not let them cool down completely, or they may crack when the hot vinegar is poured in.

DESSERTS

After a spicy Thai meal, it is customary to serve a platter of fresh fruits, often carved into the most beautiful shapes, to cleanse the palate. Ices are popular too, especially when based on watermelon or fresh lime juice. However, Thais also love sticky sweetmeats, and will often pick up their favourite treats from a stall at a night market, where they will be presented prettily on palm leaves or with a decoration of tiny flowers. Fried bananas and pineapple are also widely enjoyed.

WATERMELON ICE

AFTER A HOT AND SPICY THAI MEAL, THE ONLY THING MORE REFRESHING THAN ICE-COLD WATERMELON IS THIS WATERMELON ICE. MAKING IT IS SIMPLICITY ITSELF.

SERVES FOUR TO SIX

INGREDIENTS
- 90ml/6 tbsp caster (superfine) sugar
- 105ml/7 tbsp water
- 4 kaffir lime leaves, torn into small pieces
- 500g/1¼lb watermelon

1 Put the sugar, water and lime leaves in a pan. Heat gently until the sugar has dissolved. Pour into a large bowl and set aside to cool.

2 Cut the watermelon into wedges with a large knife. Cut the flesh from the rind, remove the seeds and chop.

3 Spoon the watermelon into a food processor. Process to a slush, then mix with the sugar syrup. Chill the mixture in the refrigerator for 3–4 hours.

4 Strain the mixture into a freezerproof container. Freeze for 2 hours, then remove from the freezer and beat with a fork to break up the ice crystals. Return the mixture to the freezer and freeze for 3 hours more, beating the mixture at half-hourly intervals. Freeze until firm.

5 Alternatively, use an ice cream maker. Pour the chilled mixture into the machine and churn until it is firm enough to scoop. Serve immediately, or scrape into a freezerproof container and store in the freezer.

6 About 30 minutes before serving, transfer the ice to the refrigerator so that it softens slightly. This allows the full flavour of the watermelon to be enjoyed and makes it easier to scoop.

COCONUT AND LEMON GRASS ICE CREAM

THE COMBINATION OF CREAM AND COCONUT MILK MAKES FOR A WONDERFULLY RICH ICE CREAM. THE LEMON GRASS FLAVOURING IS VERY SUBTLE, BUT QUITE DELICIOUS.

SERVES FOUR

INGREDIENTS
- 2 lemon grass stalks
- 475ml/16fl oz/2 cups double (heavy) cream
- 120ml/4fl oz/½ cup coconut milk
- 4 large (US extra large) eggs
- 105ml/7 tbsp caster (superfine) sugar
- 5ml/1 tsp vanilla essence (extract)

1 Cut the lemon grass stalks in half lengthways. Use a mallet or rolling pin to mash the pieces, breaking up the fibres so that all the flavour is released.

2 Pour the cream and coconut milk into a pan. Add the lemon grass stalks and heat gently, stirring frequently, until the mixture starts to simmer.

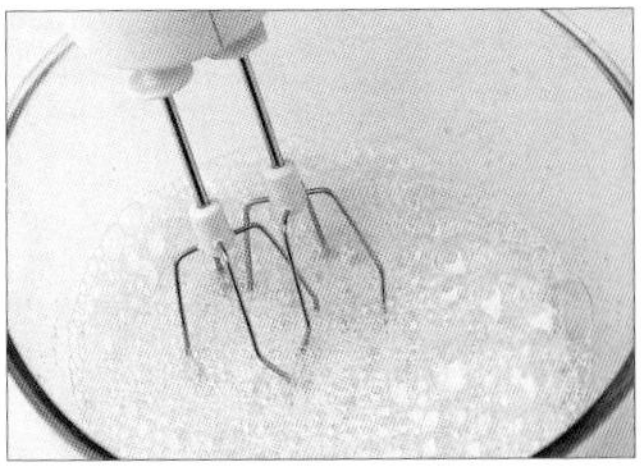

3 Put the eggs, sugar and vanilla essence in a large bowl. Using an electric whisk, whisk until the mixture is very light and fluffy.

4 Strain the cream mixture into a heatproof bowl that will fit over a pan of simmering water. Whisk in the egg mixture, then place the bowl over the pan and continue to whisk until the mixture thickens. Remove it from the heat and leave to cool. Chill the coconut custard in the refrigerator for 3–4 hours.

5 Pour the mixture into a plastic tub or similar freezerproof container. Freeze for 4 hours, beating two or three times at hourly intervals with a fork to break up the ice crystals.

6 Alternatively, use an ice cream maker. Pour the chilled mixture into the machine and churn until it is firm enough to scoop. Serve immediately, or scrape into a freezerproof container and place in the freezer.

7 About 30 minutes before serving, transfer the container to the refrigerator so that the ice cream softens slightly. Serve in scoops.

VARIATION

To make Coconut and Mango Ice Cream, purée the contents of two 400g/14oz cans of mangoes in syrup and add to the coconut custard before chilling it in the refrigerator. An ice cream made in this way will serve six.

Papayas in Jasmine Flower Syrup

The fragrant syrup can be prepared in advance, using fresh jasmine flowers from a house plant or the garden. It tastes fabulous with papayas, but it is also good with all sorts of desserts. Try it with ice cream or spooned over lychees or mangoes.

SERVES TWO

INGREDIENTS

- 105ml/7 tbsp water
- 45ml/3 tbsp palm sugar or light muscovado (brown) sugar
- 20–30 jasmine flowers, plus a few extra, to decorate (optional)
- 2 ripe papayas
- juice of 1 lime

COOK'S TIP

Although scented white jasmine flowers are perfectly safe to eat, it is important to be sure that they have not been sprayed with pesticides or other harmful chemicals. Washing them may not remove all the residue.

1 Place the water and sugar in a small pan. Heat gently, stirring occasionally, until the sugar has dissolved, then simmer, without stirring, over a low heat for 4 minutes.

2 Pour into a bowl, leave to cool slightly, then add the jasmine flowers. Leave to steep for at least 20 minutes.

3 Peel the papayas and slice in half lengthways. Scoop out and discard the seeds. Place the papayas on serving plates and squeeze over the lime.

4 Strain the syrup into a clean bowl, discarding the flowers. Spoon the syrup over the papayas. If you like, decorate with a few fresh jasmine flowers.

MANGO AND LIME FOOL

CANNED MANGOES ARE USED HERE FOR CONVENIENCE, BUT THE DISH TASTES EVEN BETTER IF MADE WITH FRESH ONES. CHOOSE A VARIETY LIKE THE VOLUPTUOUS ALPHONSO MANGO, WHICH IS WONDERFULLY FRAGRANT AND TASTES INDESCRIBABLY DELICIOUS.

SERVES FOUR

INGREDIENTS
- 400g/14oz can sliced mango
- grated rind of 1 lime
- juice of ½ lime
- 150ml/¼ pint/⅔ cup double (heavy) cream
- 90ml/6 tbsp Greek (US strained plain) yogurt
- fresh mango slices, to decorate (optional)

COOK'S TIP

When mixing the cream and yogurt mixture with the mango purée, whisk just enough to combine, so as not to lose the lightness of the whipped cream mixture. If you prefer, fold the mixtures together lightly, so that the fool is rippled.

1 Drain the canned mango slices and put them in the bowl of a food processor. Add the grated lime rind and the lime juice. Process until the mixture forms a smooth purée. Alternatively, mash the mango slices with a potato masher, then press through a sieve into a bowl with the back of a wooden spoon. Stir in the lime rind and juice.

2 Pour the cream into a bowl and add the yogurt. Whisk until the mixture is thick and then quickly whisk in the mango mixture.

3 Spoon into four tall cups or glasses and chill for 1–2 hours. Just before serving, decorate each glass with fresh mango slices, if you like.

STEWED PUMPKIN IN COCONUT CREAM

FRUIT STEWED IN COCONUT MILK IS A POPULAR DESSERT IN THAILAND. PUMPKINS, BANANAS AND MELONS CAN ALL BE PREPARED IN THIS SIMPLE BUT TASTY WAY.

SERVES FOUR TO SIX

INGREDIENTS
- 1kg/2¼lb kabocha pumpkin
- 750ml/1¼ pints/3 cups coconut milk
- 175g/6oz/¾ cup granulated sugar
- pinch of salt
- 4–6 fresh mint sprigs, to decorate

COOK'S TIP
To make the decoration, wash the pumpkin seeds to remove any fibres, then pat them dry on kitchen paper. Roast them in a dry frying pan, or spread them out on a baking sheet and grill (broil) until golden brown, tossing them frequently to prevent them from burning.

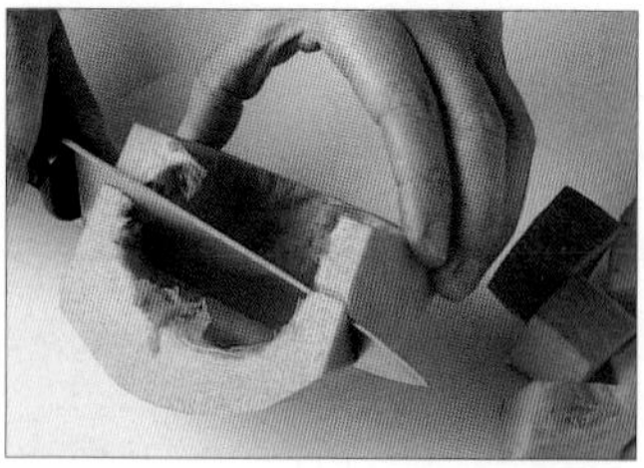

1 Cut the pumpkin in half using a large, sharp knife, then cut away and discard the skin. Scoop out the seed cluster. Reserve a few seeds and throw away the rest. Using a sharp knife, cut the pumpkin flesh into pieces that are about 5cm/2in long and 2cm/¾in thick.

2 Pour the coconut milk into a pan. Add the sugar and salt and bring to the boil. Add the pumpkin and simmer for about 10–15 minutes, until it is tender. Serve warm, in individual dishes. Decorate each serving with a mint sprig and toasted pumpkin seeds (see Cook's Tip).

MANGOES WITH STICKY RICE

STICKY RICE IS JUST AS GOOD IN DESSERTS AS IN SAVOURY DISHES, AND MANGOES, WITH THEIR DELICATE FRAGRANCE AND VELVETY FLESH, COMPLEMENT IT ESPECIALLY WELL. YOU NEED TO START PREPARING THIS DISH THE DAY BEFORE YOU INTEND TO SERVE IT.

SERVES FOUR

INGREDIENTS
- 115g/4oz/⅔ cup white glutinous rice
- 175ml/6fl oz/¾ cup thick coconut milk
- 45ml/3 tbsp granulated sugar
- pinch of salt
- 2 ripe mangoes
- strips of pared lime rind, to decorate

1 Rinse the glutinous rice thoroughly in several changes of cold water, then leave to soak overnight in a bowl of fresh cold water.

COOK'S TIP
Like cream, the thickest and richest part of coconut milk always rises to the top. Whenever you open a can or carton, spoon off this top layer and use it with fruit or to enrich a spicy savoury dish just before serving.

2 Drain the rice well and spread it out evenly in a steamer lined with muslin or cheesecloth. Cover and steam over a pan of simmering water for about 20 minutes, or until the rice is tender.

3 Reserve 45ml/3 tbsp of the cream from the top of the coconut milk. Pour the remainder into a pan and add the sugar and salt. Heat, stirring constantly, until the sugar has dissolved, then bring to the boil. Remove the pan from the heat, pour the coconut milk into a bowl and leave to cool.

4 Tip the cooked rice into a bowl and pour over the cooled coconut milk mixture. Stir well, then leave the rice mixture to stand for 10–15 minutes.

5 Meanwhile, peel the mangoes, cut the flesh away from the central stones (pits) and cut into slices.

6 Spoon the rice on to individual serving plates. Arrange the mango slices on one side, then drizzle with the reserved coconut cream. Decorate with strips of lime rind and serve.

Thai Fried Pineapple

A very simple and quick Thai dessert – pineapple fried in butter, brown sugar and lime juice, and sprinkled with toasted coconut. The slightly sharp taste of the fruit makes this a very refreshing treat at the end of a meal.

SERVES FOUR

INGREDIENTS
- 1 pineapple
- 40g/1½oz/3 tbsp butter
- 15ml/1 tbsp desiccated (dry unsweetened shredded) coconut
- 60ml/4 tbsp soft light brown sugar
- 60ml/4 tbsp fresh lime juice
- lime slices, to decorate
- thick and creamy natural (plain) yogurt, to serve

1 Using a sharp knife, cut the top off the pineapple and peel off the skin, taking care to remove the eyes. Cut the pineapple in half and remove and discard the woody core. Cut the flesh lengthways into 1cm/½in wedges.

2 Heat the butter in a large, heavy frying pan or wok. When it has melted, add the pineapple wedges and cook over a medium heat for 1–2 minutes on each side, or until they have turned pale golden in colour.

3 Meanwhile, dry-fry the coconut in a small frying pan until lightly browned. Remove from the heat and set aside.

4 Sprinkle the sugar into the pan with the pineapple, add the lime juice and cook, stirring constantly, until the sugar has dissolved. Divide the pineapple wedges among four bowls, sprinkle with the coconut, decorate with the lime slices and serve with the yogurt.

FRIED BANANAS

THESE DELICIOUSLY SWEET TREATS ARE A FAVOURITE WITH CHILDREN AND ADULTS ALIKE. IN THAILAND, YOU WILL FIND THEM ON SALE FROM PORTABLE ROADSIDE STALLS AND MARKETS AT ALMOST EVERY HOUR OF THE DAY AND NIGHT.

SERVES FOUR

INGREDIENTS

- 115g/4oz/1 cup plain (all-purpose) flour
- 2.5ml/½ tsp bicarbonate of soda (baking soda)
- pinch of salt
- 30ml/2 tbsp granulated sugar
- 1 egg, beaten
- 90ml/6 tbsp water
- 30ml/2 tbsp shredded coconut or 15ml/1 tbsp sesame seeds
- 4 firm bananas
- vegetable oil, for deep-frying
- fresh mint sprigs, to decorate
- 30ml/2 tbsp clear honey, to serve (optional)

1 Sift the flour, bicarbonate of soda and salt into a large bowl. Stir in the granulated sugar and the egg, and whisk in just enough of the water to make quite a thin batter.

2 Whisk the shredded coconut or sesame seeds into the batter so that they are evenly distributed.

3 Peel the bananas. Carefully cut each one in half lengthways, then in half crossways to make 16 pieces of about the same size. Don't do this until you are ready to cook them because, once peeled, bananas quickly discolour.

VARIATIONS

This recipe works just as well with many other types of fruit, such as pineapple rings or apple wedges.

4 Heat the oil in a wok or deep-fryer to a temperature of 190°C/375°F or until a cube of bread, dropped in the oil, browns in about 45 seconds. Dip the banana pieces in the batter, then gently drop a few into the oil. Deep-fry until golden brown, then lift out and drain well on kitchen paper.

5 Cook the remaining banana pieces in the same way. Serve immediately with honey, if using, and decorated with sprigs of fresh mint.

STEAMED CUSTARD IN NECTARINES

STEAMING NECTARINES OR PEACHES BRINGS OUT THEIR NATURAL COLOUR AND SWEETNESS, SO THIS IS A GOOD WAY OF MAKING THE MOST OF UNDERRIPE OR LESS FLAVOURFUL FRUIT.

SERVES FOUR TO SIX

INGREDIENTS
- 6 nectarines
- 1 large (US extra large) egg
- 45ml/3 tbsp palm sugar or light muscovado (brown) sugar
- 30ml/2 tbsp coconut milk

COOK'S TIP

Palm sugar, also known as jaggery, is made from the sap of certain Asian palm trees, such as coconut and palmyrah. It is available from Asian food stores. If you buy it as a cake or large lump, grate it before use.

1 Cut the nectarines in half. Using a teaspoon, scoop out the stones (pits) and a little of the surrounding flesh.

2 Lightly beat the egg, then add the sugar and the coconut milk. Beat until the sugar has dissolved.

3 Transfer the nectarines to a steamer and carefully fill the cavities three-quarters full with the custard mixture. Steam over a pan of simmering water for 5–10 minutes. Remove from the heat and leave to cool completely before transferring to plates and serving.

Coconut Pancakes

These light and sweet pancakes are often served as street food by the hawkers in Bangkok and they make a delightful dessert.

MAKES EIGHT

INGREDIENTS

- 75g/3oz/¾ cup plain (all-purpose) flour, sifted
- 60ml/4 tbsp rice flour
- 45ml/3 tbsp caster (superfine) sugar
- 50g/2oz/⅔ cup desiccated (dry unsweetened shredded) coconut
- 1 egg
- 275ml/9fl oz/generous 1 cup coconut milk
- vegetable oil, for frying
- lime wedges and maple syrup, to serve

1 Place the plain flour, rice flour, sugar and coconut in a bowl, stir to mix and then make a small well in the centre. Break the egg into the well and pour in the coconut milk.

2 With a whisk or fork, beat the egg into the coconut milk and then gradually incorporate the surrounding dry ingredients, whisking constantly until the mixture forms a batter. The mixture will not be entirely smooth, because of the coconut, but there shouldn't be any large lumps.

3 Heat a little oil in a 13cm/5in non-stick frying pan. Pour in about 45ml/3 tbsp of the mixture and quickly spread to a thin layer with the back of a spoon. Cook over a high heat for about 30–60 seconds, until bubbles appear on the surface of the pancake, then turn it over with a spatula and cook the other side until golden.

4 Slide the pancake on to a plate and keep it warm in a very low oven. Make more pancakes in the same way. Serve warm with lime wedges for squeezing and maple syrup for drizzling.

COOK'S TIP

Maple syrup is not, of course, indigenous to Thailand, but then nor are chillies. It is an international favourite for serving with pancakes. Make sure that you buy the pure syrup for the best flavour.

VARIATION

Serve with honey instead of maple syrup, if you like.

COCONUT CUSTARD

THIS TRADITIONAL DESSERT CAN BE BAKED OR STEAMED AND IS OFTEN SERVED WITH SWEET STICKY RICE AND A SELECTION OF FRESH FRUIT. MANGOES AND TAMARILLOS GO PARTICULARLY WELL WITH THE CUSTARD AND RICE.

SERVES FOUR

INGREDIENTS
- 4 eggs
- 75g/3oz/6 tbsp soft light brown sugar
- 250ml/8fl oz/1 cup coconut milk
- 5ml/1 tsp vanilla, rose or jasmine extract
- fresh mint leaves and icing (confectioners') sugar, to decorate
- sliced fruit, to serve

1 Preheat the oven to 150°C/300°F/Gas 2. Whisk the eggs and sugar in a bowl until smooth. Add the coconut milk and extract and whisk well.

2 Strain the mixture into a jug (pitcher), then pour it into four individual heatproof glasses, ramekins or an ovenproof dish.

3 Stand the glasses, ramekins or dish in a roasting pan. Fill the pan with hot water to reach halfway up the sides of the ramekins or dish.

4 Bake for about 35–40 minutes, or until the custards are set. Test with a fine skewer or cocktail stick (toothpick).

5 Remove the roasting pan from the oven, lift out the ramekins or dish and leave to cool.

6 If you like, turn out the custards on to serving plate(s). Decorate with the mint leaves and a dusting of icing sugar, and serve with sliced fruit.

Coconut Cream Diamonds

Desserts like these are served in countries all over the Far East, often with mangoes, pineapple or guavas. Although commercially ground rice can be used for this dish, grinding jasmine rice yourself – in a food processor – gives a much better result.

SERVES FOUR TO SIX

INGREDIENTS

- 75g/3oz/scant ½ cup jasmine rice, soaked overnight in 175ml/6fl oz/ ¾ cup water
- 350ml/12fl oz/1½ cups coconut milk
- 150ml/¼ pint/⅔ cup single (light) cream
- 50g/2oz/¼ cup caster (superfine) sugar
- raspberries and fresh mint leaves, to decorate

For the coulis

- 75g/3oz/¾ cup blackcurrants, stalks removed
- 30ml/2 tbsp caster (superfine) sugar
- 75g/3oz/½ cup fresh or frozen raspberries

1 Put the rice and its soaking water into a food processor and process for a few minutes until the mixture is soupy.

2 Heat the coconut milk and cream in a non-stick pan. When the mixture is on the point of boiling, stir in the rice mixture. Cook over a very gentle heat for 10 minutes, stirring constantly.

3 Stir the sugar into the coconut rice mixture and continue cooking for a further 10–15 minutes, or until the mixture is thick and creamy.

VARIATION

You could use other soft fruit in the coulis, such as blackberries or redcurrants.

4 Line a rectangular tin (pan) with non-stick baking parchment. Pour the coconut rice mixture into the pan, cool, then chill in the refrigerator until the dessert is set and firm.

5 Meanwhile, make the coulis. Put the blackcurrants in a bowl and sprinkle with the sugar. Set aside for about 30 minutes. Tip the blackcurrants and raspberries into a wire sieve set over a bowl. Using a spoon, press the fruit against the sides of the sieve so that the juices collect in the bowl. Taste the coulis and add more sugar if necessary.

6 Carefully cut the coconut cream into diamonds. Spoon a little of the coulis on to each dessert plate, arrange the coconut cream diamonds on top and decorate with the fresh raspberries and mint leaves. Serve immediately.

TAPIOCA PUDDING

THIS PUDDING, MADE FROM LARGE PEARL TAPIOCA AND COCONUT MILK AND SERVED WARM, IS MUCH LIGHTER THAN THE WESTERN-STYLE VERSION. YOU CAN ADJUST THE SWEETNESS TO YOUR TASTE. SERVE WITH LYCHEES OR THE SMALLER, SIMILAR-TASTING LONGANS – ALSO KNOWN AS "DRAGON'S EYES".

SERVES FOUR

INGREDIENTS

- 115g/4oz/⅔ cup tapioca
- 475ml/16fl oz/2 cups water
- 175g/6oz/¾ cup granulated sugar
- pinch of salt
- 250ml/8fl oz/1 cup coconut milk
- 250g/9oz prepared tropical fruits
- finely shredded lime rind and shaved fresh coconut (optional), to decorate

1 Put the tapioca in a bowl and pour over warm water to cover. Leave to soak for 1 hour so the grains swell. Drain.

2 Pour the measured water in a large pan and bring to the boil over a medium heat. Add the sugar and salt and stir until dissolved.

3 Add the tapioca and coconut milk, reduce the heat to low and simmer gently for 10 minutes, or until the tapioca becomes transparent.

4 Spoon into one large or four individual bowls and serve warm with the tropical fruits. Decorate with the lime rind and coconut shavings, if using.

BAKED RICE PUDDING, THAI-STYLE

BLACK GLUTINOUS RICE, ALSO KNOWN AS BLACK STICKY RICE, HAS LONG DARK GRAINS AND A NUTTY TASTE REMINISCENT OF WILD RICE. THIS BAKED PUDDING HAS A DISTINCT CHARACTER AND FLAVOUR ALL OF ITS OWN, AS WELL AS AN INTRIGUING APPEARANCE.

SERVES FOUR TO SIX

INGREDIENTS

- 175g/6oz/1 cup white or black glutinous rice
- 30ml/2 tbsp soft light brown sugar
- 475ml/16fl oz/2 cups coconut milk
- 250ml/8fl oz/1 cup water
- 3 eggs
- 30ml/2 tbsp granulated sugar

1 Combine the glutinous rice and brown sugar in a pan. Pour in half the coconut milk and the water.

2 Bring to the boil, reduce the heat to low and simmer, stirring occasionally, for 15–20 minutes, or until the rice has absorbed most of the liquid. Preheat the oven to 150°C/300°F/Gas 2.

3 Spoon the rice mixture into a single large ovenproof dish or divide it among individual ramekins. Beat the eggs with the remaining coconut milk and sugar in a bowl.

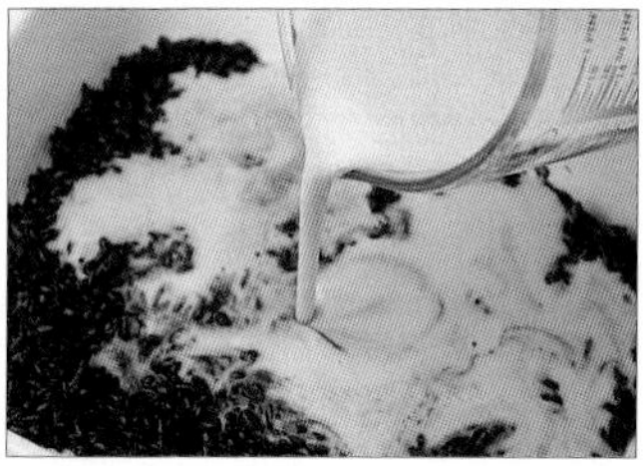

4 Strain the egg mixture into a jug (pitcher), then pour it evenly over the par-cooked rice in the dish or ramekins.

5 Place the dish or ramekins in a roasting pan. Carefully pour in enough hot water to come halfway up the sides of the dish or ramekins.

6 Cover with foil and bake for about 35–60 minutes, or until the custard has set. Serve warm or cold.

COOK'S TIP

Throughout South-east Asia, black glutinous rice is usually used for sweet dishes, while its white counterpart is more often used in savoury recipes.

Food and Shopping

AUSTRALIA

Asian Food 4U
25-27 Plaza Parade
Maroochudore QLD 4558
Tel: (617) 5443 8109

Emart Asian Supermarket
45 W Row
Canberra AU 2600
Tel: (614) 0121 1088

Kim Wang Asian Grocery
62-63 Grote Street
Adelaide SA 5000
Tel: (618) 8410 1555

Minh Phat Supermarket
2-8 Nicholson STreet
Abbotsford VIC 3067
Tel: (613) 9429 4028

Ming Mei Supermarket
G073/42 Marine Parade
Southport QLD 4215
(617) 5591 5516

OK Asian Supermarket
154 Glynburn Road
Tranmere SA 5073
Tel: (618) 8336 1237

Tan Hung Long Supermarket
90-95 The Crescent
Homebush West NSQW 2140
Tel: (612) 9746 1074

White Lotus Market
379 Anzac Parade
Kingsford NSW 2032
Tel: (612) 9662 7736

CANADA

Asian Food Centre
2120 N Park Drive
Brampton, Ontario L6S OC9
Tel: (905) 793 1338

Hong Kong Emporium
364 Young Street
Toronto
Ontario M5B 1S5
Tel: (416) 977-3386

Tan Thanh Supermarket
115 Park Street North
Hamilton
Ontario ON L8R 2N2
Tel: (905) 528 8181

SOUTH AFRICA

Akhalwaya and Sons
13 Central Road
Fordsburg
Johannesburg
Tel: (27) 833-1068

Kashmiri Spice Centre
102 Church Street
Mayfair, Johannesburg
Tel: (11) 839-3833

Spice Emporium
33 Monty Naicker Road
Durban 4001
Tel: (31) 332 5888

UNITED KINGDOM

Chung Wah Supermarket
Hardy Street
Liverpool L15 5JN
Tel: 0151 707 8488

Hang Seng Supermarket
120 Corporation St
Preston PR1 2HE

Hang Sing Supermarket
21 Blenheim Terrace
Woodhouse, Leeds
LS2 9HS
Tel: 0113 243 0500

Hoang Yen
18 Holyhead Road
Birmingham B21 0LT
Tel: 0121 515 1236

Loon Fung Supermarket
Stratford Shop Centre
London E15 1XD
Tel: 020 3598 3888

Manila Supermarket
11–12 Hogarth Road
London SW5 0QT
Tel: 07951 100028

Rum Wong Supermarket
16 London Road
Guildford GU1 2AF
Tel: 01483 599499

Spice Land
65 Dereham Road
Norwich NR2 4HU
Tel: 01603 621412

Thai Supermarket
45 Camden High Street
London NS1 7JH
Tel: 02 7383 5002

The Vietnamese Store
80-86 Oldham Road
Manchester M4 5EB
Tel: 0161 228 2387

Wing Tai
393 Edgware Road
London NW2 6LN
Tel: 020 8452 2333

Wing Yip
395 Edgware Road
London NW2 6LN
Tel: 020 8450 0422
also at
Oldham Road
Ancoats
Manchester M4 5HU
Tel: 0161 832 3215
and
375 Nechells Park Road
Nechells
Birmingham B7 5NT
Tel: 0121 327 6618

Mail Order Companies

Fiddes Payne Herbs and Spices Ltd
Unit 3A, Thorpe Way, Banbury
Oxfordshire OX16 4SP
Tel: 01295 253 888
www.fiddespayne.co.uk

Fox's Spices
Mason's Road
Stratford-upon-Avon
Warwickshire CV37 9XN
Tel: 01789 266 420

UNITED STATES

Ai Hoa
860 North Hill Street
Los Angeles, CA 90026
Tel (213) 629 8121

Asia Market
71 1/2 Mulberry St
New York NY 10013
Tel: (212) 962 2020

Asian Market
5360 Walzem Road
San Antonio TX 78218
Tel: (210) 653 9911

Bangrak Market
2319 2nd Avenue
Seattle, WA 98121
Tel: (206) 735 7352

Fu Wah Mini Market
810 S 47th St
Philadelphia PA 19143
Tel: (215) 729 2993

Hanmi Oriental Food & Gifts
1008 State Street
New Haven CT 06511
Tel: (203) 782 2009

Hong Tan Oriental Food
816 Pennsylvania Avenue
Savannah, GA 31404
Tel: (912) 233 9184

Hung Phat Grocery
11315 Fern Street
Wheaton DC 20902
Tel: (301) 929 0725

Hung Phong Oriental Market
243 Remount Drive
San Antonio TX 78218
Tel: (210) 655 8448

Hung Vuong Supermarket
1122 Washington Avenue
Philadelphia
PA 19147
Tel: (215) 336 2803

Huy Fong Foods Inc.
4800 Azure Canyon Road
Irwindale CA 91706
Tel: (626) 286 8328

Khanh Tam Oriental Market
4051 Buford Highway NE
Atlanta, GA 30345
Tel: (404) 728 0393

Little Saigon Supermarket
375 South Federal Boulevard
Denver CO 80219
Tel: (303) 937 8860

My Foa Food Market
13201 Bellaire Boulevard
Houston TX 77083
Tel: (281) 498 6699

Palengke Oriental Market
5051 Stewart Ave No 106
Los Angeles NV 89110
Tel: (702) 438 8211

Po Tung Oriental Grocery
321 Park Avenue
Baltimore MD 21201
Tel: (410) 962 1510

Saigon Asian Market
476 Union Street
Manchester NH 03103
Tel: (603) 935 9597

Saigon Market
15705 Hawthorne Boulevard A
Lawndale
CA 90260
Tel: (310) 679 2661

Thien Thank Supermarket
1080 S 10th St
San Jose CA 95112
Tel: (408) 295 1043

Vingh Loi Supermarket
867 North 8th Street
Reading PA 19604
Tel: (610) 375 8637

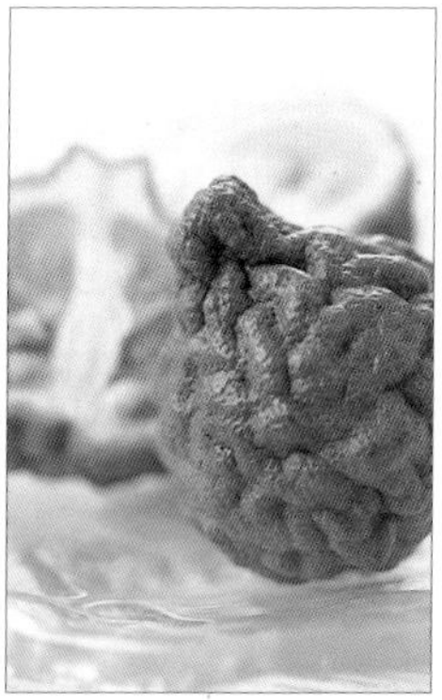

Author's Acknowledgements
I would like to thank the following people and organisations for their invaluable help in researching this book: Charles Bradley, Pat Checkley (Tourist Authority of Thailand), Jonathan Hart, Chris Lee, Alissra Sinclair-Knopp (Language and Culture Consultant, The Thai Consulting Group), The Tourist Authority of Thailand, The Thai Embassy and a special thank you to Prisana Smith of the Tammag Thai Restaurant, 50–54 Westow Hill, London, SE19 1RX who has been an invaluable source of advice and information. I would also like to give a special thanks to Clare Spurrell for her assistance with research and her editorial contribution and to my editor Susannah Blake who has made this project a joy to work on.

Publisher's Acknowledgements
All photographs are by Nicki Dowey expect the following: pages 7, 16, 17, 19 and 21, which were reproduced with the permission of Corbis Picture Agency.

We would like to thank Magimix UK and New Classic Limited for the use of equipment for photography.

INDEX